Goethe's *Faust* and Cultural Memory

Goethe's *Faust* and Cultural Memory

Comparatist Interfaces

Lorna Fitzsimmons

LEHIGH UNIVERSITY PRESS
Bethlehem

Published by Lehigh University Press
Co-published with The Rowman & Littlefield Publishing Group, Inc.
4501 Forbes Boulevard, Suite 200, Lanham, Maryland 20706
www.rowman.com

10 Thornbury Road, Plymouth PL6 7PP, United Kingdom

British Library Cataloguing in Publication Information Available

Library of Congress Cataloging-in-Publication Data

Fitzsimmons, Lorna, 1957–
  Goethe's Faust and cultural memory : comparatist interfaces / Lorna Fitzsimmons.
      p. cm.
  Includes bibliographical references and index.
  ISBN 978-1-61146-122-0 (cloth : alk. paper)—ISBN 978-1-61146-123-7 (electronic)
  1. Faust, d. ca. 1540—Appreciation. 2. Faust, d. ca. 1540—Adaptations. 3. Faust, d. ca. 1540—In literature. I. Title.
  PN6071.F33F58 2012
  809'.93351—dc23   2012012407

∞™ The paper used in this publication meets the minimum requirements of American National Standard for Information Sciences—Permanence of Paper for Printed Library Materials, ANSI/NISO Z39.48-1992.

Printed in the United States of America

Contents

List of Figures

Introduction

Magian Mnemotechny

Lorna Fitzsimmons

> —what has disappeared becomes reality.
> (Und was verschwand wird mir zu Wirklichkeiten.)[1]

During the present era of apparent globalization and transnationalism, the memory of the magus Faustus returns, out of the labyrinthine past, its seasoned imaginings still engaging. Rooted in the turbulence of sixteenth-century German society, the counterintuitive figure of the iconoclastic savant has a lengthy history of periodic disappearances and revivals, as if journeying to hell, in Karl Shapiro's verse,[2] only to reappear with a persistence that bespeaks its utility. During the Romantic era, Goethe's masterwork *Faust* (1808, 1832) arose to become the canonic treatment of the legend in the modern era.

This book takes both a canonic and archival approach to Goethe's *Faust* in studies of adaptations, performances, appropriations, sources, and the translation of the drama contextualized within cultural environments ranging from Gnosticism to artificial intelligence. Its focus is upon forms of Goethean transtextual[3] interplay, including artificial memory, as mnemonic environments. The titular concept of interface has broad resonance within contemporary intertextual studies, cultural studies, linguistics, and computer science in reference to loci of interaction.[4] The term serves here to designate the comparatist approach to Goethe's *Faust* by which this book relates the drama to anterior and posterior mnemonic spaces.

The concept of magian mnemotechny encapsulates the mnemonic role of Goethe's canonic work as a fulcral matrix of cultural memory and a paradigm for artificial intelligence. Interest in mnemotechny, the ancient art of memory, has undergone a revival within contemporary memory studies, an interdisciplinary field bridging the sciences and humanities. Cultural memory scholarship, increasingly prominent since the 1980s, draws on Maurice Halbwachs' studies of *mémoire collective* in engaging the social mediation of memory. Collective memory, in Halbwachs' work, "does not preserve the past but reconstructs it with the aid of material traces, rites, texts, and traditions left behind by the past, and with the aid, moreover, of recent psychological and social data, that is to say, with the present."[5] Jan Assmann defines the concept of cultural memory as comprising "that body of reusable texts, images, and rituals specific to each society in each epoch, whose 'cultivation' serves to stabilize and convey that society's self-image."[6] As Patrick Greaney observes, however, memory can also be an "alienating and productive force"—"[m]emory estranges," creating an "alienating discontinuity."[7] Recognizing the contested status of the concept, Astrid Erll suggests a broad definition of cultural memory as "the interplay of present and past in socio-cultural contexts."[8]

Within recent memory studies, Renate Lachmann's theory of intertextuality provides an insightful framework for understanding literature as "culture's memory." Lachmann suggests that literature is "the mnemonic art par excellence. Literature supplies the memory for a culture and records such a memory. It is itself an act of memory. Literature inscribes itself in a memory space made up of texts, and it sketches out a memory space into which earlier texts are gradually absorbed and transformed."[9] Marvin Carlson similarly suggests that "every play is a memory play"—the theater is "the repository of cultural memory," which, "like the memory of each individual . . . is also subject to continual adjustment and modifications as the memory is recalled in new circumstances and contexts."[10] The magian mnemotechny of which Goethe's *Faust* remains the canonic exemplar of our era is architecturally voluminous in being both a rich repository of memories from the distant past and a polyphonic interface for the negotiation of modernity. The Spenglerian figure of the Faustian as "limitless space"[11] anticipates the sense of intercultural sublimity encountered at the Goethean interface, reaching back to antiquity (chapter 2) and forward to research on artificial intelligence (chapter 9).

To conceive of Goethe's *Faust* as a form of cultural mnemotechny points to the drama's function as a means, both external and internal, by which memories are reconstructed and negotiated and new information processed. Whilst signs of external mnemonics, such as wood or bone inscriptions, have been traced to the Upper Paleolithic period,[12] evidence of cultivated mnemonics descends from the Greeks. Writings such as "Dialexeis" (c. 400 BCE) provide a record of how the Greeks developed memory by way of internal mnemonics—cognitive strategies that enhance the initial processing of information.[13]

> A great and beautiful invention is memory, always useful both for learning and for life.
>
> This is the first thing. if you pay attention (direct your mind), the judgment will better perceive the things going through it (the mind).
>
> Secondly, repeat again what you hear: for by often hearing and saying the same things, what you have learned comes complete into your memory.
>
> Thirdly, what you hear, place on what you know. For example, *Chrysippus* is to be remembered; we place it on *gold* and *horse*. Another example: we place *glow-worm* on *fire* and *shine*. So much for names. For things (do) thus: for courage (place it) on Mars and Achilles; for metal-working, on Vulcan; for cowardice, on Epeus.[14]

The strategies enumerated by the ancients anticipate in some respects the stress upon the interdependence of encoding, storage, and retrieval processes in contemporary mnemonology.[15] As Frances A. Yates perceives, in the example above, "the images for words are formed from primitive etymological dissection of the word. In the examples given of images for things, the 'things' virtue and vice are represented (valour, cowardice), also an art (metallurgy). They are deposited in memory with images of gods and men (Mars, Achilles, Vulcan, Epeus)."[16]

In a well-known passage from Cicero's *De oratore*, the invention of mnemotechny is attributed to the poet Simonides, who is said to have been able to identify the guests of a banquet after their faces were rendered unrecognizable:

> The story goes that Simonides was enabled by his recollection of the place in which each of them had been reclining at table to identify them for separate interment; and that this circumstance suggested to him the discovery of the truth that the best aid to clearness of memory consists of orderly arrangement. He inferred that persons desiring to train this faculty must select localities and form mental images of the facts they wish to remember and store those images in the localities, with the result that the arrangement of the localities will preserve the order of the facts, and the images of the facts will designate the facts themselves, and we shall employ the localities and images respectively as a wax writing tablet and the letters written on it.[17]

This influential passage illustrates the mnemonic of loci and *imagines*, widely practiced and taught until the print revolution of the early modern period.[18] To memorize an oration, for instance, one engaged in mental simulation of a series of places, such as the rooms of a building, wherein an image for each topic would be envisaged.[19] The simulated place served as the basis of encoding and retrieval, utilizing the association of to-be-remembered information with familiar memories.[20] The *Ad Herennium* (c. 86 BCE) advised that the imagines will be most memorable if beautified or ornamented, disfigured, or rendered comic:

> We ought, then, to set up images of a kind that can adhere longest in memory. And we shall do so if we establish likenesses as striking as possible; if we set up images that are not many or vague, but doing something; if we assign to them exceptional beauty or singular ugliness; if we dress some of them with crowns or purple cloaks, for example, so that the likeness may be more distinct to us; or if we somehow disfigure them, as by introducing one stained with blood or soiled with mud or smeared with red paint, so that its form is more striking, or by assigning certain comic effects to our images, for that, too, will ensure our remembering them more readily.[21]

The exceptional beauty of Helen, the grotesque transformation of the black poodle (Figure 1), or the animating appearance of the ornamented noble squire, bedecked with cloak, sword, and feather: such images from Goethe's *Faust* readily replay in the mind's eye, and, in turn, lend themselves as a series of loci for the encoding and retrieval of to-be-remembered information, such as the tenets of anthroposophy (chapter 6) or contemporary

Figure 1. ***Faust in His Study.*** **Reproduced from Moritz Retzsch,** ***Illustrations of Goethe's Faust.*** **London: Tilt and Bogue, 1843.**

Canadian aesthetic and societal concerns (chapter 7). The trope of magian mnemotechny enframes this book to help conceptualize the Faustian thematic as a set of palimpsestic mnemonic spaces in which a spectrum of associated images have been emplaced for varying rhetorical purposes during the course of the myth's adaptation across the centuries.

Since its first appearance in the sixteenth century, the cultural selection of the Faustus legend owes much to the type of counterintuitiveness to which key elements of the tale belong, facilitating recollection of the plot. As cognitive studies demonstrate, "a concept that is easily remembered . . . will be transmitted more successfully and thus be more common than concepts that are difficult to remember or represent."[22] On the whole, the human mind demonstrates better retrieval of concepts that are *minimally* incongruent with expectations, such as a "dog composing a symphony," which is counterintuitive in that it contradicts assumptions about ontological categories (person, animal, inanimate object), with minimal incongruity, resulting from attribute transferral between the close categories of person and animal, in fact two mammals.[23] Similarly, Mephistopheles' metamorphosis from animal (poodle, hippopotamus) ("*Pudel,*" "*Nilpferd*") (*F,* 1250–55) to person in Goethe's *Faust* is less counterintuitive than would be a transformation to or from something inanimate. Another widely remembered example occurs in "Bergschluchten" as the transfigured Faust ("Faustens Unsterbliches") ascends under the sway of the Eternal-Feminine ("das Ewig-Weibliche") (*F,* 12110) (chapter 2). Such minimally incongruent violations increase the salience of the counterintuitive concept, enhancing recollection.[24] Minimally counterintuitive concepts "achieve a cognitive optimum by being non-natural (or, in the case of religion, 'supernatural') but learnable, i.e., distinctive but still easy enough to represent, process and code in memory by maintaining the remaining inferential expectations natural kinds possess."[25]

If the Faustian matter thus shares minimal counterintuitiveness with many religious concepts, it differs crucially in lacking the principle of invariance that distinguishes ritual from myth.[26] Whereas ritual constitutes a formal kind of collective remembrance the "metamessage" of which "flaunts" pre-ordained orders, encoding a conformant congregation, mythic recitation is less formal and less participatory on the part of the audience.[27] As Paul Connerton observes, "To recite a myth is not necessarily to accept it. What the telling of a myth does not do, and what the performance of a ritual essentially does do, is to specify the relationship that obtains between the performers of the ritual and what it is that they are performing."[28] Reflecting on the principle of mythic variance, Connerton recalls the nineteenth-century debates over the extent to which major myths of Western culture such as that of Faustus could be reworked into variant forms.[29] Some assumed that, over the centuries, the Faustian matter had been subject to multiple adaptations until it attained definitive form in Goethe's *Faust*, at which point the process of variance would cease.

Today, the canonic status of Goethe's *Faust* is widely acknowledged, yet it would be unrealistic, perhaps ritualistic, to preclude or overlook further variation of the Faustus theme, or, indeed, to assume that the Goethean play itself is a static object.[30] Since Goethe's era, the cultural diffusion of *Faust* has produced an unparalleled proliferation of Faustian discourse in the form of metonymic intertexts, bound to the source in varying relations of contiguity, as well as more creative or metaphorical variants of the Goethean in the form of adaptations or appropriations.[31] Currently received as a canonic text of the foremost rank, the Goethean *Faust* is a mnemonic treasure house that interfaces with a vast network of related artifacts, some of which are also canonic in being part of the working or active cultural memory, whilst others are part of the passive cultural memory, represented by the archive or "reference memory," including many intercultural hybridizations that have been neglected because of lack of translation or cultural bias. This book recognizes the need for further scholarship on the Faustian archive and contributes to that end in a number of chapters. Such scholarship not only enhances knowledge of the Goethean *Faust* but also enriches our understanding of intercultural mnemonic relationships. As Aleida Assmann suggests,

> The reference memory . . . provides a rich background for the working memory, which means that elements of the canon may be 'estranged' and reinterpreted by framing them with elements of the archive. . . . Elements of the canon can also recede into the archive, while elements of the archive may be recovered and reclaimed for the canon. It is exactly this interdependence of the different realms and functions that creates the dynamics of cultural memory and keeps its energy flowing.[32]

As Herbert Grabes observes, canons play a major role in the "shaping and sustenance" of cultural memory, with educational institutions contributing significantly to the process of canon formation, maintenance, and reformation.[33] In recent years, the canonic status of Goethe's *Faust* has been reinforced, and elements of the Faustian archive activated, within the academic market for Faust studies, which has grown, at least in part, in response to budgetary considerations.[34] Such curricular selection broadens working memory of the Faustian thematic in intercultural and interdisciplinary directions. As high-school educators Matt Copeland and Chris Goering show, tapping students' interest in the Faust theme in blues music, for instance, can serve as a "scaffold" by which to introduce other variants of the theme.[35]

Commemorative activities associated with the "Goethe Year" in 1999 and the bicentenary of *Faust I* in 2008 have also intensified interest in Faust studies in the academy, including a number of non-Western institutions, as indicated by "The Reception of *Faust* in Non-Christian Cultures" conference at McGill University in 2006 and publications such as Jochen Golz and Adrian Hsia's *Orient und Okzident. Zur Faustrezeption in nicht-christlichen Kulturen* (2008).[36] Other commemorative symposia, such as "A Work of Art of the Highest Artistic Order: Text and Context of Gustav Mahler's Eighth Symphony," presented by the National Arts Centre and Carleton University in 2010, further contribute to the currency of *Faust* in working cultural memory.

The recent upsurge of academic interest in globalization and modernization has been reflected in the invigoration of readings of *Faust* as a canonic emblem of modernity.[37] Thematically, the centrality of Faustian "amnesia" within the Goethean plot has contributed to the play's currency in working memory as representatively modern. Western commentators such as David Gross have observed that late modern culture evinces a "pronounced tilt toward present-centeredness":

> Our orientation today has increasingly become less diachronic and more synchronic (now even on a global scale), and hence we have lost much of our interest in the past, along with the reasons we once had for remembering it. . . . [W]e in the West have dramatically shifted our attention from the old to the new, and in the process have shown a willingness to throw out the old with hardly a second thought when it is judged to have lost its utility. . . . We seem persuaded now that in being too wedded to memory we only repeat but cannot initiate, whereas with forgetting we can become free, innovative, experimental, and multifaceted (if not necessarily "whole") human beings.[38]

Susannah Radstone and Bill Schwartz contend that the "current fascination—or even obsession—with memory is ineluctably associated with the idea of its absence, atrophy, collapse, or demise."[39] At the same time, they perceive an "unprecedented politicization of memory"—"memory has become the site of, or the sign for, many intersecting issues: the temporal imaginings of past, present, and future; subjectivity and identification; the passage from the inner life to the outer world; even the politics of being in the world and of recognition."[40]

A number of studies of Goethe's *Faust* have begun to explore the play's problematicization of memory. Fred Hagen and Ursula Mahlendorf link Faust's denial of memory to his denial of concern.[41] The resurrection of youthful memories, evoked by the sound of the Easter bells, counterpoise the Faustian self-destructiveness, whilst Faust's preparation for the pact includes "a curse on memory" for frustrating "his escape from life" and "haunting him with painful recollections of failure and suffering."[42] Faust is categorized as "pathological" in his attempts to deny concerns and memories that continue to haunt him involuntarily. Hagen and Mahlendorf posit Homunculus (chapter 9) as a memory-endowed "counter-image of Faust" who illustrates "what is required for salvation or transcendence of self: charity, commitment, and self-sacrifice."[43] Memory loss, to Hagen and Mahlendorf, is represented after the phases of sleep or unconsciousness that follow the protagonist's moments of failure. The authors conclude that Faust is perpetually forgetful, "from one moment to the next," the deaths of Philemon and Baucis, in the fifth act, being one of the tragic results of this.[44]

In *Goethe's Faust and European Epic: Forgetting the Future*, Arnd Bohm suggests that the Goethean *Faust* dramatizes an aspect of the modern "crisis of memory" that has arisen from the "dispersal of topics."[45] Bohm finds the "loss of systematic information storage and retrieval capacities" to be "nothing less than the collapse of the coherent memory system of the sciences."[46] Faust thus represents "modern man" in lacking a "reliable guide to the stored knowledge of the past," which renders him "disoriented, unable to remember the sorts of things that would have satisfied previous generations."[47] Given to the "amnesia" indicative of the melancholic, the protagonist is seen as a "gravely ill" modern departure from the classical epic hero, Odysseus—"Faust errs aimlessly because he wants to abandon the sites of memory, wants to forget what *he* learned from *his* father, and therefore will never be able to make productive use of his knowledge, will never arrive at his goal."[48]

Among other recent memory studies of *Faust*, Wolf-Daniel Hartwich considers Faust's "chronic oblivion" in relation to the redemptive role of remembrance in Christianity as well as research on amnesia from Goethe's epoch.[49] Hartwich identifies parallels between Goethe's depiction of Faust as "a great forgetter" and a case study of amnesia by Johann Werner Streithorst published by Goethe's friend Karl Philipp Moritz, who shared the dramatist's interest in mnemotechnics.[50] As Ulrich Gaier observes, Goethe perceived himself as a "collective being" and was quite interested in recording collective memory.[51] Nor should it be forgotten that Goethe was fascinated by the Sanskrit drama *Sakuntala*,[52] a canonic meditation on the problem of memory that remains but one outstanding example of the rich interculturality of the Goethean *Faust* interface.

* * *

The reception of Goethe's *Faust* presented in this book falls into relations of contiguity or similarity along a metonym/metaphor continuum ranging from preservationist criticism to transformational analogy. Chapter 1 comprises metacommentary on the Faustian contest with the authority of the word which foregrounds the iconoclastic memory crucial for the fissive metaphorical space of the canonic text. Similarly metonymic, whilst extending the scope of the mnemonic space to antiquity, chapter 2 traces the elusive Eternal-Feminine trope to figures such as that of Sophia. Chapter 3 engages the metaphorical turns of the Faustian in cultural memory of Herder. Chapter 4 examines Coleridge's ambivalent reception of *Faust* for both metonymic and metaphorical purposes in the form of translation and a prospectus for a Faust story by his own hand. Chapter 5 discusses a metaphorical turn away from the Goethean source to encode memory of the gauchos in a neglected Argentinean adaptation. Chapter 6 provides a comparative examination of two recent metonymic exercises in performance of the entire *Faust* in Germany. In contrast, chapter 7 illustrates the increasingly metaphorical and intercultural directions of recent Canadian reception of the drama. Chapter 8 examines avant-garde artist Werner Fritsch's metaphorical use of the Faustian to encode multicultural memory. Chapter 9 comprises a far-reaching interdisciplinary metacommentary exploring the pertinence of Goethe's *Faust* for advances in artificial intelligence. The book as a whole therefore extends our understanding of the multifarious and increasingly intercultural mnemonic functions of Goethe's canonic text.

NOTES

1. Johann Wolfgang von Goethe, *Faust: Texte,* vol. 7, pt. 1, *Sämtliche Werke. Briefe, Tagebücher und Gespräche,* ed. Albrecht Schöne (Frankfurt: Deutscher Klassiker Verlag, 2005) [hereafter *F*]. Translations, unless otherwise noted, are the author's.
2. Karl Shapiro, "The Progress of Faust," in *Lives of Faust: The Faust Theme in Literature and Music. A Reader,* ed. Lorna Fitzsimmons (Berlin and New York: De Gruyter, 2008), 479–80.
3. Gérard Genette defines transtextuality as "all that sets the text in a relationship, whether obvious or concealed, with other texts," *Palimpsests: Literature in the Second Degree,* trans. Channa Newmann and Claude Doubinsky (Lincoln: University of Nebraska Press, 1997), 1.
4. Johanna Drucker, for instance, suggests that a "book is an interface, so is a newspaper page, a bathroom faucet, a car dashboard, an ATM machine. An interface is not so much a 'between' space as it is the mediating environment that makes the experience, a 'critical zone that constitutes a user experience,'" "Humanities Approaches to Interface Theory," *Culture Machine* 12 (2011): 10, www.culturemachine.net (accessed August 15, 2011).
5. Maurice Halbwachs, *On Collective Memory,* ed. and trans. Lewis A. Coser (Chicago: University of Chicago Press, 1992), 119.
6. Jan Assmann, "Collective Memory and Cultural Identity," *New German Critique* 65 (1995): 132.
7. Patrick Greaney, "Estranging Memory in Ilse Aichinger," *German Quarterly* 80, no. 1 (2007): 42, 54.
8. Astrid Erll, "Cultural Memory Studies: An Introduction," in *A Companion to Cultural Memory Studies,* ed. Astrid Erll and Ansgar Nünning (Berlin and New York: De Gruyter, 2010), 2.

9. Renate Lachmann, *Memory and Literature: Intertextuality in Russian Modernism*, trans. Roy Sellars and Anthony Wall (Minneapolis and London: University of Minnesota Press, 1997), 15.

10. Marvin Carlson, *The Haunted Stage: The Theatre as Memory Machine* (Ann Arbor: University of Michigan Press, 2001), 2.

11. Oswald Spengler, *The Decline of the West*, trans. Charles Francis Atkinson, ed. Helmut Werner (Oxford: Oxford University Press, 1991), 97.

12. James B. Worthen and R. Reed Hunt, *Mnemonology: Mnemonics for the 21st Century* (New York and London: Psychology Press, 2011), 2.

13. Worthen and Hunt, *Mnemonology*, 2.

14. "Dialexeis," in *Memory in Historical Perspective: The Literature before Ebbinghaus*, ed. Douglas J. Herrmann and Roger Chaffin (New York and Berlin: Springer, 1988), 23; Frances A. Yates, *The Art of Memory* (Chicago: University of Chicago Press, 1966), 29–30.

15. Worthen and Hunt, *Mnemonology*, 38.

16. Yates, *The Art of Memory*, 30.

17. Cicero, *De oratore*, in *Memory in Historical Perspective*, 78.

18. See Mary Carruthers, "How to Make a Composition: Memory Craft in Antiquity and the Middle Ages," and Peter Sherlock, "The Reformation of Memory in Early Modern Europe," in *Memory: Histories, Theories, Debates*, ed. Susannah Radstone and Bill Schwarz (New York: Fordham University Press, 2010), 15–29, 30–40.

19. Yates, *The Art of Memory*, 3.

20. Worthen and Hunt, *Mnemonology*, 55–58.

21. Anonymous, *Ad Herennium*, in *Memory in Historical Perspective*, 90.

22. Justin L. Barrett and Melanie A. Nyhof, "Spreading Non-Natural Concepts: The Role of Intuitive Conceptual Structures in Memory and Transmission of Cultural Materials," *Journal of Cognition and Culture* 1, no. 1 (2001): 70.

23. See Pascal Boyer, *Religion Explained: The Evolutionary Origins of Religious Thought* (New York: Basic Books, 2001), 85; Pascal Boyer and Charles Ramble, "Cognitive Templates for Religious Concepts: Cross-Cultural Evidence for Recall of Counter-Intuitive Representations," *Cognitive Science* 25 (2001): 558; Michael H. Kelly and Frank C. Keil, "The More Things Change . . . : Metamorphoses and Conceptual Structure," *Cognitive Science* 9 (1985): 415; Barrett and Nyhof, "Spreading Non-Natural Concepts," 72, 83, 91.

24. See Boyer, *Religion Explained*, 79–80; Boyer and Ramble, "Cognitive Templates for Religious Concepts," 538; Barrett and Nyhof, "Spreading Non-Natural Concepts," 72.

25. D. Jason Slone, Lauren Gonce, Afzal Upal, Kristin Edwards, and Ryan Tweney, "Imagery Effects on Recall of Minimally Counterintuitive Concepts," *Journal of Cognition and Culture* 7 (2007): 357.

26. See Paul Connerton, *How Societies Remember* (Cambridge: Cambridge University Press, 1989), 54, 57; Roy A. Rappaport, *Ritual and Religion in the Making of Humanity* (Cambridge: Cambridge University Press, 1999), 23–41.

27. Rappaport, *Ritual and Religion in the Making of Humanity*, 31, 36, 39, 41.

28. Connerton, *How Societies Remember*, 54.

29. Connerton, *How Societies Remember*, 54.

30. Margaret Jane Kidnie suggests that "a play, for all that it carries the rhetorical and ideological force of an enduring stability, is not an object at all, but rather a dynamic *process* that evolves over time in response to the needs and sensibilities of its users," *Shakespeare and the Problem of Adaptation* (Abingdon and New York: Routledge, 2009), 2.

31. See Lachmann, *Memory and Literature*, 18, 32.

32. Aleida Assmann, "Canon and Archive," in *A Companion to Cultural Memory Studies*, 104–105.

33. Herbert Grabes, "Cultural Memory and the Literary Canon," in *A Companion to Cultural Memory Studies*, 311.

34. See Simon Richter, "Help from the Devil in Boosting Course Enrollments," *Chronicle of Higher Education*, July 14, 2000: A56.

35. Matt Copeland and Chris Goering, "Blues You Can Use: Teaching the Faust Theme through Music, Literature, and Film," *Journal of Adolescent and Adult Literacy* 46, no. 5 (2003): 439, 441.

36. Jochen Golz and Adrian Hsia, eds., *Orient und Okzident. Zur Faustrezeption in nicht-christlichen Kulturen* (Cologne: Böhlau, 2008).

37. See, for example, Hans Christoph Binswanger, *Money and Magic: A Critique of the Modern Economy in the Light of Goethe's Faust* (Chicago: University of Chicago Press, 1994); Franco Moretti, *Modern Epic: The World System from Goethe to García Márquez* (London: Verso, 1996); Ian Watt, *Myths of Modern Individualism: Faust, Don Quixote, Don Juan, Robinson Crusoe* (Cambridge and New York: Cambridge University Press, 1996); Ulrich Gaier, *Fausts Modernität* (Stuttgart: Reclam, 2000); Ludger Scherer, *"Faust" in der Tradition der Moderne: Studien zur Variation eines Themas bei Paul Valéry, Michel de Ghelderode, Michel Butor und Edoardo Sanguineti: Mit einem Prolog zur Thematologie* (Frankfurt and New York: Peter Lang, 2001); Osman Durrani, *Faust: Icon of Modern Culture* (Mountfield, East Sussex: Helm Information, 2004); Michael Jaeger, *Fausts Kolonie. Goethes kritische Phänomenologie der Moderne* (Würzburg: Verlag Königshausen and Neumann, 2004); "Faust in the 21st Century: Modernity, Myth, Theatre," conference, University of Toronto, 2004; Martin Swales,"Goethe's *Faust* and the Drama of European Modernity," *Publications of the English Goethe Society* 74 (2005): 83–94; John K. Noyes, "Goethe on Cosmopolitanism and Colonialism: *Bildung* and the Dialectic of Critical Mobility," *Eighteenth-Century Studies* 39, no. 4 (2006): 443–62; Arnd Bohm, *Goethe's "Faust" and European Epic: Forgetting the Future* (Rochester: Camden House, 2007); Michael Jaeger, *Global Player Faust, oder, Das Verschwinden der Gegenwart: Zur Aktualität Goethes* (Berlin: Wolf Jobst Siedler, Jr., 2008); Ulrich Gaier, "Helena, Then Hell: *Faust* as Review and Anticipation of Modern Times," *Goethe Yearbook* 17 (2010): 3–20; Hans Schulte, John Noyes, and Pia Kleber, eds., *Goethe's Faust: Theatre of Modernity* (Cambridge: Cambridge University Press, 2011). At the same time, current interest in postcolonialism and transcultural reception studies is reflected in the broadening and politicization of Faust studies within work on the international reception of *Faust*, such as Kimura Naoji, "Probleme der japanischen *Faust*-Übersetzung," *Goethe Jahrbuch* 105 (1993): 333–43; Adrian Hsia, ed., *Zur Rezeption von Goethes "Faust" in Ostasien* (Bern: Peter Lang Verlag, 1993); Anne Bohnenkamp, "Variationen eines Mythos: 'Faust' in Europa," in *Faust: Annäherung an einen Mythos*, ed. Frank Möbus,

Friederike Schmidt-Möbus, and Gerd Unverfehrt (Göttingen: Wallstein Verlag, 1996), 97–108; Galina Viktorovna Jakuševa, *Faust v iskušenijach XX veka: Gëtevskij obraz v russkoj i zarubežnoj literature* (Moscow: Nauka, 2005); Inez Hedges, *Framing Faust: Twentieth-Century Cultural Struggles* (Carbondale: Southern Illinois University Press, 2005); "Reception of Faust in Non-Christian Cultures," conference, McGill University, 2006; Paolo Orvieto, *Il mito de Faust. L'uomo, Dio, il diavolo* (Rome: Salerno, 2006); Michael Mitchell, *Hidden Mutualities: Faustian Themes from the Gnostic to the Postcolonial* (Amsterdam and New York: Rodopi, 2006); David Hawkes, *The Faust Myth: Religion and the Rise of Representation* (New York and Basingstoke: Palgrave Macmillan, 2007); Frederick Burwick and James C. McKusick, eds., *Faustus, from the German of Goethe. Translated by Samuel Taylor Coleridge* (Oxford: Oxford University Press, 2007); J. M. van der Laan, *Seeking Meaning for Goethe's* Faust (London and New York: Continuum, 2007); Golz and Hsia, eds., *Orient und Okzident. Zur Faustrezeption in nicht-christlichen Kulturen*; Marianneli Sorvakko-Spratte, *Der Teufelspakt in deutschen, finnischen und schwedischen Faust-Werken: Ein unmoralisches Angebot?* (Würzburg: Verlag Königshausen and Neumann, 2008); Lorna Fitzsimmons, ed., *International Faust Studies: Adaptation, Reception, Translation* (London and New York: Continuum, 2008); Paul Goetsch, *Machtphantasien in englishsprachigen Faust-Dichtungen: Funktionsgeschichtliche Studien* (Paderborn: Ferdinand Schöningh, 2008); Lea Marquart, *Goethes Faust in Frankreich: Studien zur dramatischen Rezeption im 19. Jahrhundert* (Heidelberg: Universitätsverlag Winter, 2009); and David G. John, *Bennewitz, Goethe,* Faust. *German and Intercultural Stagings* (Toronto: University of Toronto Press, 2011).

38. David Gross, *Lost Time: On Remembering and Forgetting in Late Modern Culture* (Amherst: University of Massachusetts Press, 2000), 134–35.

39. Susannah Radstone and Bill Schwartz, eds., "Introduction: Mapping Memory," in *Memory: Histories, Theories, Debates* (New York: Fordham University Press, 2010), 1.

40. Radstone and Schwartz, "Introduction: Mapping Memory," 2.

41. Fred Hagen and Ursula Mahlendorf, "Commitment, Concern and Memory in Goethe's *Faust*," *Journal of Aesthetics and Art Criticism* 21, no. 4 (1963): 475.

42. Hagen and Mahlendorf, "Commitment, Concern and Memory in Goethe's *Faust*," 475.

43. Hagen and Mahlendorf, "Commitment, Concern and Memory in Goethe's *Faust*," 477–78.

44. Hagen and Mahlendorf, "Commitment, Concern and Memory in Goethe's *Faust*," 479.

45. Arnd Bohm, *Goethe's "Faust" and European Epic: Forgetting the Future*, 213.

46. Bohm, *Goethe's "Faust" and European Epic*, 214.

47. Bohm, *Goethe's "Faust" and European Epic*, 215.

48. Bohm, *Goethe's "Faust" and European Epic*, 220, 222. Also see Bohm's reading of "Auerbachs Keller" as "memory theatre," 177–79.

49. Daniel Hartwich, "Amnesia and Anamnesis in Goethe's *Faust*," in *Goethe's Faust: Theatre of Modernity*, 68–77. Also see Harald Weinrich, *Lethe: The Art and Critique of Forgetting*, trans. Steven Rendall (Ithaca: Cornell University Press, 2004), 118–24; Dieter Borchmeyer, *Goethe, der Zeitbürger* (Munich: C. Hanser, 1999).

50. Hartwich, "Amnesia and Anamnesis in Goethe's *Faust*," 70–73.

51. Gaier, "Helena, Then Hell," 12.

52. See, for example, Ekbert Faas, "*Faust* and *Sacontalá*," *Comparative Literature* 31, no. 4 (1979): 367–91; Lalita Pandit, "Orientalism and Anxiety of Influence: Seeking *Sakuntula* in Goethe's *Faust*," *Journal of Commonwealth and Postcolonial Studies* 11, no. 1–2 (2004): 114–42.

BIBLIOGRAPHY

Anonymous. *Ad Herennium*. In Herrmann and Chaffin, *Memory in Historical Perspective*, 85–91.

Anonymous. "Dialexeis." In Herrmann and Chaffin, *Memory in Historical Perspective*, 23.

Assmann, Aleida. "Canon and Archive." In Erll and Nünning, *A Companion to Cultural Memory Studies*, 97–107.

Assmann, Aleida, and Sebastian Conrad, eds. *Memory in a Global Age: Discourses, Practices and Trajectories*. Basingstoke: Palgrave Macmillan, 2010.

Assmann, Jan. "Collective Memory and Cultural Identity." *New German Critique* 65 (1995): 125–33.

Barrett, Justin L., and Melanie A. Nyhof. "Spreading Non-natural Concepts: The Role of Intuitive Conceptual Structures in Memory and Transmission of Cultural Materials." *Journal of Cognition and Culture* 1, no. 1 (2001): 69–100.

Binswanger, Hans Christoph. *Money and Magic: A Critique of the Modern Economy in the Light of Goethe's Faust*. Chicago: University of Chicago Press, 1994.

Bohm, Arnd. *Goethe's "Faust" and European Epic: Forgetting the Future*. Rochester: Camden House, 2007.

Bohnenkamp, Anne. "Variationen eines Mythos: 'Faust' in Europa." In *Faust: Annäherung an einen Mythos*, edited by Frank Möbus, Friederike Schmidt-Möbus, and Gerd Unverfehrt, 97–108. Göttingen: Wallstein Verlag, 1996.

Borchmeyer, Dieter. *Goethe, der Zeitbürger*. Munich: C. Hanser, 1999.

Bowker, Geoffrey C. *Memory Practices in the Sciences*. Cambridge: MIT Press, 2005.

Boyer, Pascal. *Religion Explained: The Evolutionary Origins of Religious Thought*. New York: Basic Books, 2001.

Boyer, Pascal, and Charles Ramble. "Cognitive Templates for Religious Concepts: Cross-Cultural Evidence for Recall of Counter-Intuitive Representations." *Cognitive Science* 25 (2001): 535–64.

Burwick, Frederick, and James C. McKusick, eds. *Faustus, from the German of Goethe. Translated by Samuel Taylor Coleridge*. Oxford: Oxford University Press, 2007.

Carlson, Marvin. *The Haunted Stage: The Theatre as Memory Machine*. Ann Arbor: University of Michigan Press, 2001.

Carruthers, Mary. "How to Make a Composition: Memory Craft in Antiquity and the Middle Ages." In Radstone and Schwartz, *Memory: Histories, Theories, Debates*, 15–30.

Cicero, Marcus Tullius. *De oratore*. In Herrmann and Chaffin, *Memory in Historical Perspective*, 77–82.

Connerton, Paul. *How Societies Remember*. Cambridge: Cambridge University Press, 1989.

Copeland, Matt, and Chris Goering. "Blues You Can Use: Teaching the Faust Theme through Music, Literature, and Film." *Journal of Adolescent and Adult Literacy* 46, no. 5 (2003): 436–41.

Drucker, Johanna. "Humanities Approaches to Interface Theory." *Culture Machine* 12 (2011): 1–20. www.culturemachine.net (accessed August 15, 2011).

Durrani, Osman. *Faust: Icon of Modern Culture*. Mountfield, East Sussex: Helm Information, 2004.

Erll, Astrid, and Ansgar Nünning, eds. *A Companion to Cultural Memory Studies*. Berlin and New York: De Gruyter, 2010.

Faas, Ekbert. "*Faust* and *Sacontalá*." *Comparative Literature* 31, no. 4 (1979): 367–91.

"Faust in the 21st Century: Modernity, Myth, Theatre." Conference, University of Toronto, 2004.

Fitzsimmons, Lorna, ed. *International Faust Studies: Adaptation, Reception, Translation*. London and New York: Continuum, 2008.

——, ed. *Lives of Faust: The Faust Theme in Literature and Music. A Reader*. Berlin: De Gruyter, 2008.

Gaier, Ulrich. *Fausts Modernität: Essays*. Stuttgart: Reclam, 2000.

——. "Helena, Then Hell: *Faust* as Review and Anticipation of Modern Times." *Goethe Yearbook* 17 (2010): 3–20.

Genette, Gérard. *Palimpsests: Literature in the Second Degree*. Translated by Channa Newmann and Claude Doubinsky. Lincoln: University of Nebraska Press, 1997.

Goethe, Johann Wolfgang von. *Faust: Texte*. Vol. 7, pt.1, *Sämtliche Werke. Briefe, Tagebücher und Gespräche*. Edited by Albrecht Schöne. Frankfurt: Deutscher Klassiker Verlag, 2005.

Goetsch, Paul. *Machtphantasien in englishsprachigen Faust-Dichtungen: Funktionsgeschichtliche Studien*. Paderborn: Ferdinand Schöningh, 2008.

Golz, Jochen, and Adrian Hsia, eds. *Orient und Okzident. Zur Faustrezeption in nicht-christlichen Kulturen*. Cologne: Böhlau, 2008.

Grabes, Herbert. "Cultural Memory and the Literary Canon." In Erll and Nünning, *A Companion to Cultural Memory Studies*, 311–19.

Greaney, Patrick. "Estranging Memory in Ilse Aichinger." *German Quarterly* 80, no. 1 (2007): 42–58.

Gross, David. *Lost Time: On Remembering and Forgetting in Late Modern Culture*. Amherst: University of Massachusetts Press, 2000.

Hagen, Fred, and Ursula Mahlendorf. "Commitment, Concern and Memory in Goethe's *Faust*." *Journal of Aesthetics and Art Criticism* 21, no. 4 (1963): 473–84.

Halbwachs, Maurice. *On Collective Memory*. Edited and translated by Lewis A. Coser. Chicago: University of Chicago Press, 1992.

Hartwich, Wolf-Daniel. "Amnesia and Anamnesis in Goethe's *Faust*." In Schulte, Noyes, and Kleber, *Goethe's Faust: Theatre of Modernity*, 68–77.

Hawkes, David. *The Faust Myth: Religion and the Rise of Representation*. New York and Basingstoke: Palgrave Macmillan, 2007.

Hedges, Inez. *Framing Faust: Twentieth-Century Cultural Struggles*. Carbondale: Southern Illinois University Press, 2005.

Herrmann, Douglas J., and Roger Chaffin, eds. *Memory in Historical Perspective: The Literature before Ebbinghaus*. New York and Berlin: Springer, 1988.

Hsia, Adrian, ed. *Zur Rezeption von Goethes "Faust" in Ostasien*. Bern: Peter Lang Verlag, 1993.

Jaeger, M. *Fausts Kolonie. Goethes kritische Phänomenologie der Moderne*. Würzburg: Verlag Königshausen and Neumann, 2004.

——. *Global Player Faust, oder, Das Verschwinden der Gegenwart: Zur Aktualität Goethes*. Berlin: Wolf Jobst Siedler, Jr. , 2008.

Jakuševa, Galina Viktorovna. *Faust v iskušenijach XX veka: Gëtevskij obraz v russkoj i zarubežnoj literature*. Moscow: Nauka, 2005.

John, David. G. *Bennewitz, Goethe,* Faust. *German and Intercultural Stagings*. Toronto: University of Toronto Press, 2011.

Kelly, Michael H., and Frank C. Keil. "The More Things Change . . . : Metamorphoses and Conceptual Structure." *Cognitive Science* 9 (1985): 403–16.

Kidnie, Margaret Jane. *Shakespeare and the Problem of Adaptation*. Abingdon and New York: Routledge, 2009.

Lachmann, Renate. *Memory and Literature: Intertextuality in Russian Modernism*. Translated by Roy Sellars and Anthony Wall. Minneapolis and London: University of Minnesota Press, 1997.

Mahl, Bernd. *Goethes Faust auf der Bühne (1806–1998): Fragment, Ideologiestück, Spieltext*. Stuttgart: Metzler, 1999.

Marquart, Lea. *Goethes Faust in Frankreich: Studien zur dramatischen Rezeption im 19. Jahrhundert*. Heidelberg: Universitätsverlag Winter, 2009.

Mitchell, Michael. *Hidden Mutualities: Faustian Themes from Gnostic Origins to the Postcolonial*. Amsterdam and New York: Rodopi, 2006.

Moretti, Franco. *Modern Epic: The World System from Goethe to García Márquez*. London: Verso, 1996.

Nalantian, Suzanne, Paul M. Matthews, and James L. McClelland, eds. *The Memory Process: Neuroscientific and Humanistic Perspectives*. Cambridge: MIT Press, 2011.

Naoji, Kimura. "Probleme der japanischen *Faust*-Übersetzung." *Goethe Jahrbuch* 105 (1993): 333–43.

Noyes, John K. "Goethe on Cosmopolitanism and Colonialism: *Bildung* and the Dialectic of Critical Mobility." *Eighteenth-Century Studies* 39, no. 4 (2006): 443–62.

Olick, Jeffrey K., Vered Vinitzky-Seroussi, and Daniel Levy, eds. *The Collective Memory Reader*. Oxford: Oxford University Press, 2011.

Orvieto, Paolo. *Il mito de Faust. L'uomo, Dio, il diavolo*. Rome: Salerno, 2006.

Pandit, Lalita. "Orientalism and Anxiety of Influence: Seeking *Sakuntala* in Goethe's *Faust*." *Journal of Commonwealth and Postcolonial Studies* 11, no. 1–2 (2004): 114–42.

Radstone, Susannah, and Bill Schwartz, eds. *Memory: Histories, Theories, Debates*. New York: Fordham University Press, 2010.

Rappaport, Roy A. *Ritual and Religion in the Making of Humanity*. Cambridge: Cambridge University Press, 1999.

"Reception of Faust in Non-Christian Cultures." Conference, McGill University, 2006.

Richter, Simon. "Help from the Devil in Boosting Course Enrollments." *Chronicle of Higher Education*, July 14, 2000: A56.

Scherer, Ludger. *"Faust" in der Tradition der Moderne: Studien zur Variation eines Themas bei Paul Valéry, Michel de Ghelderode, Michel Butor und Edoardo Sanguineti: Mit einem Prolog zur Thematologie*. Frankfurt and New York: Peter Lang, 2001.

Schulte, Hans, John Noyes, and Pia Kleber, eds. *Goethe's Faust: Theatre of Modernity*. Cambridge: Cambridge University Press, 2011.

Shapiro, Karl. "The Progress of Faust." In Fitzsimmons, *Lives of Faust*, 479–80.

Sherlock, Peter. "The Reformation of Memory in Early Modern Europe." In Radstone and Schwartz, *Memory: Histories, Theories, Debates*, 30–40.

Simm, Hans-Joachim, and Christian Lux, eds. *Zweihundert Jahre Goethes "Faust."* Frankfurt: Insel Verlag, 2007.

Slone, D. Jason, Lauren Gonce, Afzal Upal, Kristin Edwards, and Ryan Tweney. "Imagery Effects on Recall of Minimally Counterintuitive Concepts." *Journal of Cognition and Culture* 7 (2007): 355–67.

Sorvakko-Spratte, Marianneli. *Der Teufelspakt in deutschen, finnischen und schwedischen Faust-Werken: Ein unmoralisches Angebot?* Würzburg: Verlag Königshausen and Neumann, 2008.

Spengler, Oswald. *The Decline of the West*. Translated by Charles Francis Atkinson. Edited by Helmut Werner. Oxford: Oxford University Press, 1991.

Swales, Martin. "Goethe's *Faust* and the Drama of European Modernity." *Publications of the English Goethe Society* 74 (2005): 83–94.

Van der Laan, J. M. *Seeking Meaning for Goethe's* Faust. London and New York: Continuum, 2007.

Watt, Ian. *Myths of Modern Individualism: Faust, Don Quixote, Don Juan, Robinson Crusoe*. Cambridge and New York: Cambridge University Press, 1996.

Weber, Albrecht. *Goethes "Faust" Noch und Wieder? Phänomene—Probleme—Perspektiven*. Würzburg: Verlag Königshausen and Neumann, 2005.

Weinrich, Harald. *Lethe: The Art and Critique of Forgetting*. Translated by Steven Rendall. Ithaca: Cornell University Press, 2004.

Worthen, James B., and R. Reed Hunt. *Mnemonology: Mnemonics for the 21st Century*. New York and London: Psychology Press, 2011.

Yates, Frances A. *The Art of Memory*. Chicago: University of Chicago Press, 1966.

1

The Faustian Contest with the Authority of the Word

Alan Corkhill

The "Night" ("Nacht") scene in Act I of Goethe's *Faust* offers an appropriate point of departure for a close textual and contextual reading of the ways in which the theological/ecclesiastical, epistemological, linguistic, legal, and gendered *auctoritas* of the written word is directly or implicitly critiqued at various junctures throughout the drama. The sites of contestation encompass primarily scholarly books, necromantic writings, sacred scripture, canon law, and the devil's pact. The drama also opens up perspectives on the reliability of written and non-verbal modes of communication, such as the physiognomic dependability of gestural and facial language. Faust three times over (*F*, 354–60)[1] is disenchanted from the outset with the dead weight of scholarly tradition, symbolized by the dusty manuscripts, parchments, and scrolls that vie for space with scientific paraphernalia within the cluttered confines of his gloomy study (*F*, 399–407). Unlike Marlowe's protagonist, Faust does not question the scholarly canon by naming the specific books to be consigned to oblivion.[2] Rather, the time-honored disciplines of philosophy, jurisprudence, medicine, and law themselves come under fire—first in the opening soliloquy (*F*, 354–56), and later in the "Freshman's Scene" ("Studierzimmer II"), that is to say, during Mephistopheles' satirical diatribe against academia (*F*, 1868–2049, esp. 1911–2036). Additionally, historiography is thrown into question when, in dialogue with Wagner, Faust derides the annals of history so revered by his doting famulus as the self-projections and self-inscriptions of individuals rather than the repository of cultural memory:

> My friend, for us the alluring times of old
> Are like a book that's sealed-up sevenfold.

And what you call the Spirit of the Ages
Is but the spirit of your learned sages,
Whose mirror is a pitiful affair

(Mein Freund, die Zeiten der Vergangenheit
Sind uns ein Buch mit sieben Siegeln;
Was ihr den Geist der Zeiten heißt,
Das ist im Grund der Herren eigner Geist,
In dem die Zeiten sich bespiegeln) (*F*, 575–79)

Far from viewing human history as a continuum of accumulating wisdom, Faust sees only chaos and disconnectedness in every direction. Faust appears petulantly iconoclastic at this point in the drama, perhaps with the express purpose of spiting his famulus. Yet, as the custodian, archivist, and transmitter of historical scholarship—however personally distasteful this calling has become—Faust participates, wittingly or unwittingly, in the maintenance and perpetuation of European cultural memory. One might add that *Faust II*, in particular, is all about the poetics of cultural memory through its charting of the iconography of mythical prehistory.

It could be argued that the Faustian impulse to abandon the hallowed halls of academe for power, wealth, worldly fame, and the promise of illicit knowledge (*Doctor Faustus*) and for the totality of experience (*Faust I*)[3] attests in part to an underlying fear of vocational obsolescence in the Republic of Scholars. Although neither text makes explicit mention of the revolution in print technology unleashed by Gutenberg's innovations with movable type, a topical undercurrent is the challenge posed by mass-produced and widely disseminated books to both the exclusivity of the (painstakingly copiable) illuminated manuscript and the academy's historically uncontested sole rights to intellectual ownership and exegetical analysis. Needless to say, advances in printing spawned a lay scribal culture that made serious inroads into a hierarchically organized orthodoxy of erudition. The upside of print hegemony was undoubtedly the provision of a more reliable repository for the documentation of historical truth than pre-literate oral cultures could ever have offered. A further advantage of reproducibility through print was the minimization, if not total elimination, of knowledge lost through the post-Reformation burning of heretical, blasphemous, or seditious writings.[4] Technically, then, Faustus' anguished biblioclasmic reflex to his impending doom, "I'll burn my books" (*DF*, V.ii.191), would have been to no avail.

As Lewis Mumford rightly states, "printing broke the class monopoly of the written word, and it provided the common man with a means of gaining access to the culture of the world."[5] Moreover, according to Marshall McLuhan, the ensuing process of sociological leveling was no less dramatic than the accompanying psychological changes occurring in the predominant representation systems of the late sixteenth and early seventeenth century.[6] In turn, the introduction of the cylinder printing press and the art of lithography had parallel ramifications for the status of books in the Age of Goethe.

While the sacrosanct nature of the print medium was something Goethe believed the Elizabethan world had highly prized ("Printing had been invented a century beforehand, and yet a book still seemed like a sacred object") ("Die Druckerkunst war schon über hundert Jahre erfunden; demohngeachtet erschien ein Buch noch als ein Heiliges"),[7] popular superstition in Marlovian times identified the duplicable book—one that was totally indistinguishable from the next—with devilish trickery.[8] It is noteworthy in this regard that the title of Spies' original chapbook *Historia von D. Johann Fausten* (1587), from which Marlowe borrowed so heavily, ascribes to the sorcerer Faustus the secondary appellation "black magician" ("*Schwarzkünstler*"). Significantly, this is also translatable as "printer," a user of black ink.

In the area of biblical scholarship, the print revolution of early modern England and Reformation Germany encouraged the rapid proliferation of Protestant writings such as vernacular Bibles, to which even moderately literate laity now gained ready access. The new technology facilitated a shift in the custodianship of the printed word by placing sacred texts in the hands of ordinary people, thereby opposing "the claims of the traditional ecclesiastical elite to control the meaning of the sacred words."[9] But technology was not the only threat to the entrenched interests of the practitioners of scriptural exegesis. Reformation divinity itself was instrumental in putting an end to the exclusivity of ecclesiastical scholasticism. It raised the vexed question as to whether the single meaning of the sacred text would continue to be mediated and revealed "by the Holy Spirit through the devotional life of the pious reader" or whether it would be henceforth "defined by the new class [created] by the print culture."[10]

Both Goethe's and Marlowe's response to this historical watershed is to theatricalize the ramifications of an emergent Lutheran hermeneutics designed to liberalize the theocratic interpretive practices of late medievalism.[11] Marlowe, for his part, uses Faustus' deliberate misreading of scripture, that is to say, his willful distortion of context in unfinished citations from the New Testament, to critique the arbitrariness of intuitive theological hermeneutics.[12] Subjectivism also underlies Faust's anthropological reconceptualization of logos as "Thought" ("*Sinn*"), "Power" ("*Kraft*"), and "Deed" ("*Tat*") (*F*, 1229–37) while he sets about transliterating the Hebrew original of St. John's account of the Creation Story into his native tongue. If Faustus, as one commentator suggests, is both a "bad Christian" and a "bad humanist,"[13] at least Goethe's Promethean heaven-stormer is hardly classifiable as the latter, having approached the notoriously difficult Gospel text with intellectual rigor and earnestness. By comparison, Marlowe's

Faustus comes across to the reader/critic as a superficial humanist whose inquisitiveness barely extends beyond a series of lame and largely rhetorical cosmological and metaphysical questions fired at and evasively answered by Mephistopheles (*DF*, I.iii.61–69; II.iii.31–75).[14]

Faust I is informed by a double historical frame of reference, given that the titular protagonist is at once a man of the Renaissance *and* a Goethean contemporary. Thus in addition to an exegetical problematic specific to (post-)Reformation theology, Faust's ad hoc redefinitions of the divine mysteries of the Inspired Word also mirror Kantian epistemological doubts about the knowability of a reality outside the realm of the senses.[15] At the same time, they intimate a solution to Kant's "*Erkenntniskrise*" ("crisis of knowledge") insofar as Faust's intuitive reading of John 1:1[16] is analogous to the German Romantics' trust in intuition and personal insight as a means of reconnecting with the *Dinge an sich*, the noumena beyond the reach of *Verstand* ("cognition").

Faust and his literary progenitor are equally one voice as empirical pantheists dedicated to the scientific analysis of the laws (*Gesetzmäßigkeiten*) governing the physical world. In this respect they seek the fingerprints of the divine predominantly in the Book of Nature rather than in holy writ or in the sealed books of history. Goethe describes such (partially) decodable hieroglyphics thus: "Behold, Nature is a living book, / Not understood, yet not incomprehensible" ("Sieh, so ist Natur ein Buch lebendig, / Unverstanden, doch nicht unverständlich").[17] Faustus, by contrast, trains his gaze outward on the heavens in order to "know the secrets of astronomy / Graven in the book of Jove's high firmament" (*DF*, III. Ch. 2–3). The breadth of vision captured by Faustus' inquiring scientific eye in the course of his aerial travels contrasts with the narrowness of ecclesiastic dogma encountered during the subsequent visit to the Roman Curia.

The anti-Papist tenor of Act III, which critics have attributed largely to Marlowe's alleged, if not totally proven, anti-Catholicism, encompasses not only the hegemonic politics of centralized ecclesiastical power and its suppression of German sovereignty (Faustus emerges as a fervent patriot in the manner of the Christian humanist Ulrich von Hutten); it is equally directed at the Roman Church's "superstitious books" (*DF*, III.i.114)—in all likelihood a reference to the privileging of the "authority apostolical" (*DF*, III.i.144) of canon law over the primordial auctoritas of the scriptural Word. Marlowe also satirizes the arbitrariness of synodic decrees (*DF*, III.i.106–7) orchestrated by the Council of Trent (1545–1563) at the behest of the Papal Prince to discredit and marginalize the Saxon usurper pope Bruno.

Faust I likewise contains several undercurrents of anti-Catholic polemics, poignantly exemplified by Gretchen's unquestioning surrender of her newly acquired jewelry to the Church thanks to the persuasive rhetoric of a "damned old parson" (*F,* 2814), or, in the "Witch's Kitchen" ("Hexenküche"), by the parodic mimicry of the Gradual of the Mass as a book of magic is carried in Procession, flanked by apes as torchbearers substituting for acolytes (*F,* stage directions between 2531 and 2532).

NECROMANTIC WRITINGS AND INCANTATIONS

By privileging a necromantic knowledge base identifiable with "appearance, change and deceit," over a scholastic orthodoxy of "sic probo" (*DF,* I.i.2) predicated on "substance, permanence and truth,"[18] the renegade Wittenberg sage enters dangerous, unchartered waters. Faustus' thirst for unprocessed knowledge might have been quenched by the study of Hermetic and Cabbalist writing, yet even prior to the sealing of a covenant with the powers of darkness, Faustus finds himself drawn almost irresistibly to the esotericism of books of magic, most notably to the coded semiotics of their "[l]ines, circles, letters, characters—" (*DF,* I.i.51). Just as Faustus' predilection for Latin phraseology over the vernacular could be said to constitute an in-principle stand against the march of secular culture, so mastery of these signifiers may well compensate psychologically for the power and authority wielded by books prior to their commodification in a democratized marketplace. Ironically, Faustus' learned authority is undermined by the facility of less educated figures like the clown Robin, who learn magic from a conjuring book. In Renaissance and Reformation Europe the fear of magic "descending to the popular level" was shared by magi and astrologers alike, who considered the "rich and evocative" symbolic language of their trade the sole preserve of "a few highly literate and learned scholars."[19]

Faust's exemplar for engagement with the world of magic is an (unnamed) "secret book / From Nostradamus' very hand" ("geheimnisvolle Buch, / Von Nostradamus eigner Hand") (*F,* 419–20), whose "sacred sign[s]" ("*heil'gen Zeichen*") (*F,* 427) he now sets about deciphering in a Swedenborgian bid to commune with the spirit kingdom. That the Wittenberg professor should seek inspiration from yet another book, having disparaged the written word, seems self-contradictory. Yet this is no ordinary tome, for it contains "etchings which, unlike words, seem to him complete . . . and without ambiguity."[20] Whereas Marlowe's Good Angel cautions Faustus not to gaze at the "damnèd book" (*DF,* I.i.69) of charms lest it tempt his soul, Faust knows of no metaphysical harm that could accrue to his person from the optical lure of the strange lines and shapes on the book's pages. The Sign of the Macrocosm holds a sensory appeal not dissimilar to Faustus' bewitchment by the aesthetics of "[l]ines, circles, letters, characters" (*DF,* I.i.51) in books of conjuration and invocation.

Uppermost in Faust's mind at this juncture is the desire to fathom "Nature's wisdom" ("Und wenn Natur dich unterweist") (*F*, 423) and "[t]he hidden drive" ("*geheimnisvolle[n] Trieb*") (*F*, 437) of "Nature's force" ("*Kräfte der Natur*") (*F*, 438) from signs and signifiers indecipherable via "dusty logic" ("*trocknes Sinnen*") (*F*, 423). This is consonant with the *ratio* tenet of sixteenth-century Humanism and the eighteenth-century Enlightenment. Yet the Sign reveals a Platonic sphere of holistic ideality that for mortals trapped in the world of appearance, Kant's "*Erscheinungswelt*," is tantamount to a spectacle; hence Faust's exclamation: "O endless pageant!—But a pageant still, / A show, that mocks my touch or grasp or will!" ("Welch Schauspiel! aber ach! ein Schauspiel nur! / Wo fass'ich dich, unendliche Natur?") (*F*, 454–55). In the German original the noun "*Schauspiel*" (454) conveys the double meaning of theater and visual game. While the tricks that appearance (*Schein*) plays on the senses constitute an existential and epistemological quandary for Goethe's introspective protagonist, Marlowe's more extraverted, puppet-show necromancer thrives on theatricality and showmanship during the four-and-twenty years of "pleasure and . . . dalliance" (*DF*, III.i.61) at his disposal.

The agendas of both Faust figures differ markedly in relation to the employment of black and white magic as a means to an end. In Marlowe's play the professional sorcerers Valdes and Cornelius tempt Faustus into devoting his oral skills of disputation and *eloquentia* to a more self-serving cause than the mere advancement of higher learning (*DF*, I.i.130–37).

Faustus, as we know, turns his new facility to base ends at the papal court. The litany of curses chanted by the Vatican clergy to ward off the evil spirits that have thrown their patronal festival into sheer disarray (*DF*, III.iii.95–106) proves futile. Marlowe seems to be taking a satirical swipe at the hegemonic authority and efficacy of liturgical language. In the Middle Ages a litany of curses was regarded as particularly useful against magic users because it robbed them of their spell-casting abilities. Yet in this scene it fails to counter a very potent form of devilish witchcraft.

Faust, for his part, does not treat magic and the language-games that activate it as an (aesthetic) end in itself. In fact, he exhibits no interest in dabbling in the "concealèd arts" (*DF*, I.i.101), never allowing himself to be initiated into the rites and rituals of magic by his satanic companion. In the "Witch's Kitchen" he watches in cynical bemusement as the magic potion is brewed to the accompaniment of the hag's One-Times-One incantation (*F*, 2540–42), a pseudo-form of "mathematical" magic (Agrippa) performed in gibberish. Of course, the rejuvenating "juice" ("*Saft*") (*F*, 2519) does take effect, but Faust has learned via "Squire Satan" ("Junker Satan") (*F*, 2504) that there are more natural and honest, if more strenuous, ways of stripping away the years.[21] Yet clearly by the end of Part Two, Faust's integrity has been severely tainted, however involuntarily, by magical practice.

His grandiose land reclamation projects, which rely for their implementation on the primacy of a male-centered language of control and coercion ("The master's word alone gives weight" ["Des Herren Wort es gibt allein Gewicht"]) (*F*, 11502), have sacrificed the lives of the dispossessed elderly cottagers Philemon and Baucis (*F*, 11239–40), and only the approach of his own death elicits from him a remorseful abjuration of all forms of sorcery (*F*, 11405–6; 11423).

PLEDGES, OATHS, AND DEEDS OF "TRUST"

The signed and sealed pact between both sets of parties raises multifaceted issues of authority over which Faustian scholarship has spilled much ink.[22] Central to the argumentation of this chapter is the degree to which the spoken/written binarism plays out in terms of the legality and the morality of the transaction. Were a legally binding and enforceable agreement of purchase and sale to be drawn up, as Nishan Swais has ingeniously done in redrafting in contemporary legalese the terms and stipulations negotiated in each play,[23] the loopholes and contradictions of the covenants would become more transparent. This is particularly so in *Faust* where the vagueness and linguistic ambiguity of the exchanged pledges enable the octogenarian to escape damnation on a series of technicalities.

In *Faust I* an oral wager or bet replaces the deed of gift, one that stipulates no given length of service for Mephistopheles. Instead, the expiration of the employment agreement[24] and the accompanying surrender of Faust's soul are made contingent upon the arrival of a hazily and arbitrarily defined "beautiful moment" of total self-completion ("Werd' ich zum Augenblicke sagen: / Verweile doch! du bist so schön!") (*F*, 1699–1700). When Faustus at the end of his twenty-four years of riotous living is suddenly made acutely conscious of the dreaded hour of reckoning, it is because he harbors no doubts as to the enforceability of the pact's binding clauses which he solemnly recites (*DF*, II.i.105–111) as though swearing an oath in a court of law.[25] Not so with the less superstition-prone Faust who, as both a forward-looking Reformation humanist and a proxy Enlightenment progressive, refuses to take the pact seriously from the very start. His minimalist approach to legal formalities is evidenced by his preference for an oral pledge, a so-called gentlemen's agreement, over a formal promissory note. In short, Faust respects the spirit of the understanding over the letter.[26] Yet ironically, his indignation at Mephistopheles' unwillingness to strike a bargain solely on the strength of his word of honor (*F*, 1717) proves unwarranted, for it is not the devil, a legendary trickster, who ultimately reneges on the purchase deal.

Mephistopheles' fallback position is the acceptance of "any scrap of paper" ("Ist doch ein jedes Blättchen gut") (*F*, 1736), as long as it is signed.

Since it would not be in the devil's interests to risk any transaction for the purchase of his victim's soul that was not absolutely watertight, one might query the motive for Mephistopheles' casualness and obliging bonhomie at this critical juncture. Arguably, it is predicated on a fatalistic acquiescence in the undefeatability of the cosmic wager initiated by the Lord in the "Prologue in Heaven" ("Prolog im Himmel") to safeguard his beloved "servant" ("*Knecht*") (*F*, 299) from everlasting damnation. Such a safe bet could be formalized in writing, but the Lord chooses not to bind his adversary in this way. Marlowe's devil, on the other hand, is quick to exploit ruthlessly the reprobate's wish for the verbal renewal of the purchase contract in exchange for the object of his "heart's desire" (*DF*, V.i.86). If Mephistopheles is outmaneuvered by the angelic host in his attempt to claim Faust's soul (*F*, 11825–31), Marlowe's succubus becomes the final means of Faustus' irreversible, eternal perdition.

A cavalier attitude to legalities is nowhere more pronounced than in the scene "Neighbour's House" ("Der Nachbarin Haus"), where Faust's "word of honor" is tainted by his complicity in Mephistopheles' lies over the alleged death of Martha's husband in Padua and the absence of an inheritance and certificate of death. The untrustworthiness of a spoken testimony is epitomized by the sophist's utter fabrication of the dying man's last words. However, it is the moral questionability of Mephistopheles' verbal fiction that irks Faust most of all, as evidenced by his unwillingness to perjure himself (*F*, 3039) in bearing false witness (Exodus 20:16).

But to return to the original pact, the signing of which constitutes an enactment of far greater gravitas for Marlowe than for Goethe, Faust sardonically proposes several methods of making his mark, including etching into bronze or chiseling into marble (*F*, 1731–32). Whereas Goethe's Mephistopheles demands a signature in blood on the deed of trust—ironically, a finite and thus theoretically retractable record of transaction given the perishability of parchment—Marlowe's gives the vendor no choice in the matter.[27] The bloodletting is patently a blasphemous transgression against Christ's injunction, "This is my blood of the new covenant that is being poured out for many people for the forgiveness of sins" (Matthew 26:28). On the other hand, the Goethean option of a testament in stone is a discreet allusion to the tablets of stone Moses received on Mount Sinai (Exodus 31:18) to perpetuate the (old) covenant betwixt Yahweh and his (chosen) people (Genesis 17:7)—the Word made law as opposed to the Word made flesh.

The ritual shedding of blood in *Doctor Faustus* has received a good deal of scholarly attention,[28] but one perspective has been all but ignored, namely the nexus between the coagulation of blood in Faustus' arm ("My blood congeals, and I can write no more") (*DF*, II.i.62) and what we might call graphophobia. This phenomenon pertains literally to a fetishized angst over writing in one's own hand and is not necessarily linked to creative paralysis or writer's block (scriptophobia).[29] But it can equally signal a dread of commitment to a course of action of ethical questionability. The latter scenario certainly underlies Faustus' uneasy inkling that the "staying" of his blood is a "portend" (*DF*, II.i.64) of moral self-imperilment. The visual corroboration of a taint of sin is the inscription "Homo, fuge!" (*DF*, II.i.77), which appears on his arm and vanishes without trace. In Christian demonology the diabolical imprint, a counterpart to the biblical mark of Cain, was an indelible mark inscribed by Satan or any other demon on the flesh of those who had entered into a pact with the denizens of hell. Goethe's Mephistopheles does not resort to this "branding" ritual as an extra insurance policy against the vendor defaulting on the deal. Faust's autographobic complex has little to do with moral or theological scruples. Rather, the vendor's reluctance to negotiate a non-verbal agreement is more indicative of an existential and epistemological resistance to textuality ("The word expires, in passing to the pen") ("Das Wort erstirbt schon in der Feder") (*F*, 1728).

AUTHORITY AND THE CRITIQUE OF LANGUAGE

Both playwrights import a linguistic and semiotic dimension to the issue of the efficacy of the written and spoken word: the questionable capacity of language to represent, describe, or express the signified accurately. Goethe turns this problematic into a recurring subtext that reflects the wider trajectory of the ongoing philosophy-of-language debates of his own day, such as those spearheaded by Condillac, Herder, Hamann, and Friedrich Schlegel.[30] *Faust* criticism has focused largely on the improvised re-translation of John 1:1 as a crucial starting point for interrogating the disjuncture between language and meaning. The logocentric or hermetic view of language that ideas exist outside the language we use to articulate them was not a formalized discourse in either Marlowe's or Goethe's era. However, there is a noteworthy correlation between poststructuralist signification theory, according to which words refer only to other words (Derrida), and Faust's linguistic predicament as he attempts to define his religiosity (or lack thereof) to his God-fearing paramour in "Martha's Garden II" ("Marthens Garten"). Here Gretchen's interrogation of his Christian convictions is countered by Faust's denial of a single concept of faith to which words might give adequate meaning, if indeed any. The issue is not simply a theological one: the preference for heterodoxy over orthodoxy ("Give it what name you will") ("Nenn' es dann wie du willst") (*F*, 3453). The naming process has linguistic implications besides. The inter-referentiality of language (Derrida) is evidenced by a string of random, interchangeable synonyms ("joy," "heart," "love," "God") ("Glück! Herz! Liebe! Gott!") (*F*, 3454), serving as surrogates for an indefinable concept of faith.[31]

Faust's skepticism toward naming ("Names are but noise and smoke") ("Name ist Schall und Rauch") (*F*, 3457) is rearticulated in the witch's incantation ritual during the brewing of the rejuvenation potion. Here the critique of language is entrusted to Mephistopheles: "And when the people hear a sounding word / They stand convinced that somewhere there's a meaning" ("Gewöhnlich glaubt der Mensch, wenn er nur Worte hört, / Es müsse sich dabei doch auch was denken lassen") (*F*, 2565–66). Mephistopheles effectively reiterates Derrida's deconstructivist approach to signification: the idea that we think only in signs and that consequentially words refer to other words rather than functioning as metalinguistic descriptors of meaning-producing concepts. Whereas Marlowe's Faustus is less conspicuously bothered about the communicability of language systems than his Goethean counterpart, integral to both texts is an ethically founded concern over the potentiality of language to distort or fabricate "truth" and to blur the boundaries between reality and appearance.

In *Faust* the power of language to shape and transform is not solely a male prerogative, as the witch's necromantic praxis clearly confirms. It also holds true for the revelries of the witches' Sabbath ("Walpurgisnacht") and for Gretchen's intercessional function in the operatic finale of Part Two. By comparison, in Marlowe the female voice is all but silent. Whereas the only utterance emanating from Marlowe's "she"-devil is the crude aurality of the "suck[ing] forth" (*DF*, V.i.97) of Faustus' soul, Goethe accords Helen of Troy a considerable speaking role. However, in contradistinction to Scheherazade whose storytelling serves as an exemplum of creative empowerment over narration, Helena's récit is largely confined to the reconstruction of her own story (oral history), supplemented by the testimony of the chorus (biography). For all that, in both plays the female voice is essentially barred from the symbolic order of male scribal authority. The orality of women's language is such that Gretchen's cultural literacy is confined to knowledge of the breviary and prayer book, while her singing/recitation of folkloric ballads (*F*, 2759–82; 3374–409) attests to an immersion in oral tradition. Although recreational reading by literate women increased toward the end of the sixteenth century, patriarchy subsumed popular fiction under forbidden books on the spurious grounds "that from secular literature, especially romances, [women] would learn promiscuity."[32]

BEYOND WORDS: THE METALANGUAGE OF PERFORMATIVITY

An offshoot of linguistic discourse that is decidedly more pronounced in Goethe's drama than in *Doctor Faustus* is the metalanguage of bodily appearance. Such is Faustus' aesthetic aversion to Mephistopheles' hideous looks during the initial encounter that he commands the devil to return in the guise of a Franciscan friar (*DF*, I.iii.26–27). We might then quite justifiably view the substitution of a drag queen for the regal "face that launched a thousand ships" (*DF*, V.i.94) as a vengeful quid pro quo.

In *Faust I* the trope of physical appearance can be read within the topical context of physiognomics. In short: what can gestures and facial expressions tell us about the character or (emotional) disposition of others, and how scientifically or morally reliable is this metalanguage? Gretchen is the principal mouthpiece for physiognomic typecasting, instinctively recoiling as she does from the sinister omnipresence of Mephistopheles whose inner being she purports to be able to read like a book: "One sees he cares for nothing: it stands forth / Writ on his forehead, clear as on a scroll, / That he can never love a living soul" ("Man sieht, daß er an nichts keinen Anteil nimmt; / Es steht ihm an der Stirn' geschrieben, / Daß er nicht mag eine Seele lieben") (*F*, 3488–90). Physiognomics was a fringe science that had fluctuated in popularity since its adoption by Hellenistic philosophers. Having fallen into disrepute during the Middle Ages, the discipline was given a new lease on life by the Renaissance scholar Giambattista della Porta (1535–1615), who argued in his book *De humana physiognomia* (1586) against the ancient and medieval astrological view of a stellar influence on appearance and character. The perceived correlation between temperament and physical makeup was pursued further by the Swiss pastor Johann Kaspar Lavater (1741–1801), an early friend and collaborative partner of Goethe. Lavater's findings were published in 1772 in a series of essays.

It is noteworthy by way of comparison that Maximilian Klinger introduces an artisan community of self-proclaimed physiognomists into the narrative of his prose romance *Fausts Leben, Thaten und Höllenfahrt* (*Faustus: His Life, Death, and Doom*) (1791) as a parodic foil. While the conjectured legibility of the soul proves accurate in the case of the beautiful physician's daughter whose eyes are construed as "the very mirror of chastity,"[33] the misreading of the Devil's character on the strength of phrenological data makes a mockery of the dependability of physiognomic evaluation:

> PHYSIOGNOMIST. Permit me, with my measure, to ascertain the height of your brow? Yes; I see unshaken courage in that forehead, as clearly as I do steadfast friendship, fidelity, love of God and man, in those lips. What a nobleness in the whole! Thy face is the physiognomy of an extraordinary man, who thinks deeply, who holds fast to whatever he undertakes, works, flies, triumphs, finds few men in whom he will confide, but many who will rely on him.[34]

In both plays language as performance accounts for a noticeable shift from the scholastic study of words to their enactment. With Goethe the reorientation is much more protracted and is only really discernible in Part Two, where Faust seeks fame via a culture of action (*F*, 10188). Marlowe's figure, not unlike his forebear in the *Historia*, is content to prostitute *curiositas* to the performance of coarse tricks and tomfoolery more reminiscent of the alleged sorcery and miracle-working of the historical Dr. Georg (later Johann) Faust (ca. 1480–ca. 1540), a celebrity entertainer at fairs and royal courts. Faust, on the other hand, remains consistently aloof from and at times contemptuous of Mephistopheles' quackery and charlatanic practices.[35]

Faustus' increasingly audacious performance antics move the focus away from a written/spoken binarism to scenarios in which non-verbal performativity not only eclipses or even supplants iterative speech acts but is equally "seen" to be a more exact measure of trustworthiness than the power of words alone. A case in point is the Emperor's insistence that the "learnèd Faustus" (*DF*, IV.i.10) provide firsthand evidence of his reputedly wondrous skills before the assembled court.[36] The dumb show in which the ghosts of Helen of Troy, Alexander the Great, and the Persian warrior Darius are raised attests to the extraordinary "magic art" (*DF*, IV.i.11) of the renowned "German conjurer" (*DF*, IV.i.9). The unfolding pantomime is an aesthetic illusion, a performative commemoration of ancient history in which gestural language, substituting for speech, enacts on stage the violent and passionate emotions of the silent players.

Faustus' command of magic is not confined to resurrecting the dead, but extends to paralyzing the speech function of others, such as the impish act of silencing the horse-courser, the carter, and the clowns Robin and Dick (*DF*, IV.iv.110–20). By contrast, in *Faust I and II* word magic relates predominantly to the aesthetics of sonority, be it Gretchen's susceptibility to the beguiling flow of her paramour's speech (*F*, 3398–99) or Helena's surrender to the intoxicating rhythms of the foreign tongue in which the medieval knight woos her (*F*, 9365–71).[37] In both instances orality functions as the guarantor of moral trustworthiness. It is worthy of note that, compared to *Faust I*, Part Two privileges oral culture over book knowledge. Although the mythological spaces Faust enters on his odyssey into the ancient world (Acts II and III) are not populated by pre-literate figures, no mention is ever made of specific books or other written records. Nevertheless, at the beginning of Act II Goethe juxtaposes the rich orality of Homeric poetics with the pragmatic literacy of the brave new world of futuristic genetic engineering. The Baccalaureus, whom Mephistopheles had once "lectured" on the flaws in the epistemology of scholastic jargon (*F*, esp. 1993–2002) and who is now a member of Wagner's laboratory team, appears to have taken earnest heed of this counsel. Indeed, the headstrong researcher impresses upon his erstwhile academic advisor the untenability of linguistic ambiguity or dialectical rhetoric for the empirical sciences (*F*, 6738–39).[38] Implicit in his sharp rebuke of humanist logicians ("We sharpen wits in quite another style") ("Wir passen nun ganz anders auf") (*F*, 6740) is a deconstructivist critique of the content and methodologies of the Western scholastic canon. Mephistopheles had himself ("Studierzimmer II") attributed the bankruptcy of orthodox wisdom to the outworn pedagogy of learned professors who "never deviate[d] from the book" ("Daß er nichts sagt, als was im Buche steht") (*F*, 1961), thereby failing to push back the frontiers of knowledge. Undoubtedly, Faustus had "deviated" from his tools of trade through an outright rejection of them, but even so his swapping of one mode of bookishness (scholastic) for another (necromantic) inevitably proves to be existentially, morally, and culturally retrogressive. As for the so-called progressiveness of new generation science, Mephistopheles' complicity in the creation of Homunculus in the laboratory suggests that the clonability of the human species is no less diabolical a procedure than is the superstition-bound duplication of printed books.

OUTCOMES

This chapter suggests that a central concern of both Goethe's *Faust I and II* and Marlowe's *The Tragical History of Doctor Faustus* is the reliability, power, and value of the written word, which encompasses the pact, scholarly works, magical books, Scripture, and canon law. Equally, both playwrights contest the linguistic and ethical trustworthiness of speech. In order to contextualize these trajectories I have attempted to account for the various ways in which the respective moral, theological/ecclesiastical, epistemological, legal, and gender-exclusive authority of the word is directly or implicitly critiqued. I have linked a close reading of text-specific issues of spoken and written communication to the broader social and cultural discourses in which they are historically embedded (e.g., sixteenth-century superstition and sorcery, the post-Gutenbergian democratization of book knowledge, or the eighteenth-century scholarly debate on oral versus literary traditions in the context of language theory), as well as to more recent critical positions on logocentrism (Derrida), graphophobia, orality, and literateness.

Both Goethe and Marlowe were born into times of historically significant upheavals: the astronomical heresy of Copernicus and the Gutenbergian communications revolution on the one hand, and the French Revolution and the Kantian epistemological revolution on the other. The questioning of hegemonic orthodoxy in every quarter emboldens both Fausts to stand their ground against Satan's ambassador, indeed to "reason" with the Devil's Advocate as erudite and highly literate mortals even at the risk of eternal perdition. Not only is knowledge shown to be equitable with power in both plays, the mastery of the spoken and written word equally sets Marlowe's

Faustus apart from the underclasses as yet untouched by the proliferation of print and thus unable from their unenlightened default position of ignorance and superstition to contest the Devil's rhetoric and scriptural authority and to throw the proverbial ink-pot at him. In turn, the fearlessness of Goethe's Faust toward Mephistopheles, with whom admittedly the quester enjoys a protracted earthly "co-existence," derives in considerable measure from the knowledge and confidence that his rhetorical skills are a match for, even superior to, his adversary's. In the end, he is saved from eternal hell fires not merely upon divine intervention, but arguably on a verbal and written technicality as well.

NOTES

1. Johann Wolfgang von Goethe, *Faust. Part One,* trans. Philip Wayne (Hammondsworth: Penguin, 1949), and *Faust. Part Two,* trans. Philip Wayne (Hammondsworth: Penguin, 1962). *Faust: Texte,* vol. 7, pt. 1, *Sämtliche Werke. Briefe, Tagebücher und Gespräche,* ed. Albrecht Schöne (Frankfurt: Deutscher Klassiker Verlag, 2005) [hereafter *F*].

2. Doctor Faustus' first soliloquy positions him as an intellectual iconoclast, a rebel against medieval scholasticism and an upholder of the Renaissance's spirit of free inquiry (*curiositas*). Hardly surprising, then, is Faustus' disillusionment with the limitations of the written word, whether it be Jerome's Vulgate Bible or Aristotle's logic, the mathematics of Galen or the jurisprudential treatises of the Byzantine emperor Justinian. See Christopher Marlowe, *Doctor Faustus,* ed. David Bevington and Eric Rasmussen (Manchester: University of Manchester Press, 1993), I.i.1–36 [hereafter *DF*].

3. Goethe wrote in defense of the experiential realm over oratory and book knowledge, for which his famulus Wagner displays a pedantic predilection in *Faust I*: "Trust in life; it teaches better than the orator or the book" ("Glaube dem Leben; es lehrt besser als Redner und Buch" (my translation). Johann Wolfgang von Goethe, *Neunundzwanzig Distichen,* vol. 1, *Werke. Weimarer Ausgabe in 143 Bänden,* ed. Paul Raabe (Munich: dtv., 1987), 352. Marlowe's Wagner, hardly more than a boy, is a sketchy and limited figure in the play. The sum total of wisdom that he requires for goodly living is unlikely to exceed the precepts of the Book of Common Prayer which he quotes in paraphrase (*DF,* I.ii.27–28). Goethe's Wagner, on the other hand, has far greater personal ambitions: "I've learnt a deal, made books my drink and meat, / But cannot rest till knowledge is complete" ("Mit Eifer hab'ich mich der Studien beflissen; / Zwar weiß ich viel, doch möcht'ich alles wissen") (*F,* 600–1).

4. The topicality of biblioclasm is self-evident. Pope Leo personally supervised the consignment of Luther's works to the flames at the Diet of Worms in 1521, while Giordano Bruno's unwillingness to recant the charge of heresy brought against him resulted in the ecclesiastical authorities torching both the heretic and his books at the stake in early 1600. Goethe also makes mention in *Faust I* of historical martyrs burned to death for daring to voice unorthodox truths (*F,* 590–93).

5. Lewis Mumford, "The Invention of Printing," in *Communication in History: Technology, Culture, Society*, ed. David Crowley and Paul Heyer (New York: Longman, 1999), 88. For all that, Marlowe's allegorical figure Envy, presented in the guise of an illiterate commoner, remonstrates: "I cannot read, and therefore wish all books burned" (*DF*, II.iii.137).

6. Marshall McLuhan, *The Gutenberg Galaxy: The Making of Typographic Man* (Toronto: University of Toronto Press, 1962), 28.

7. Johann Wolfgang von Goethe, "*Maximen und Reflexionen*," vol. 9, *Gedenkausgabe der Werke, Briefe und Gespräche*, ed. Ernst Beutler (Zurich and Stuttgart: Artemis, 1948–1971), no. 252, 523. My translation.

8. The superstitious association of books with sorcery and demonism has been commented on by, among others, Sarah Wall-Randell, "*Doctor Faustus* and the Printer's Devil," *Studies in English Literature 1500–1900* 48, no. 2 (2008): 261–62.

9. David Lochhead, "Technology and Interpretation: A Footnote to McLuhan," http://www.religion-research.org/irtc/martin.htm (accessed February 23, 2009).

10. Lochhead, "Technology and Interpretation."

11. Luther termed his biblical hermeneutics *sola scriptura*, by which he meant an interpretive method that was not reliant on external commentaries. According to Kevin Sharpe and Steven N. Zwicker, *Reading, Society and Politics in Early Modern England* (New York and Cambridge: Cambridge University Press, 2003): "For the literate and learned [during the Protestant Reformation] the Bible became not only an authority, but a text to be edited, emended, retranslated, glossed, interrogated and, in fine, deconstructed" (4).

12. The most widely discussed of these passages is the syllogism (*DF*, 39–47) Faustus constructs around the half-verse "the wages of sin are death" (Romans 6: 23), one that conveniently neglects its corollary "but the gift of God is eternal life in Christ Jesus our Lord" (ibid.).

13. Bevington and Rasmussen, introduction to *Doctor Faustus*, 17.

14. See, for example, H. W. Matalene, "Marlowe's *Faustus* and the Comforts of Academicism," *Journal of English Literary History* 39, no. 4 (1972): "To Faust, books are not to be read; they are proposed for a ritual to make you feel smart. And the Bible turns out to be just another book to skim and put down" (507).

15. See on the link between Kantian epistemology and the problematic of language in *Faust I* Alan Corkhill, "Sprachphilosophische Fragestellungen in Goethes *Faust I*," *Neophilologus* 79, no. 3 (1995): 452, 453, and 462.

16. Faust is described by Durrani as coming increasingly "to rely . . . on his own intuition . . . and [to] resort to new renderings." Osman Durrani, *Faust and the Bible: A Study of Goethe's Use of Scriptural Allusions and Christian Religious Motifs in Faust I and II* (Berne: Peter Lang, 1977), 60.

17. Goethe, *Sendeschreiben*, vol. 2, *Werke. Weimarer Ausgabe*, 191. In *Wilhelm Meisters Lehrjahre* (1795–1796) we find distinct echoes of Goethe's own skepticism toward the revealed word, namely in Therese's rejection of devotional writings: "I cannot understand at all how one could believe that God speaks to us through books and stories" ("Ich kann überhaupt nicht begreifen, wie man hat glauben können, daß Gott durch Bücher und Geschichten zu uns spreche") (my translation). Goethe, *Wilhelm Meisters Lehrjahre. Siebtes—Achtes Buch*, vol. 23, *Werke. Weimarer Ausgabe*, 286.

18. Thomas McAlindon, "The Ironic Vision: Diction and Theme in Marlowe's *Doctor Faustus," Review of English Studies* 32, no. 126 (1981): 135.

19. Filomena Vasconcelos, "Occult Philosophy and the Philosophy of Language in Renaissance Europe and Elisabethan England," *Revista da Faculdade de Letras – Línguas e Literaturas* 21 (2004): 204.

20. Debra A. Faszer, "Luther and Interpretation in Marlowe and Goethe's Faustian Dramas," *Direction* 25, no. 1 (1996), http://www.directionjournal.org/article/?907 (accessed February 15, 2009).

21. Mephistopheles' recommendation of an unnamed book (*F*, 2349) as a guide to healthy living may refer to *Über die Verlängerung des Lebens* (On the prolongation of life) (1792). This was a best-selling treatise by Goethe's physician, C. W. Hufeland, who "engaged in medical practices bordering on quackery but classifiable today as branches of alternative medicine." Alan Corkhill, "Charlatanism in Goethe's *Faust I* and Tieck's *William Lovell," Forum for Modern Language Studies* 42, no. 1 (2006): 84.

22. Studies of the satanic blood pact in Goethean and Marlovian scholarship include, apart from its widely researched religious and demonological dimensions (e.g., E. M. Butler, *The Fortunes of Faust* [Cambridge: Cambridge University Press, 1979]), socio-cultural readings (e.g., Neil Brough, *New Perspectives of Faust: Studies in the Origins and Philosophy of the Faust Theme in the Dramas of Marlowe and Goethe* [Frankfurt and New York: Peter Lang, 1994]), the compact's function as a performative speech act formalized in writing (see Andrew Sofer, "How to Do Things with Demons: Conjuring Performatives in *Doctor Faustus," Theatre Journal* 61, no. 1 [March 2009]: 1–21), as well as a focus on its legal and jurisprudential complexities (see Nishan Swais, "Putting It in Writing: Drafting Faust's Contract with the Devil," *Canadian Journal of Law and Jurisprudence* 14, no. 2 [2001]: 227– 47).

23. Swais, "Putting It in Writing."

24. Employment agreements are also struck elsewhere. Wagner pressures the clown Robin into his service (*DF*, I.iv.1–50), but there are no mutual indemnity clauses in what is essentially a verbal pledge underpinned by the threat of bullying and harassment. A hiring arrangement also exists in "Prelude in the Theatre" ("Vorspiel auf dem Theater") (*Faust I*). The poet is bound to the theater director by unspecified contractual obligations that could be verbal, written, or even unspoken. The employer demands his pound of flesh, as it were, in his request for stage plays with popular entertainment value (*F*, 89–103).

25. Integral to Faustus' formal declaration, "I, John Faustus, of Wittenberg, Doctor, by these presents, do give both body and soul to Lucifer, Prince of the East, and his minister Mephistopheles [etc.]" (*DF*, II.i.105–10), is the Lyotardian grammatological proposition that the first-person subject in a sentence "is the one who intends, who gives birth to, and controls (or tries to control) the meaning of the statement." See in this respect Jeff Noonan, *Critical Humanism and the Politics of Difference* (Montreal and Kingston: McGill-Queen's University Press, 2004), 43. However, Faustus' autonomous linguistic control ultimately proves defenseless against the powers of darkness.

26. One of the factors contributing to Goethe's disillusionment with his prewriting legal career was his aversion to having to master a "juristic catechism" at odds with his advocacy of natural law and its complete absence of formalism. See

on this point Edmond N. Cahn, "Goethe's View of Law—With a Gloss out of Plato," *Columbia Law Review* 49 (1949): 904.

27. The modern-day equivalent of the blood signature is the small red seal affixed to legal documents.

28. Apart from attempts to explain Faust's blood clotting medically, his congealing blood is read predominantly within the framework of the play's conventional theology. See, for instance, Ruth Lunney, *Marlowe and the Popular Tradition: Innovation in the English Drama before 1595* (Manchester: Manchester University Press, 2002): "[T]hat the signing is against both heaven and Nature is seen in the recalcitrant blood" (58). However, other critics see the coagulating blood as an essential ingredient of the visual and performance rhetoric of early modern theatrical spectacle. See in this respect Christa Knellwolf King, *Faust and the Promises of the New Science, ca. 1580–1730. From the Chapbooks to Harlequin Faustus* (Farnham: Ashgate, 2008), 76.

29. The most systematic treatment of literary representations of graphophobia is by Aníbal González, *Killer Books: Writing, Violence, and Ethics in Modern Spanish American Narrative* (Austin: University of Texas Press, 2001), who, in his reading of texts from classical times through to contemporary Hispanic letters, identifies this condition as one extending beyond the fear of writing "to an attitude towards the written word that mixes respect, caution, and dread with revulsion and contempt" (3).

30. See in relation to Goethe's indebtedness to eighteenth- and nineteenth-century language philosophy in *Faust*, Alan Corkhill, "Language Discourses in Goethe's *Faust II*," in *Unravelling the Labyrinth: Decoding Text and Language*, ed. Kerry Dunne and Ian R. Campbell (Berne: Peter Lang, 1997), 58, 61, and 69–72; Alan Corkhill, "'Why all this noise?': Reading Sound in Goethe's *Faust I and II*," in *International Faust Studies: Adaptation, Reception, Translation*, ed. Lorna Fitzsimmons (London and New York: Continuum, 2008), 59.

31. Goethe wrote in this respect: "Unfortunately, words are for people usually surrogates. They can generally think . . . better than they can express themselves" ("[L]eider sind dem Menschen die Worte gewöhnlich Surrogate: Er denkt . . . meistenteils besser, als er sich ausspricht" [my translation]). Goethe, *Maximen und Reflexionen*, vol. 9, *Gedenkausgabe der Werke, Briefe und Gespräche*, no. 589, 674. For an overview of the key facets of Goethe's philosophy of language see Alan Corkhill, "Goethes Sprachdenken in beziehungsgeschichtlicher Hinsicht," *Neophilologus* 75, no. 2 (1991): 239–51.

32. Alison Findlay, *A Feminist Perspective on Renaissance Drama* (Oxford: Wiley-Blackwell, 1999), 16.

33. Friedrich M. Klinger, *Faustus: His Life, Death, and Doom. A Romance in Prose. Translated from the German* (London: W. Kent, 1864), http://www.gutenberg.org/etext/25468 (accessed February 14, 2009). A person's character, especially the "quickness of . . . thoughts" (168) is also judged to be readable on the authority of handwriting and signatures. Klinger's Faustus is a typical Storm and Stress libertarian—a rebel against authority and a defender of just social causes.

34. Klinger, *Faustus*, 175.

35. See in this regard Corkhill, "Charlatanism in Goethe's *Faust I* and Tieck's *William Lovell*," 82, 84–86.

36. In the A-text we find that hearsay, i.e., the spoken word, is not sufficient for the emperor: "let me see some proof of thy skill, / that mine eyes may be witnesses to confirm what mine eyes have heard reported" (IV.i.6–8).

37. See with respect to phonosemantics and the aesthetics of acoustical transfer Corkhill, "Language Discourses in Goethe's *Faust II*," 62, and Corkhill, "'Why all this noise?'" 60–63.

38. As a natural scientist, Goethe was fully conscious of the need for linguistic precision in the analysis and classification of empirical data.

BIBLIOGRAPHY

Brough, Neil. *New Perspectives of Faust: Studies in the Origins and Philosophy of the Faust Theme in the Dramas of Marlowe and Goethe*. Frankfurt and New York: Peter Lang, 1994.

Butler, E. M. *The Fortunes of Faust*. Cambridge: Cambridge University Press, 1979.

Cahn, Edmond N. "Goethe's View of Law—With a Gloss out of Plato." *Columbia Law Review* 49 (1949): 904–6.

Corkhill, Alan. "Charlatanism in Goethe's *Faust I* and Tieck's *William Lovell*." *Forum for Modern Language Studies* 42, no. 1 (2006): 80–92.

———. "Goethes Sprachdenken in beziehungsgeschichtlicher Hinsicht." *Neophilologus* 75, no. 2 (1991): 239–51.

———. "Language Discourses in Goethe's *Faust II*." In *Unravelling the Labyrinth. Decoding Text and Language*, edited by Kerry Dunne and Ian R. Campbell, 57–73. Berne: Peter Lang, 1997.

———. "Sprachphilosophische Fragestellungen in Goethes *Faust I*." *Neophilologus* 79, no. 3 (1995): 451–63.

———. "'Why all this noise?': Reading Sound in Goethe's *Faust I and II*." In *International Faust Studies: Adaptation, Reception, Translation*, edited by Lorna Fitzsimmons, 55–69. London and New York: Continuum, 2008.

Durrani, Osman. *Faust and the Bible: A Study of Goethe's Use of Scriptural Allusions and Christian Religious Motifs in Faust I and II*. Berne: Peter Lang, 1977.

Faszer, Debra A. "Luther and Interpretation in Marlowe and Goethe's Faustian Dramas." *Direction* 25, no. 1 (1996). http://www.directionjournal.org/article/?907 (accessed February 15, 2009).

Findlay, Alison. *A Feminist Perspective on Renaissance Drama*. Oxford: Wiley-Blackwell, 1999.

Goethe, Johann Wolfgang von. *Faust. Part One*. Translated by Philip Wayne. Hammondsworth: Penguin, 1949.

———. *Faust. Part Two*. Translated by Philip Wayne. Hammondsworth: Penguin, 1962.

———. *Faust: Texte*. Vol. 7, pt.1, *Sämtliche Werke. Briefe, Tagebücher und Gespräche*. Edited by Albrecht Schöne. Frankfurt: Deutscher Klassiker Verlag, 2005.

———. *Gedenkausgabe der Werke, Briefe und Gespräche*. Edited by Ernst Beutler. 24 vols. and 3 suppl. vols. Zurich and Stuttgart: Artemis, 1948–1971.

———. *Werke. Weimarer Ausgabe in 143 Bänden*. Edited by Paul Raabe. Munich: dtv, 1987.

González, Aníbal. *Killer Books: Writing, Violence, and Ethics in Modern Spanish American Narrative*. Austin: University of Texas Press, 2001.

Klinger, Friedrich M. *Faustus: His Life, Death, and Doom. A Romance in Prose. Translated from the German*. London: W. Kent, 1864. http://www.gutenberg.org/etext/25468 (accessed February 14, 2009).

Knellwolf King, Christa. *Faust and the Promises of the New Science, ca. 1580–1730. From the Chapbooks to Harlequin Faustus*. Farnham: Ashgate, 2008.

Lehrich, Christopher I. *The Language of Angels and Demons: Cornelius Agrippa's Occult Philosophy*. Leiden and Boston: Brill, 2003.

Lochhead, David. "Technology and Interpretation: A Footnote to McLuhan." http://www.religion-research.org/irtc/martin.htm (accessed February 23, 2009).

Lunney, Ruth. *Marlowe and the Popular Tradition: Innovation in the English Drama before 1595*. Manchester: Manchester University Press, 2002.

Marlowe, Christopher. *Doctor Faustus*. Edited by David Bevington and Eric Rasmussen. Manchester: University of Manchester Press, 1993.

Matalene, H. W. "Marlowe's *Faustus* and the Comforts of Academicism." *Journal of English Literary History* 39, no. 4 (1972): 495–519.

Matthews, Michelle M. "Magician or Witch? Christopher Marlowe's *Doctor Faustus*." MA diss., Bowling Green State University, 2006.

McAlindon, Thomas. "The Ironic Vision: Diction and Theme in Marlowe's *Doctor Faustus*." *Review of English Studies* 32, no. 126 (May 1981): 129–41.

McLuhan, Marshall. *The Gutenberg Galaxy: The Making of Typographic Man*. Toronto: University of Toronto Press, 1962.

Mumford, Lewis. "The Invention of Printing." In *Communication in History: Technology, Culture, Society*, edited by David Crowley and Paul Heyer, 85–88. New York: Longman, 1999.

Sharpe, Kevin, and Steven N. Zwicker. *Reading, Society and Politics in Early Modern England*. New York and Cambridge: Cambridge University Press, 2003.

Sofer, Andrew. "How to Do Things with Demons: Conjuring Performatives in *Doctor Faustus*." *Theatre Journal* 61, no. 1 (2009): 1–21.

Swais, Nishan. "Putting It in Writing: Drafting Faust's Contract with the Devil." *Canadian Journal of Law and Jurisprudence* 14 (July 2001): 227–47.

Vasconcelos, Filomena. "Occult Philosophy and the Philosophy of Language in Renaissance Europe and Elisabethan England." *Revista da Faculdade de Letras – Línguas e Literaturas* 21 (2004): 199–208.

Wall-Randell, Sarah. "*Doctor Faustus* and the Printer's Devil." *Studies in English Literature 1500–1900* 48, no. 2 (2008): 259–81.

2

The Enigmatic Eternal-Feminine

J. M. van der Laan

Goethe's famous Faust-play remains memorable and challenging not least because its ending is in so many ways so unsatisfactory and unacceptable. The vision of an uncertain, utopian future begs for comment; the protagonist surrenders to a moment he has not yet experienced; the antagonist is deprived of his rightful prize; angels utter a perplexing declaration of salvation; everything dissolves into symbolism and metaphysics; and something called the Eternal-Feminine ("das Ewig-Weibliche") appears for the first and only time in the very last lines of the entire play.

Although he does not expressly introduce the Eternal-Feminine until the play's conclusion, Goethe prepared for its appearance from the outset. Especially pertinent in this regard are Gretchen and Helen, who alternate with each other from start to finish and ultimately combine with others to constitute the Eternal-Feminine. In Part I, Faust initially sees Helen in Gretchen. As Mephistopheles remarks sotto voce in the "Witch's Kitchen" ("Hexenküche"), "You'll see, with this drink in your body, / Soon Helen in every woman" ("Du siehst, mit diesem Trank im Leibe, / Bald Helenen in jedem Weibe") (*F*, 2603–4).[1] In Part II and with roles reversed, Faust sees Gretchen in Helen, so to speak, after he recognizes the recently departed Helen in the clouds: "Does a charming image deceive me, / As youth's first, long-surrendered, highest possession?" ("Täuscht mich ein entzückend Bild, / Als jugenderstes, längstentbehrtes höchstes Gut?") (*F*, 10058–59). Gretchen and Helen trade places with each other throughout the play, but most significantly merge with additional female figures in the finale and culminate in the enigmatic Eternal-Feminine.

When, as Act IV opens, Faust glimpses "a godlike female form" ("ein göttergleiches Fraungebild") (*F*, 10049) in the passing clouds, he discerns

Juno, Leda, and Helen, tokens of majesty, beauty, love, and divinity: "like Juno, Leda, Helena," Faust declares, "How majestically lovely I see it sway to and fro" ("Ich seh's! Junonen ähnlich, Leda'n, Helenen, / Wie majestätisch lieblich mir's im Auge schwankt") (*F*, 10050–51). Yet, as noted in the paragraph above, he also perceives Gretchen's form in the cloudscape (*F*, 10058–59), another expression of beauty and love, but also loss. Finally, he adds a brief, personal interpretation: "The earliest treasures of the deepest heart well up: it represents to me a gentle rise, Aurora's love" ("Des tiefsten Herzens frühste Schätze quollen auf: / Aurorens Liebe, leichten Schwung bezeichnet's mir") (*F*, 10060–61). Aurora, the dawn, holds the promise of the new day, but especially renewal for Faust.

While Cyrus Hamlin considers Galatea, who appears in Act II of Part II, and the Mater Gloriosa of the play's last scene to be "embodiments of the Eternal-Feminine," he asserts that "the Eternal-Feminine as a concept of force in the drama should not be identified with any of the actual episodes or experiences of Faust the character, least of all with either Gretchen or Helena."[2] The text itself contradicts such a view, however. As Faust himself attests, "the lovely form, / Does not dissolve, rises up into the aether / And draws the best of my soul forth with itself" ("die holde Form, / Löst sich nicht auf, erhebt sich in den Äther hin / Und zieht das Beste meines Innern mit sich fort" (*F*, 10064–66). Gretchen, Helen, and the other goddesses who appear to Faust in the cloudscape draw him onward, like the Eternal-Feminine yet to appear in the couplet, "The Eternal-Feminine / Draws us onward" ("Das Ewig-Weibliche / Zieht uns hinan") (*F*, 12110–11).

The figure those women form in the clouds clearly anticipates the last lines of the play. As a godlike feminine form ("ein göttergleiches Fraungebild") (*F*, 10049), Juno, Leda, Helena, Aurora, and Gretchen pre-conceive the configuration of five other women who appear at the conclusion of Part II, Act V: Magna Peccatrix (or Maria Magdalena whom Christian legend typically identified as a prostitute), Mulier Samaritana (the Samaritan woman in John 4 who had had many husbands and was living with yet another man, not her husband, when she spoke with Jesus), Maria Aegyptiaca (or Mary of Egypt, the patron saint of penitence, who had led a dissolute life in Alexandria), Una Poenitentium (once called Gretchen), and the Mater Gloriosa (who is virgin, mother, queen, and goddess ["Jungfrau, Mutter, Königin, / Göttin"], and calls yet another Mary, Jesus' mother, to mind) (*F*, 12102–3).

Ellis Dye likens the Eternal-Feminine to an "agent and vessel of mixing and mingling, the universal solvent—the *menstruum universale*, the maternal *Wunderschoß* [or miraculous womb]" (*F*, 8665).[3] Certainly, a multitude of feminine characters and meanings mix and mingle in Goethe's construct. As Michael Neumann notes in his study *Das Ewig-Weibliche in Goethes Faust*, Doctor Marianus prepares for the naming of the Eternal-Feminine with his song of praise for the Mater Gloriosa (*F*, 12102–3).[4] The words of Doctor Marianus here echo several of those used previously in Part II, Act III to describe Helen—"goddess" ("*Göttin*") (*F*, 9237), "queen" ("*Königin*") (*F*, 8592, 8640, 9191, 9258), "mother" ("*Mutter*") (*F*, 9600, 9607, 9615)—but also Gretchen in Part I—"godlike" ("*göttergleich*") (*F*, 2707), "image of the gods" ("*Götterbild*") (*F*, 2716), "sweet face of heaven" ("holdes Himmelsangesicht") (*F*, 3182)—who as virgin mothered her little sister ("And so I brought it up [the child] all alone, / With milk and water; thus it became mine" ["Und so erzog ich's [das Kind] ganz allein, / Mit Milch und Wasser; so ward's mein"]) (*F*, 3132–33). Of course, Gretchen the innocent virgin also became the unwed mother of Faust's first child. The images of the virgin mother, Mother Nature, even the Magna Mater and Urmother all coalesce in the Eternal-Feminine.[5]

While the Eternal-Feminine is by name certainly gendered as female, it is not defined by all the women or female figures who appear in the play, despite their identification as feminine. For instance, Lieschen, who gossips about the misfortune of Barbara, pregnant out of wedlock, does not possess the qualities later to be associated with the Eternal-Feminine. These qualities are also lacking in the witches of the Walpurgis Night. Only a select number of the play's many feminine figures contribute something of themselves to the construction of the ideality Goethe finally reveals at the end of the play.

A synthesis of Gretchen, Helen, and the Mater Gloriosa, the Eternal-Feminine also includes the Graces Aglaia, Hegemone, and Euphrosyne; Galatea, Leda, Aurora, and Juno; and even the Mothers ("die Mütter") whom Faust visited in order to conjure Helen for the emperor and his entourage. Although the only reference to the Eternal-Feminine occurs in the last two lines of the play, all those feminine figures along with their diverse significations first prefigure, then combine, and culminate in that final grand symbol. Dye identifies a range of connotations for the Eternal-Feminine: "physicality, eros, domesticity, and divinity; also fertility, agency, origin, and destiny."[6] Given the various female figures associated with the Eternal-Feminine, those meanings certainly obtain.

A host of female figures all contribute something of themselves and their various symbolic possibilities to the Eternal-Feminine. The relation of the three Graces of the Masked Ball to the Eternal-Feminine is admittedly marginal, but even so deserves consideration. Aglaia represents beauty; Hegemone, fertility; Euphrosyne, joy. Although mentioned only briefly, but defined above all by "*Anmut*" (*F*, 5299), they here embody giving (*F*, 5300), receiving (*F*, 5301), and thankfulness (*F*, 5304) as well, indicating something of the potential attraction the Eternal-Feminine will be said to exert. Galatea, in turn, appears as a Venus or Aphrodite figure at the end of Part II, Act II and prefigures the Eternal-Feminine in her love and beauty, but also in the magnificent union of male and female, order and chaos, mind and body, when Homunculus smashes his crystalline orb on her shell. Thanks to its relation to Juno as well as Gretchen, Galatea, and Helen, the Eternal-Feminine signifies fertility, childbirth, and marriage. As the daughter of Leda and Zeus, Helen invests the Eternal-Feminine with a certain divine quality as well. Aurora, the personification of the dawn, is also present in the Eternal-Feminine, and symbolizes rebirth and renewal. In addition, the women of the last scene who prepare for the appearance of and are associated with the Eternal-Feminine—Magna Peccatrix, Mulier Samaritana, Maria Aegyptiaca, Una Poenitentium—convey sexuality, albeit illicit sexuality, but, more important, repentance and forgiveness received, a repentance Faust never confessed, but a forgiveness he requires and receives from or through the feminine love expressed throughout the finale. As the sum of these highly symbolic women, the Eternal-Feminine represents forgiveness, renewal or rebirth, divinity, and harmonious union.

Like Helen, the Eternal-Feminine is the "form of all forms" ("Gestalt aller Gestalten") (*F*, 8907). Significantly, the friend and mentor of Goethe's youth, Johann Gottfried Herder, used similar language in his "Erläuterungen zum Neuen Testament" (1775), where he invokes God as the "being of beings" ("Wesen der Wesen") and goal of all human inquiry. "You [God] elevated the human being," wrote Herder, "so that he himself, without knowing and wanting it, would carefully look for the causes of things, would guess their correlation, and therefore find You, you the great correlation of all things, being of beings" ("Den Menschen erhobst du, daß er selbst ohne daß ers weiß und will, Ursachen der Dinge nachspähe, ihren Zusammenhang errathe und Dich also finde, du großer Zusammenhang aller Dinge, Wesen der Wesen").[7] So, too, the Eternal-Feminine can be understood to embody everything Faust had ever sought to discover.

According to Hans Urs von Balthasar, Faust travels "from Gretchen and Helen through Sophia . . . up higher to Mary."[8] Although Sophia (the Greek word for wisdom or knowledge) per se never appears in *Faust*, she is nevertheless subtly present in Helen, not to mention the other women and the Eternal-Feminine. Konrad Burdach (1932) links the Eternal-Feminine as well to Gnosticism and to the mystical tradition, in particular to the thought of Friedrich Christoph Oetinger (1702–1782), Paracelsus (1493/4–1541), and Plato (ca. 428–347 BCE). In Goethe's concept of the Eternal-Feminine, moreover, Burdach discerns the maternal vocation and care which presents itself both in Gretchen's characteristics and the idea of the Mothers from whom Faust obtained access to Helen or at least her specter during his time at the emperor's court.[9] To include the concepts represented by the Mothers with those represented by Helen, Gretchen, and the Gnostic Sophia in the Eternal-Feminine is not unwarranted. After all, Mephistophiles defined the Mothers as "Formation, transformation, / Eternal upholding of the eternal mind" ("Gestaltung, Umgestaltung, / Des ewigen Sinnes ewige Unterhaltung") (*F*, 6287–88), words which echo in the description of Helen as the "form of all forms" ("Gestalt aller Gestalten") (*F*, 8907), but which also suggest Sophia and anticipate the Eternal-Feminine.

Characterized by a striving for transcendent knowledge, contempt for this world, and a radical dualism, Gnosticism contains the seeds for many elements of the Faust myth. Thanks to the Gnostic strata of the Faust tradition and as told in a late Gnostic saga, a woman sometimes called Helena, but also Sophia, was connected at one time with the memory of Simon Magus (or Simon the Sorcerer), the man who in the biblical book of Acts wanted to purchase the divine power of the Holy Spirit from the apostles Peter and John, but who also later came to be the individual identified with Gnosticism.[10]

According to Hans Jonas, moreover, Simon Magus reportedly used the surname Faustus—meaning "the favored one" (from "*favustus*")—in Latin surroundings. "This in connection with his permanent cognomen 'the Magician,'" writes Jonas, "and the fact that he was accompanied by a Helena whom he claimed to be the reborn Helen of Troy shows clearly that we have here one of the sources of the Faust legend of the early Renaissance."[11] Another Gnostic story tells of a being named Homunculus to which Helena (or Sophia) either gave birth or conjured up. Of course, both Helena and Homunculus figure prominently in Goethe's version of the Faust story as well.

Gnostic legends indicate that Helena—the companion of Simon Magus—was often identified with "the fallen divinity also known as Sophia."[12] As documented in *The Apocryphon of John*, the Gnostics considered Sophia a divine being, the Noble Virgin of Divine Wisdom, who created angels and then together with them created human beings. While he considers Faust the descendant of the Gnostic sectary, Simon Magus, Jonas identifies Helen as "the fallen Thought of God [that is, Sophia] through whose raising mankind was to be saved."[13] The salvation Goethe grants his Faust in which a divine female principle, not to mention a once-fallen woman, plays so central a role owes at least some of its character to such Gnostic lore.

Personified as the feminine figure Sophia, the wisdom or knowledge of God has long been identified with the divine activity of creation. Not only the New Testament understanding of the logos,[14] but also the ancient wisdom literature of the Hebrews, both canonical and apocryphal, emphasize such a correlation. The biblical book of Proverbs, for example, articulates the essential unity of both the mind and will of God, of divine wisdom and action in the creation of the heavens and the earth: "By wisdom the Lord laid the earth's foundations, by understanding he set the heavens in place; by his knowledge the deeps were divided, and the clouds let drop the dew" ("Der Herr hat die Erde durch Weisheit gegründet und nach seiner Einsicht die Himmel bereitet. Kraft seiner Erkenntnis quellen die Wasser der Tiefe hervor und triefen die Wolken von Tau") (Proverbs 3:19–20, NIV). According to S. H. Ringe, creation is the self-disclosure of Wisdom, "not simply something God has done, but a glimpse into the very heart and nature of God."[15]

In a subsequent passage in Proverbs, Wisdom herself speaks. Echoing passages in Job, a personified Wisdom declares: "I was there when he gave the sea its boundary / so the waters would not overstep his command, / and when he marked out the foundations of the earth. / Then I was the craftsman at his side" ("Als er dem Meere seine Grenze setzte und den Wassern, daß sie nicht überschreiten seinen Befehl; als er die Grundfesten der Erde legte, da war ich als sein Liebling bei ihm" (8:29–30, NIV). (Note that the German uses the word "*Liebling*," or favorite, here, in contrast to the English "craftsman.") Wisdom actively participates in the very act of creation. Here, we recognize moreover the object of Faust's desire, even the outline of the great undertaking he would eventually conceive. He, too, wants to "mark the foundations of the earth" and "give the sea its boundary." Already in his opening monologue, he announces that as his goal: "That I know what holds the world / In its innermost together" ("Daß ich erkenne, was die Welt / Im Innersten zusammenhält") (*F*, 382–83). Near the end of the play, he is finally able to focus his energies on one specific task: "To shut out the imperious sea from the shore, / To contract the borders of the watery reaches, / And to drive them back deep into themselves" ("Das herrische Meer vom Ufer auszuschließen, / Der feuchten Breite Grenzen zu verengen / Und, weit hinein, sie in sich selbst zu drängen") (*F*, 10229–31). To do so would allow him to attain divine wisdom, to know the very mind of God himself. As the creator of a world, Faust could become the master, the god, he has always striven to be, and so finally usurp God's power and authority, indeed, God's knowledge.

The Wisdom of Solomon, a book of the Biblical apocrypha, suggests further associations among Helen, Sophia, or Wisdom, and the Eternal-Feminine.

> There is in her [Wisdom/Sophia] a spirit that is intelligent, holy, unique, loving the good, keen, irresistible, sure, free from anxiety, all-powerful, overseeing all, and penetrating through all spirits that are intelligent, pure and altogether subtle . . . For she is a breath of the power of God . . . For she is a reflection of eternal light.[16]

As enumerated here—manifold, irresistible, eternal, all-powerful—her attributes recall the feminine figures manifested in the cloud and give an outline of the principle that exerts such attraction on Faust. His repeated references to eternal light throughout the play now take on new significance as subtle allusions to Sophia and the Eternal-Feminine.

As Richard Ilgner points out, Gnostics considered Sophia "the goddess of wholeness, of the Pleroma" (Greek for "that which fills") ("die Göttin der Ganzheit, des Pleromas").[17] To reach Sophia would be to attain divine knowledge, but also to achieve wholeness, fullness or completion, a union of everything which had been separated: mind and body, male and female, sky and earth. The Gnostic Sophia, also known as the "Pearl of Wisdom," may have, in addition to Helen, another hidden presence in *Faust*, for Gretchen's full name Margareta means "pearl of the sea." After all, the quest for Sophia, for the pearl of wisdom, first led Faust to another pearl, Margareta, from whom he initially sought a new path to transcendent knowledge.[18] Indeed, in the scene "Forest and Cave" ("Wald und Höhle") Faust characterizes the ecstasy he experienced with Gretchen as "bliss, / Which brings me close and closer to the gods" ("Wonne, / Die mich den Göttern nah und näher bringt") (*F*, 3241–42).

While it symbolizes forgiveness, grace, and love, the Eternal-Feminine also personifies the transcendent realm of ultimate being, of divine wisdom and creative power which forever exceeds human reach, but at the same time ever draws us unto itself. As a fusion of Gretchen, Helen, Galatea, Leda, Aurora, Juno, Mary, and Sophia, Goethe's Eternal-Feminine is able to signify everything, or I should say the one and only prize, Faust has been seeking all along. In the opinion of Hans Arens, the Eternal-Feminine is not simply to be equated with love. Rather, it is the eternal or divine which reveals itself in the feminine.[19] According to Michael Neumann, the last song of Doctor Marianus (*F*, 12096–103; quoted above) is a hymn to the Eternal-Feminine which there reveals itself to be divinity per se.[20]

The concluding, cryptic reference to "das Ewig-Weibliche" (*F*, 12110–11) provides a final and subtle commentary on Faust's lifelong quest and infinite striving. In his afterlife, Faust does not find himself in heaven, nor even on a mountaintop, but in the mountain gorges, awaiting a possible ascent of some kind about which he has no say. The famous last lines of the play with their mysterious reference to the Eternal-Feminine likewise contain no language referring specifically to an upward (*"hinauf," "aufwärts,"* or *"nach oben"*), but only to a forward or onward trajectory (*"hinanziehen"*), in other words, to a never-finished, never-perfected Faust, never in possession of an ultimate knowledge.

As the symbolic representation of divine wisdom and creative power, of the eternal and quintessential, the Eternal-Feminine can never be grasped or possessed. Beyond all human reach and comprehension, the eternal and divine always draws Faust and humanity onward toward itself. As Arens observes, the Eternal-Feminine represents "the secret or mysterium of yearning."[21] Indeed, the mysterious symbol of the play's concluding verses represents all Faust had ever so ardently longed to know. It signifies everything toward which Faust from beginning to end has been ineluctably and irresistibly drawn and toward which he has been relentlessly striving: divine wisdom, divine creative power, the will and mind of God, the divine principle, divinity, in other words, ultimate being and meaning. It is the alluring, yet elusive goal which draws him and people ever onward, all the while remaining just beyond his and our reach.

According to Nicholas Vazsonyi, Jean-François Lyotard's famous attempt to answer the question "What is Postmodernism?" was already explicit in *Faust II* (that he excludes *Faust I* seems to me unwarranted). If the postmodern is, as formulated by Lyotard, that which "puts forward the *unpresentable* in presentation itself; that which denies the solace of good forms, the consensus of a taste which would make it possible to share collectively the nostalgia for the *unattainable*; that which searches for new presentations, not in order to enjoy them but in order to impart a stronger sense of the *unpresentable*,"[22] then *Faust* already exemplifies such an attitude. As Vazsonyi points out, Goethe's own conclusion to *Faust*, specifically its closing remarks about "the inadequate" ("das Unzulängliche") and "the indescribable" ("das Unbeschreibliche"), but especially an Eternal-Feminine ever beyond our reach, echoes in Lyotard's words.

In the way *Faust* resists the production of meaning, the play resists "the 'human' desire to *understand* and to *categorize*" it.[23] The contradictions and paradoxes in *Faust* and especially its conclusion persist despite our best efforts to resolve them. The meanings of the text remain indeterminate and thwart our attempts to construct a coherent and definitive interpretation. *Faust* paints a picture of the world in all its chaos and complexity, a picture of life in all its immense and unmanageable disharmony and ambiguity. If the contradictions of Faust's closing monologue and the play's finale can be harmonized at all, it is with the unsolvable paradoxes and ironies of life itself.

Maybe the question about Faust's knowledge as well as our own knowledge of *Faust* is moot. In the same way Gretchen is to lead Faust, the Eternal-Feminine is said to draw us onward. Each remains beyond reach, however, probably in perpetuity, so that the answers Faust, the protagonist, wants and we desire for *Faust*, the play, always exceed our grasp. Meaninglessness for Faust (the character) and an overabundance of meaning for *Faust* (the text) persist to the very end of the play. The only escape from it is in a salvation which is utterly out of place, senseless and illogical, at odds with the rest of the play, not to mention our empirical experience of objective reality.

The last verses of the play assert that there is no final union with an eternal principle nor ultimate comprehension of eternity. Neither Faust nor we ever attain that goal in the context of the play. Eternity remains beyond Faust's reach, but he has been released and relieved of the desperate need to comprehend and possess it. After all the language and imagery of ascension and transcendence, the last lines of the play bring us back to immanence: "*Here* it occurs . . . *Here* it is done") ("*Hier* wird's Ereignis . . . *Hier* ist's getan") (*F*, 12107, 12109—emphasis added). Dorothea Hölscher-Lohmeyer deserves credit for noting the emphasis placed on *here* in the play's last verses.[24] To paraphrase the song of the Chorus Mysticus, the unattainable and the indescribable are not attained or described in any hereafter, but only *here*. Faust was hardly wrong to declare, "The view to the other side is denied us" ("Nach drüben ist die Aussicht uns verrannt") (*F*, 11442). The Chorus Mysticus specifies, reiterates, and emphasizes the here (and now), the human realm, in its final strophe. We do well to remember that the final scene of the play, Faust's final resting place, as it were, is not in hell, where previous Fausts had ended up, nor in heaven, where the audience for this "saved" Faust might expect to see him, but "here," on earth, that is, in the Mountain Gorges. He has neither descended unto the depths nor risen up to the heights, has not moved on to some supernatural realm, but remains here in the in-between, which is all the audience has and knows as well. The divine, the eternal, the infinite can only be conceived of here, that is, only in the human, the temporal, the finite—and only vicariously, approximately, metaphorically. In the end, it is only metaphor, literally a *carrying over*, which allows for any transcendence at all in *Faust*.

NOTES

1. Unless otherwise noted, all translations are my own. In the case of *Faust* itself, my translations hold as close to the original German as possible. All references to Goethe's *Faust* indicate line numbers in Johann Wolfgang Goethe, *Goethes Werke* (Hamburger Ausgabe), ed. E. Trunz., 12th ed., vol. 3 (Munich: C. H. Beck, 1982), and are abbreviated *F*.

2. Cyrus Hamlin asserts that "the Eternal-Feminine as a concept of force in the drama should not be identified with any of the actual episodes or experiences of Faust the character, least of all with either Gretchen or Helena," "Tracking the Eternal-Feminine in Goethe's *Faust II*," in *Interpreting Goethe's Faust Today*, ed. Jane K. Brown, Meredith Lee, and Thomas P. Saine (Columbia, SC: Camden House, 1994), 145, 151.

3. Ellis Dye, "Figurations of the Feminine in Goethe's *Faust*," in *A Companion to Goethe's Faust Parts I and II*, ed. Paul Bishop (Rochester, NY: Camden House, 2001), 109.

4. Michael Neumann, *Das Ewig-Weibliche in Goethes Faust* (Heidelberg: Carl Winter, 1985), 102.

5. In addition to the studies by Ellis, Hamlin, and Neumann, four others deserve specific acknowledgment, even though they have little bearing on the present interpretation. They all appear in *Interpreting Goethe's Faust Today*: Hannelore Schlaffer, "Paradies und Parodie: Die letzten Szenen in Goethes letzten Werken," 102–111; Gail K. Hart, "Das Ewig-Weibliche nasführet dich: Feminine Leadership in Goethe's

Faust and Sacher-Masoch's *Venus*," 112–22; Herbert Lindenberger, "Closing Up *Faust*: The Final Lines According to Schumann, Liszt, and Mahler," 123–32; and Christoph E. Schweitzer, "Gretchen and the Feminine in Goethe's *Faust*," 133–41. Readers may be interested as well in Michael Mitchell's *Hidden Mutualities: Faustian Themes from Gnostic Origins to the Postcolonial* (Amsterdam: Rodopi, 2006), although I found little, if anything, new or particularly relevant in this volume for the present study.

6. Dye, "Figurations of the Feminine in Goethe's *Faust*," 107.

7. Johann Gottfried Herder, *Sämmtliche Werke*, ed. Bernhard Suphan (Berlin: Weidmann, 1877–1913), 13:162–63.

8. According to Hans Urs von Balthasar, Faust travels "from Gretchen and Helen through Sophia . . . up higher to Mary," *Prometheus: Studien zur Geschichte des deutschen Idealismus* (Heidelberg: F. H. Kerle Verlag, 1947), 514.

9. Konrad Burdach, "Das religiöse Problem in Goethes *Faust*," *Euphorion* 33 (1932): 83.

10. A Gnostic website labeled "The Gnostic Link" bears witness to the enduring link between Gnosticism and the Eternal-Feminine. In its electronic newsletter for May 2000, the site offers a brief note about "the Eternal Feminine Principle." There is, however, no reference to Goethe as the author of the concept. http://home.earthlink.net/~gnosisla/Mayissue.html (accessed June 27, 2008).

11 Hans Jonas, *The Gnostic Religion: The Message of the Alien God and the Beginnings of Christianity* (Boston: Beacon Hill, 1958), 111.

12. E. M. Butler, *The Myth of the Magus* (Cambridge: Cambridge University Press, 1948), 82.

13. Jonas, *The Gnostic Religion*, 111.

14. Cf. Arthur Peacocke, *Paths from Science toward God: The End of All Our Exploring* (Oxford: One World, 2002), 158.

15. S. H. Ringe, *Wisdom's Friends* (Louisville, KY: Westminster John Knox Press, 1999), 44.

16. *Wisdom of Solomon*, 7:23–26, NRSV.

17. Richard Ilgner, *Die Ketzermythologie in Goethes Faust* (Herbolzheim: Centaurus Verlag, 2001), 79.

18. Ilgner, *Die Ketzermythologie*, 149–50.

19. Hans Arens, *Kommentar zu Goethes Faust II*, Beiträge zur neueren Literaturgeschichte, 3. Folge, Bd. 86 (Heidelberg: Carl Winter, 1989), 1052.

20. Neumann, *Das Ewig-Weibliche*, 102.

21. Arens, *Kommentar zu Goethes Faust II*, 1052.

22. Jean-François Lyotard, *The Postmodern Condition: A Report on Knowledge*, trans. Geoff Bennington and Brian Massumi (Minneapolis: University of Minnesota Press, 1989), 81.

23. Nicholas Vazsonyi, "Searching for 'The Order of the Things': Does Goethe's *Faust II* Suffer from the 'Fatal Conceit'?" *Monatshefte* 88, no. 1 (1996): 88.

24. See the commentary of Dorothea Hölscher-Lohmeyer on *Faust* in the Munich edition of Goethe's works, *Letzte Jahre. 1827–1832*, ed. Gisela Henckmann and Dorothea Hölscher-Lohmeyer, vol. 18, pt. 1, *Sämtliche Werke nach Epochen seines Schaffens* (Munich and Vienna: Hanser, 1997), 1186.

BIBLIOGRAPHY

Arens, Hans. *Kommentar zu Goethes Faust II*. Beiträge zur neueren Literaturgeschichte. 3. Folge, Bd. 86. Heidelberg: Carl Winter, 1989.

Balthasar, Hans Urs von. *Prometheus: Studien zur Geschichte des deutschen Idealismus*. 2nd ed. Heidelberg: F. H. Kerle Verlag, 1947.

Brown, Jane K., Meredith Lee, and Thomas P. Saine, eds. *Interpreting Goethe's Faust Today*. Columbia, SC: Camden House, 1994.

Burdach, Konrad. "Das religiöse Problem in Goethes *Faust*." *Euphorion* 33 (1932): 3–83.

Butler, E. M. *The Myth of the Magus*. Cambridge: Cambridge University Press, 1948.

Dye, Ellis. "Figurations of the Feminine in Goethe's *Faust*." In *A Companion to Goethe's Faust Parts I and II*, edited by Paul Bishop, 95–121. Rochester, NY: Camden House, 2001.

Goethe, Johann Wolfgang von. *Goethes Werke* (Hamburger Ausgabe). Edited by E. Trunz. 12th ed. 14 vols. Munich: C. H. Beck, 1982.

——. *Letzte Jahre. 1827–1832*. Edited by Gisela Henckmann and Dorothea Hölscher-Lohmeyer. Vol. 18, pt. 1, *Sämtliche Werke nach Epochen seines Schaffens*. Munich and Vienna: Hanser, 1997.

Hamlin, Cyrus. "Tracking the Eternal-Feminine in Goethe's *Faust II*." In Brown, Lee, and Saine, *Interpreting Goethe's Faust Today*, 142–55.

Hart, Gail K. "Das Ewig-Weibliche nasführet dich: Feminine Leadership in Goethe's *Faust* and Sacher-Masoch's *Venus*." In Brown, Lee, and Saine, *Interpreting Goethe's Faust Today*, 112–22.

Herder, Johann Gottfried. *Sämmtliche Werke*. Edited by Bernhard Suphan. 33 vols. Berlin: Weidmann, 1877–1913.

Ilgner, Richard. *Die Ketzermythologie in Goethes Faust*. Herbolzheim: Centaurus Verlag, 2001.

Jonas, Hans. *The Gnostic Religion. The Message of the Alien God and the Beginnings of Christianity*. Boston: Beacon Hill, 1958.

Lindenberger, Herbert. "Closing up *Faust*: The Final Lines According to Schumann, Liszt, and Mahler." In Brown, Lee, and Saine, *Interpreting Goethe's Faust Today*, 123–32.

Lyotard, Jean-François. *The Postmodern Condition: A Report on Knowledge*. Translated by Geoff Bennington and Brian Massumi. Minneapolis: University of Minnesota Press, 1989.

Mitchell, Michael. *Hidden Mutualities: Faustian Themes from Gnostic Origins to the Postcolonial*. Amsterdam: Rodopi, 2006.

Neumann, Michael. *Das Ewig-Weibliche in Goethes Faust*. Heidelberg: Carl Winter, 1985.

Peacocke, Arthur. *Paths from Science toward God: The End of All Our Exploring*. Oxford: One World, 2002.

Ringe, S. H. *Wisdom's Friends*. Louisville, KY: Westminster John Knox Press, 1999.

Rudolph, Kurt. *Gnosis. The Nature and History of Gnosticism*. Translated by Robert McLachlan Wilson. San Francisco: Harper and Row, 1983.

Schlaffer, Hannelore. "Paradies und Parodie: Die letzten Szenen in Goethes letzten Werken." In Brown, Lee, and Saine, *Interpreting Goethe's Faust Today*, 102–11.

Schweitzer, Christoph E. "Gretchen and the Feminine in Goethe's *Faust.*" In Brown, Lee, and Saine, *Interpreting Goethe's Faust Today*, 133–41.
van der Laan, J. M. *Seeking Meaning for Goethe's Faust.* London and New York: Continuum, 2007.
Vazsonyi, Nicholas. "Searching for 'The Order of the Things': Does Goethe's *Faust II* Suffer from the 'Fatal Conceit'?" *Monatshefte* 88, no. 1 (1996): 83–94.

3

Herder as Faust

Robert E. Norton

It has been celebrated as one of the pivotal events in German intellectual history, even as a moment of far-reaching consequence for the later development of German culture as a whole. During the second week of September 1770, in the Alsatian university town of Strasbourg, a newly matriculated student by the name of Johann Wolfgang Goethe happened to meet another recent arrival to the city, Johann Gottfried Herder, as Herder was climbing up the stairs to his hotel, improbably named "Zum Geist." This chance encounter sparked a period of intense adulation on Goethe's part, forming the basis of a friendship that grew over the following weeks and months and would last a quarter century. Goethe's initial veneration of Herder was due not only to his being the younger of the two—Goethe had just turned twenty-one, and Herder was his senior by almost exactly five years—but also because Herder was then something of a minor celebrity, having already earned a precocious notoriety with several books on literature and philosophy that began to appear in the mid-1760s. They had attracted the notice and even the ire of some of the most prominent writers of the day—including Winckelmann, Lessing, and Moses Mendelssohn—whose works Herder had subjected to extensive and occasionally blunt criticism. There was, when Goethe met him, even a whiff of scandal surrounding Herder's name, for he had published his polemical essays anonymously and when confronted publicly about his authorship, he had vigorously, and perhaps foolishly, denied any association with them. In addition, in June of the previous year Herder had suddenly left his post as pastor and teacher in Riga—among other things, there were rumors about his attachment to a married woman there—whereupon he had embarked on a lengthy sea journey via Denmark and the German-speaking territories all the way to France, where he had met some of the leading lights of Paris, especially the principal editors of the *Encyclopédie,* d'Alembert and Diderot, the latter of whom Herder called "the best philosopher in France."[1] Herder kept a diary of his travels that he filled with ambitious plans both for himself and for his country, ideas for books and essays he intended to write, and reflections about almost every conceivable aspect of history, society, art, and life. Even though the *Journal meiner Reise im Jahr 1769* (Journal of my travels in 1769) was not published until 1846, it has been rightly called "the most illuminating document of the inner story of Herder's mind"[2] that we possess from the time just before he arrived in Strasbourg. In short, Herder in the autumn of 1770 cut an almost irresistibly exciting figure: he knew and was known by important people—on top of everything else, he had also studied philosophy for two years in Königsberg under Immanuel Kant—he was widely traveled, creative, prolific, and even slightly dangerous. He was the first genuine intellectual Goethe had met, and the effect on the impressionable younger man was electric.

Even the prelude to this fateful meeting seems to be the stuff of legend. Goethe had agreed to enroll at Strasbourg at the behest of his doting but ambitious father, who was eager to see his son finish his studies and finally complete the law degree he had begun in Leipzig five years before, in 1765, when he was only sixteen. Life had been a little too easy for the teenage Goethe in modern and bustling Leipzig, called "Little Paris" for its intellectual vibrancy—in addition to its university, Leipzig also possessed the distinction of being the book-publishing capital of Germany—but also for its fashionable elegance and for the relative abundance of attractive diversions on offer there. Supported by a generous allowance from his father, who remained vigilant over his son's academic progress but at a reassuringly safe distance in his native city of Frankfurt, the young Goethe had devoted much of his time to extracurricular pursuits. Quickly disenchanted and bored by the Leipzig law professors, Goethe concentrated his energies instead on art and poetry, honing his drafting and etching skills and composing verses in the gallant but rather artificial style of the Rococo, which celebrated pastoral love in Arcadian settings. Only a serious illness that struck Goethe in June 1768 put a premature end to these pleasant but ultimately trivial dalliances and Goethe spent the next six months convalescing at home in Frankfurt. But after he had finally fully recovered, the question of his future still loomed. Leipzig had proved educational, but not in the way his father had wished, and Strasbourg, he hoped, would provide a more congenial, which is to say less distracting, environment for his bright but unfocused son who, perhaps forgivably, preferred writing poetry to studying law.

It fell to Herder to jolt Goethe out of his Anacreontic complacency. While he was in Strasbourg, Herder was busy writing the work for which he is still most famous today, the *Abhandlung über den Ursprung der Sprache* (Treatise on the origin of language), which later won the prize contest announced that year by the Berlin Academy of Sciences. Over the winter, Goethe read the treatise as it was being composed, and it revealed to him a dynamic conception of language and its place within human experience. Herder placed particular emphasis on the creative power of language and on its inseparable connection to the history, culture—or, to use a then fashionable term, the "spirit"—of the people who spoke it. These were not ideas unique to Herder—Montesquieu, for one, whom Herder greatly admired, had written extensively about the particular esprit of individual peoples, and Condillac, whom Herder pretended to disdain but secretly appropriated, had applied this insight specifically to the study of language—but these ideas *were* new to Goethe, and the lesson he learned was that his native language, indeed all languages, were just as capable of expressing poetic vigor, dignity, and beauty as classical Latin and Greek, not to mention the lingua franca of educated Europeans, French.

This, then, was Herder as Goethe first saw him: already immensely learned, inexhaustibly curious, impetuous, emotionally volatile and physically restless, exuding an intellectual vitality coupled with a quick impatience, all of which formed a potent mixture that beguiled, and often enough alienated, those who encountered him. Although driven to comprehend history in all of its breadth and complexity, Herder was also very much a man of the moment, attuned to the extraordinary intellectual ferment taking place throughout Europe that was challenging long-held beliefs about every facet of human experience, from religion and art, to education and law, to politics, epistemology, and science—all of which were subjects to which Herder would devote his many essays and books during the rest of his life. Through the accident of birth, Herder thus enjoyed the good luck of coming of age just as the Enlightenment reached its zenith, making him the fortunate beneficiary of one of the most intellectually vibrant and productive periods in history. It is easy to imagine that Herder must have seemed to Goethe the very incarnation of the kind of expansive mind that all of his university professors so disappointingly were not: a seemingly endlessly inquisitive spirit who stopped at no disciplinary boundaries, in fact disdained such boundaries as obstacles to real insight, a thinker whose goal was to strive for nothing less than the achievement of the Enlightenment dream: to attain a comprehensive understanding of humanity, even more to aspire to universal knowledge. Herder personified an ardent but indefinite longing, he embodied an unquenchable yearning, a striving for something perpetually, because necessarily, beyond our grasp: in short, in the words of more than one later observer, for the young Goethe "Herder is Faust!"[3]

There is much that speaks in favor of the notion that, as someone else more cautiously suggested, "Herder became a model of Goethe's Faust,"[4] or, as another put it even more circumspectly, "Herder's desire for life is in Faust."[5] First, as I have indicated, Herder's personality, his intellectual profile, his vast ambition and insatiable drive, all find an easily identifiable resonance in the figure of the tormented scholar familiar from Goethe's drama. Too, not long after they had met and under the lingering influence of Herder's powerful example, Goethe began to write what became the first draft of the play, the so-called *Urfaust*, which, however, he abandoned unfinished in 1774. Finally, although the story of Faust had long been popular in Germany, usually transmitted in some corrupted version of Marlowe's *Doctor Faustus*, it was first in Strasbourg that, as Nicholas Boyle reminds us, "Goethe may have seen a performance of the story by strolling actors,"[6] thus perhaps forging a lasting bond in the poet's mind that fused Herder and Faust inseparably together. This connection seemed in fact so compelling that in 1911 a German scholar by the name of Günther Jacoby published a nearly five-hundred-page book, *Herder als Faust*, which set out to prove, in exhaustive—and exhausting—detail, that "Herder himself is Faust" and "that we must see in Faust the concentration of the human impression of Herder and a wealth of impulses that, at the beginning of the 1770s, passed over from Herder to Goethe."[7]

However, as intriguing as the question of Herder's possible paternity of *Faust* may be, what interests me more and will form the focus of my comments in this chapter, are not so much the eighteenth-century circumstances from which Goethe's work emerged, but rather the early-twentieth-century context in which such a claim as "Herder is Faust" could make sense. For in that statement there lies buried an entire world, a tradition and style of interpretation, a particular set of assumptions about German culture and its meaning, which rested not so much on historical as on ideological grounds. Ultimately, the claim that "Herder is Faust" entailed not a description of Herder or of Goethe—or, for that matter, of Faust—at all, but rather conforms to a broader effort to define the German past as a means of shaping the German present and future. As we will see, the meeting between Herder and Goethe was from the beginning invested with extraordinary significance, and as time went on that significance grew to encompass not just the individual lives of the two men involved, but the greater fortune and destiny of Germany itself.

Given the tremendous importance granted to Herder for having ostensibly inspired Goethe in writing his masterpiece, indeed for having helped to set modern German culture on its proper course, it is remarkable how minor and indistinct a role Herder played until relatively recently in the collective German consciousness. It was not until 1877 that a critical edition of his works began to appear—the surest sign of canonical status—and as late as 1895, in one of the few monographs then written on Herder, the author lamented the relative ignorance about Herder as compared to his other illustrious contemporaries: "If one speaks to a German about Lessing, a very definite and almost palpable figure arises before his eyes. If one mentions the name of Herder to him, nothing stirs in his soul except a vague memory. He looks at us with that minor embarrassment that befalls us when we realize that we ought to know about something and yet know nothing."[8] Paradoxically, this lack of familiarity with Herder remained a kind of topos in the literature about him for decades, so that as late as 1941, Hans-Georg Gadamer still complained that "among the very great figures of our literature, Herder is the only one who is no longer read: no poem, no work can be named by someone who has a working notion of Klopstock's odes, of Lessing's dramas and critical works, of Goethe and of Schiller."[9] Thus it remained for years thereafter, and, indeed, in no small measure continues to hold true today as well. The International Herder Society was not established until 1985—by comparison, the Goethe Society was founded a full century earlier, and the Schiller Society ten years later, in 1895—and only recently have many of his works become available in English translation.

But what was deplored as shameful negligence toward the memory of a great cultural forebear turned out in practice to be a useful advantage for his later would-be champions. For it was precisely the comparative neglect of Herder, whose works went relatively unread and whose thoughts and opinions thus remained all but unknown, that allowed his name to become a kind of empty cipher, a tabula rasa onto which successive interpreters could project their own image of Herder without fearing contradiction from readers who might know what he had actually said. So great was the ignorance about Herder prior to the early twentieth century, and so persuasive was the narrative subsequently constructed to explain what he meant, that to an unusual degree Herder is, or has become, what others have said about him and not what he actually was. In the absence of any widespread agreement or even knowledge about what Herder meant, his early-twentieth-century interpreters had extraordinary license not just in shaping his image, but in actively creating it. Thus, as odd as it sounds, the Herder many people think they know, as ill-defined as that notion may be, is in actuality not Herder at all, or is at best a partial and distorted reflection of the Herder who lived and wrote in the second half of the eighteenth century. Instead, the Herder handed down to us, and the Herder I will be focusing on here, is an artificial construction wholly invented by later critics who purported to explain Herder but really exploited him to further other ends. Herder as Faust was a fiction in every sense of the word, but it was a fiction that was treated as truth.

The process of turning the historical Herder into what one might call an ideological placeholder began as early as 1867, when Wilhelm Dilthey, the father of German *Geistesgeschichte*, held his inaugural address at the University of Basel. Called "The Poetic and Philosophical Movement in Germany 1770–1800," the title of the lecture already signals Dilthey's determination to see those thirty years as forming a coherent whole, indeed as constituting a "movement," a word that itself conveys a programmatic, even implicitly political, sense. "There arose at the time," Dilthey wrote to explain the origin of this "movement," "not only within individual people of a significant constitution, but rather within the educated classes of the nation in general the *urge to form a new ideal of life*—an inquiry into the purpose of man—into the content of a truly valuable life, into genuine culture."[10]

We already see in this brief passage a tendency toward the abstraction and generalization of concrete particulars that would become one of the hallmarks of subsequent commentary on Herder, combined with an eagerness to view him not as an individual thinker, but rather as a representative of ideas and forces much larger than himself, and indeed that were identical with German culture as a whole. And it is far from accidental that Dilthey dates the first stirrings of this "urge to form a new ideal of life" to the year Goethe met Herder. For Dilthey, that is, 1770 marks the birth of a "genuine culture" in Germany out of the spirit of Herder as Faust. As Dilthey explained it, "the transformed ideal of life of this new generation was the poetically, scientifically, morally productive genius. And I know of no more precise expression of this ideal of life in the reality of life than Herder's well-known travel journal in which he draws the line of his future existence as if into infinity, embracing the entire world, reforming all the sciences. But there is only one completely adequate representation of the same thing in literature: the oldest fragments of *Faust*."[11]

Here, then, at the beginning of Dilthey's career and, not coincidentally, just three years before the unification of the German Empire, we can make out the outlines of what would become the dominant perception, or rather the willful portrait, of Herder that would predominate in the decades to come. In this account, Herder stood as both the advocate and personification of original genius, that unfathomable, creative force of nature, inaugurating what Dilthey identified as a completely new culture that opposed and overcame the supposedly exhausted and defunct culture that had come before and had been given consummate expression in Goethe's *Faust*. Although Dilthey spoke in fairly neutral, and often rather positive terms about the Enlightenment itself—he praised Lessing's *Nathan der Weise*, for example, by saying that "the idea of the Enlightenment is transfigured in the hero of this play into perfected moral beauty"[12]—there is the unmistakable suggestion that it was precisely what Dilthey elsewhere called the "intellectual culture" (*Verstandeskultur*)[13] that defined the Enlightenment, which the new "ideal of life" came to supplant.

In the following decades, what Dilthey had merely hinted at or alluded to hardened into a sort of secular dogma among educated Germans: the "new ideal of life" represented by the generation of "poets and thinkers" during the last third of the eighteenth century was understood as having inaugurated a distinct culture, one that took shape in reaction to, or more precisely in rejection of, the Enlightenment era that preceded it. In 1908, for instance, a former student of Dilthey, the literary historian Oskar Walzel, published an essay devoted to "Goethe and the Problem of the Faustian Nature" that offers one of the first attempts to combine the themes touched on by Dilthey into a unified interpretive scheme—namely, to trace the rise of a distinctly new cultural moment, or movement, which was exemplified by the original genius Herder and codified in Goethe's *Faust*—and to argue that this shift largely consisted in repudiating the supposedly facile culture that Walzel identified with the Enlightenment. This is how Walzel, with a pronounced air of bemused condescension, characterized the social context that Herder ostensibly confronted at the end of the 1760s.

> The eighteenth century still believed it could elevate people above all difficulties through a one-sided intellectual culture. The sacred conviction of Wolff's Enlightenment philosophy that the understanding could put everything on the best path has something touching and poignant about it. The more enlightened a person is, he thought, the better he would also have to be. Intellectual culture led without fail to virtue. All natural drives were to be tamed through intellectual culture. Decent, civilized people, upright and full of healthy common sense, were the goal of the Enlightenment. They were convinced they had come wonderfully far by breeding vapid natures that had nothing to fear from their instincts. The result was a sad philistinism that, confined within the tightest boundaries, banished everything beautiful and good.

Walzel was of course not alone in regarding what he, following Dilthey, also called "intellectual culture" with suspicion and even open disdain. In the intervening years and especially around the turn of the century, a number of thinkers—most prominently Nietzsche and Bergson—had engaged in a sustained critique of the value and meaning of reason, truth, and objectivity, arguing that these very concepts were, at best, partial and naïve, serving to obscure rather than reveal the full and complex nature of reality. The Enlightenment, with its constitutive emphasis on the power of human reason to answer all questions about nature and existence, thus came to be regarded not as an exemplary period of human achievement but as an embarrassing episode of human self-delusion, shortsightedness, and smug folly. Reason did not liberate, it acted as a constraint; thinking did not disclose reality, it ensconced itself in its own self-reflexive illusions. And, in Oskar Walzel's eyes, it was none other than Herder who first recognized and repudiated what Walzel called "the narrowness of this cultural program," and that it was his "Faustian Nature" that prompted this revelation:

> The man who touched Goethe most powerfully when the idea of the Faust play germinated within him, Herder, wrestled and struggled from the beginning to

> grant equal worth to spirit and life. He wanted to embrace all of the wisdom of the earth in a Faustian manner, and simultaneously achieve a vital effect. . . .
>
> Conscious of being able to approach this lofty goal only from a distance, the young Herder repeatedly displayed the Faustian dissatisfaction and torment of the thinker who desires an actively worthwhile life and thus turns away from arid speculation full of aversion and disgust. A dissatisfied craving for knowledge also drove him to the desire to enjoy life to its fullest. The diary of his journey has become an entirely indispensible document of Faustian struggle around the time of 1770: Herder sees in himself merely an inkwell of scholarly scribbling, a dictionary of arts and sciences he has not actually seen and does not understand, a repository full of books and paper that belongs only in a study. He wants to put experience in the place of rumination, he wants to seize and grasp life where before he had only thought and pondered.[14]

In this relatively brief account, Walzel thus performed a remarkable fusion of the major themes of Herder's early life story by fashioning an integrated narrative that blends biography, literary criticism, cultural history, and philosophical analysis into a seamless, and thus convincing, amalgam. Herder as Faust literally embodied the "new ideal of life" envisioned by Dilthey, enacting in and through his own experience the very ideas he was said to espouse. Thus Herder became both the herald and the exemplar of the forces that transformed the German intellectual landscape, ushering in a development that early-twentieth-century observers felt led directly to themselves.

While we may smile at the circularity of this argument—wherein the past is read through the lens of one's own immediate preoccupations, which produces amazement at how uncannily that past prefigured the present—it would be a mistake to underestimate its influence on the perception of both Herder and of his relevance for contemporary concerns. Indeed, it was increasingly the imagined pertinence or applicability of Herder's thought to current circumstances that moved to the center of discussion. In an overview published in 1909 of "Recent Research on Herder," a literary scholar named Rudolf Unger made this intention explicit. Unger began by repeating the almost ritualistic complaint that "for a long time, too long," Herder had "stood to one side unnoticed, indeed almost invisible,"[15] but that ever since the 1860s things had begun to change for the better: "More or less simultaneously with the national ascent of his people," Unger explained, "Herder's star began slowly to rise up over the horizon of the German spiritual firmament." Unger called this belated rediscovery of Herder a "penitential act of objective historical justice for the enthusiastic prophet of German greatness."[16] "In a word, through this transformation he has been moved out of the distant perspective of history into the proximity of the current questions and struggles of our own, immediate intellectual life."[17] Similarly, Unger singled out as particularly noteworthy the new writings on Herder he was reviewing: "They have set themselves the task not merely to place Herder's thoughts and ideals in a vital relationship to ours, but rather to reveal those relationships that are already everywhere present and to make them productive for the advancement of our own intellectual life."[18]

There are several things that warrant mention here and have a bearing on the further evolution of our subject. First, in addition to putting almost exclusive stress on Herder's importance for contemporary issues, Unger even more closely associates Herder with German culture itself, or, as he puts it, with "German greatness." This linking of individual and national destinies, together with the dehistoricization that inevitably results from the desire to find meaning in the past only insofar as it is thought to be reflected or continued in the present, further intensified that tendency toward the generalization and abstraction of individual lives into grand cultural-historical developments that had already animated Dilthey's reading. That is, Herder—already regarded principally as the living personification of a literary figure—had turned into not just the starting point, but also the validation for modern German culture. Just as Goethe's *Faust* had become a kind of national secular bible, Herder as Faust thus became a national cultural prophet.

For the next decade or so, there were other aspects of the modern world other than Herder's significance for it that demanded attention—there was a world war to fight and a revolution to muddle through—but in the politically charged climate of the Weimar Republic, Herder was pressed ever more forcefully into compulsory service for his country. One of the most sophisticated and influential attempts to lend intellectual history a covert political relevance was by Hermann August Korff, who more than anyone else gave the notion of a *Goethezeit,* or "Age of Goethe," its intellectual, or rather ideological, content and justification. In 1923, Korff published the first of ultimately three volumes dedicated to elucidating what he called the "Spirit," or "*Geist,*" of the Goethezeit. Symptomatically, Korff viewed what he called "Faustian man" as "symbolic" of the entire phenomenon. "The spirit of the Age of Goethe," he wrote, "can be provisionally described as the spirit of an irrationalistic idealism" as opposed to the "questionable qualities of an interpretation of reality governed solely by the understanding"[19] that Korff also insisted characterized the Enlightenment. To his credit, however, Korff understood the Enlightenment and the Goethezeit not as discrete points along a chronological axis, but as the twin poles of an eminently dialectical struggle. As he conceded,

> it is true that the Enlightenment remains the basis of modern culture, just as the former cannot deny its origins in the completely opposite theological system of the Middle Ages. And the Age of Goethe, in which this development takes place, cannot be viewed as a world-historical epoch in the same sense as the modern culture of European humanity that begins with the Enlightenment, because it is born out of contradiction to the Enlightenment, but from

> a contradiction that not only destroys the idea of the Enlightenment, but also continues it in a higher sense.[20]

It is this same dialectical tension that Korff saw played out within Goethe's drama itself. Korff thus similarly claimed:

> Of all the imaginative realizations of this eternal problematic of the idealist who battles against reality and understanding for his very existence, none symbolizes it more powerfully that the Faust drama, which in its two great antagonists represents, in terms of the history of ideas, nothing other than the world-historical, yet basically eternally human, battle fought throughout the history of the Age of Goethe between idealism and Enlightenment.[21]

Not surprisingly, for Korff as well Herder epitomized the struggle between the new German culture and the old, mainly French, culture of the Enlightenment. But in line with his dialectical perspective, Korff also perceived elements of that other tradition, exemplified by Rousseau, as still operative within Herder, adding to the internal conflicts that supposedly beset his Faustian nature. Typically, Korff also focused on Herder's journey to France as expressive of his essential nature:

> And the diary of this journey is one of the most important documents for the emergence of Rousseauism in the German spirit. Herder considered himself to be a victim of the same intellectualism and of that entire ink-stained culture which Rousseau also felt suffocated his wild, unfettered nature. Indeed, Herder's entire youth, which had been artificially "driven" by the needs of a precocious mind, had been a life spent purely in books, and his world—"and that is called a world!" [another quote from *Faust*]—had been the world of literature. But the more he had thirstily sought the springs of life in the desert of scholarly culture, the more dissatisfied he had felt. Like Faust in the dead confines of his study, he also yearned finally to escape from his confined existence in Riga and into the freedom of creative life. And like Faust who bursts open the prison of his life with the cry "Flee! Away! Out into the open land!" and, pulled by his worldly and active genius, throws himself into the arms of a new, immediate life, so too Herder with sudden resolve liberates himself from the dungeon of his study and seeks to save himself by setting out on the open sea, which becomes symbolic for him of the open sea of life. . . . This sea journey is the symbol of the Faustian world journey and the attempt on the part of a man suffocated by culture to recuperate in nature from the curse of cultural life and to awaken from the cultural death to natural life. And the entire mood during this journey also swings in Faustian fashion between the highest expectations and deepest resignation. For just as Herder is driven out into the radiant pulsation of immediate life, so too he is simultaneously tormented by bitter regret not only over his lost youth, but rather, what was worse, by his lost youthfulness. And his diary is the chaotic testament of an impassioned, self-reproachful, forward and backward-looking, Faustian-Rousseauistic self-reflection.[22]

Korff's portrait of Herder as a tormented soul, who rejected the culture of his time as an impediment to his own self-realization, and in particular renounced reason as too partial and restrictive, turning instead to a fuller range of experience and feeling, is fully in line with the image Korff's predecessors had also elaborated. Too, the weaving together of multiple literary, philosophical, historical, and cultural perspectives within a captivating narrative has by now become familiar. And, indeed, that very familiarity was largely responsible for the enormous appeal and longevity of the story: the tale of Herder as Faust, of the intrepid traveler who turned his back on his time to embrace an uncertain future, had been told and retold so many times that it had become almost as well known as the Faust legend itself.

In 1924, one year after Korff's book appeared, another prominent literary historian, Josef Nadler, gave the by then standard version of Herder as Faust a dramatically new twist when he published an essay that posed a seemingly innocuous question in its title: "Goethe oder Herder?" (Goethe or Herder?).[23] But there was nothing innocuous about Nadler's motives. For Nadler, the question was no longer what Herder meant within the context of the eighteenth century or even what significance he might have had for Nadler's own time, but rather what role Herder might play in shaping the future. In Nadler's hands, the view of Herder as the implacable opponent of a moribund Enlightenment culture thereby metastasized into a previously unthinkable heresy: in his effort to make Herder even more relevant to the present day, Nadler relegated none other than Goethe himself to the exemplary role of representing the old, stifling order, and promoted Herder to the forefront of the national pantheon not merely as the champion of a new culture, but also as the inspirational leader of a new political order to come.

With Nadler, then, a new stage in the appropriation of Herder began, one that would have enormous consequences for the subsequent perception of Herder by both his admirers and detractors. At first glance, it appears that Nadler merely adopted some of the essential components of the established image of Herder—his elemental originality, his hostility to the Enlightenment, his craving for experience and authenticity—and raised them to an even higher level of intensity. That Nadler did, but he also added a new, even more potent ingredient to the mix. Nadler later became famous—or notorious—for his multivolume work titled *Literaturgeschichte der deutschen Stämme und Landschaften* (The literary history of the German tribes and landscapes). In it, Nadler tried to demonstrate that every region—or "landscape"—of Germany had a specific and identifiable quality that materially influenced the character and mentality of the people—or "tribe"—and hence the writers, who inhabited it. It is not quite literally a racist theory—and Nadler, who lived until 1963, always rather primly denied that it was—his ideas could and did easily converge with those of other writers who had no such scruples. This, then, is how Nadler describes Herder's lasting importance:

> With his first minor writings, the young Herder already set the reversal of his time in motion by taking up the question of the origin of language, myth, and poetry, while combining the roles of historian, natural scientist, and philosopher simultaneously. . . . Herder was the first to see the preeminent value of what is originary over what is developed, of what is growing over what has been made, of the youth of a people over its mature years. He was not concerned with the opposition between nature and culture, but rather between the culture of the lower class and the civilization of the upper class. He discovered the people [*Volk*] as the true breeding ground of great cultural processes. And if he demanded progress instead of regress, return to what is originary, that is to the people, to the youth of *"völkisch"* existence, then he was not playing a rough natural state against refined culture. He was opposing true culture to false, growth against completion and senile preservation.[24]

Not content with giving Herder credit for having discovered the meaning and value of *das Volk*, Nadler also drew up a whole catalogue of other innovations that he ascribed to Herder and were presented as a direct consequence of his presumed elevation of the Volk. "Various scientific disciplines today are breathing Herder's spirit, not still, but again," Nadler proposed. "Think of certain movements in modern geography and of what today we call geopolitics."[25] Further, Herder was, according to Nadler, "the originator of the new concept of the state that arose during Romanticism, the triumphant concept of the national state [*Volksstaat*]."[26] Likewise, Nadler claimed that Herder "laid the groundwork for ethnology [*Volkskunde*], that is, for the consciousness of a people of itself."[27] Even more, Nadler asserts that Herder anticipated the greatest political upheaval of his time: "Twenty years before the outbreak of the French Revolution," Nadler writes, "Herder was the discoverer of the people [Volk] as the producer and supporter of all social life. He is thus the originator of those insights which perhaps of all eighteenth-century ideas have most effectively influenced the reconstruction of the world from the nineteenth into the twentieth centuries."[28]

Curiously, it never seems to have occurred to Nadler to consider why, if Herder had indeed been responsible for so many and such momentous advances, it had escaped everyone else's notice but his own. But, again, Nadler was not actually interested in history at all, but rather in using history—or a version of it—to advance another cause. And that cause was the German people itself. In Nadler's deliberately provocative scheme, Goethe represented not the pinnacle of modern German culture, but rather an enervated internationalism, an individualistic cosmopolitanism that inevitably lost its vigor as it distanced itself from its specific cultural context, or landscape. Thus, Nadler wrote that "Goethe's national [*gemeinvölkisch*] attitude was that of individual to individuals and thus basically not a national attitude at all."[29] Specifically, Nadler argued that Goethean Classicism, with its center in Weimar, was nothing but a minor clique of rootless, elite aesthetes far removed from the lives of the German people. "Goethe's Europeanness," Nadler explained, "which again fundamentally was not one, was based on the last remnant of common humanistic culture. But how can one speak of Europe if a half dozen people present themselves as a class? A single individual cannot form a race with itself alone. He thus can also not step out of his race and form a higher species, for instance a 'Europe,' with others who are each in the same situation, at most he can form a class of raceless people."[30] In sum, Nadler saw Goethe essentially as a holdover from an age that had outlived itself. "Goethe represented the educated upper class of a declining age. It was the old monarchical state, the old society that had managed to save itself following 1789, the old 'International' of individual to individual, it was the age of the French encyclopedists and the Germany of the Confederation of the Rhine,"[31] the latter being the name given to the collaborationist occupational government under Napoleon.

It was on this basis, then, that Nadler concluded that despite, or perhaps precisely because of, his status as the great Olympian of Classical culture, Goethe could not serve as an inspiration or model for the present. "For how could Goethe," Nadler wrote,

> the cultural aristocrat and individualist, help where it is a matter of the decisive question of our social life? The uprooted masses who today act as a people, who lack precisely what Herder sought, namely what is primordial, undeveloped, rejuvenating, they have to be integrated in Herder's sense back into the earth. . . . These uprooted masses have to be integrated into an energizing place to live. And if today everywhere hands are in motion to make a people out of the masses who merely fill a state, then that is Herder's will that moves us.[32]

It is at this point that Nadler's political intentions become manifest. What he was most concerned with is how to shape the masses—the German people—into something more than merely inhabitants of a geographical region. More specifically—we remember that Nadler was writing only six years after the end of the war—in the wake of military defeat, revolution, an unpopular government, and economic turmoil, Nadler like many others of his generation was looking for a leader who could guide the people out of their current uncertainty and toward a better future. Nadler explains:

> The cultural type of our developing era is not Goethe, but Herder. We, a generation of swirling chaos, are fated not to preserve passed-down forms, but rather to be formless, form-free, form-liberated in the service of a creative and procreative idea. . . . We, who were condemned to experience, are called on to create a new content, but not to form where there is nothing to form. What

> our generation produces in terms of ideas, what we experience and engender in our suffering, will be the material that another great creator of form after us will once again give shape. Precursors of this form-giver live among us. But they are forward posts, destined to perish, as is the fate of forward posts. Thus we have Goethe at our backs and before us the work of a new form still to be done. . . . The destiny of Moses repeats itself in great rhythmical cycles. No age sees the form-giver it creates out of its ideas.[33]

Here the language of literary criticism has clearly ceded to the rhetoric of messianic demagoguery. No longer merely the living embodiment of a literary hero, Herder had now become a national prophet who would lead the German people toward their promised geopolitical destiny. However, contrary to Nadler's assertion, Herder did not in fact invent "geopolitics," at least not in name. It was instead the Swedish scholar Rudolf Kjellén who coined the term "geopolitics" during the First World War. As it happens, Kjellén may have also been the first person to use the term "National Socialism," whose proponents in Germany were all too eager to submit their individual lives to the service of their cause. The author of a dissertation written at the University of Jena in 1936 put it succinctly: "The essence of the Revolution in 1933 carried out by the National-Socialist movement is founded in the overcoming of individualism through National Socialism, which replaces the single person with the people [das Volk] at the center of all thought."[34]

Throughout the 1930s, numerous studies of Herder appeared in Germany that sought to align him with the aims and spirit of the new regime. Heinz Kindermann, who became head of the department of German literature at the University of Danzig in 1927 and joined the Nazi party in 1933, typified this intellectual *Gleichschaltung* or "synchronization." In an introduction to an anthology of several works by Herder published in 1935, Kindermann wrote that: "the battle against the spirit and form of life of the pan-European Enlightenment" initiated by Herder "was a first attempt to liberate the German people from the domination of Western influences and thereby to clear a path for a species-appropriate, German culture and disposition, for an organic and natural formation of German life and German art arising from the people."[35] In Kindermann's view, therefore, the Enlightenment was not just antithetical to life, but also opposite to the German character as such.

Not surprisingly, Kindermann's sketch also drew primarily on details from Herder's life, particularly from the period when he met Goethe, as indicative of the larger significance he had for German culture. But Kindermann's political allegiances also infuse his style with a shrill vehemence that, in its undisguised hostility toward the perceived opponents of "Germanness," has an unmistakably menacing ring:

> The theoretical and abstract book and encyclopedia learning of the age of reason weighs like a nightmare especially on those who have already recognized its injurious effects, its obsolescence, its corrosive influence on Germanness. It required a radical, explosive act to gain mastery over these repressive forces; but that is what Herder did through his flight from the enlightened narrowness of the philistine, bourgeois world [*Lebensraum*] into the elemental freedom and expanse of his ocean journey around half of Europe.[36]

Kindermann of course fails to mention that Herder himself regarded as one of the high points of his journey his acquaintance with that arch encyclopedist, Diderot.

But, as was the case with his fellow critics, Kindermann was fundamentally concerned not so much with Herder's stance toward or within the eighteenth century, but rather with his presumed influence on the twentieth, and particularly on the new German reality. In 1938, a colleague of Kindermann named Wolfdietrich Rasch emphasized that connection when he wrote of Herder that "we recognize in this work an often surprising proximity to our time, a deep affinity with many of the fundamental views that make Herder appear to us as a prophet, inspiration, and precursor to the forces that today are active in our people; as a man who—in the words of Alfred Rosenberg—'became a teacher particularly for our time, as only very few did among even the greatest.'"[37] As we will recall, Rosenberg was the author of *Der Mythus des zwanzigsten Jahrhunderts* (The myth of the twentieth century), published in 1930 and intended to consolidate the disparate themes within National Socialist thought into a unified theory. The apotheosis—or nadir—of the same line of reasoning was achieved in a book published a few years later whose title tells us all we need to know: written by Hans Dahmen, it is called *Die nationale Idee von Herder bis Hitler* (The national idea from Herder to Hitler).[38]

As one historian has aptly put it: "German fascism transformed not only cities and landscapes, but also the 'regions of the spirit,' into blackened fields of rubble."[39] It has taken a very long time for Herder's reputation to emerge from the ruins left by his early-twentieth-century champions, and in many respects the process of rehabilitation is far from complete. In an essay published as recently as 2006, Wolfgang Pross, one of the best scholars writing about Herder today, still found it necessary to point out the "grave injustice" done by those who have perpetuated the "erroneous identification" of Herder with the so-called "Counter-Enlightenment."[40] "Although there is scarcely a grain of truth in such perspectives," Pross rather pessimistically writes, "legends ascribing to Herder doctrines of medievalism, nationalism, and irrationalism" seem "ineradicable." "Yet," Pross goes on, "Herder was profoundly acquainted with the political, philosophical, and historical writings of contemporary European thinkers [who] helped him to frame an interpretation of man as a social being with reference to different stages of human culture."[41] Although Pross does not stress the point, one of the most bizarre after effects of the misappropriation of Herder is that those who continue to claim he was an early advocate, if not the father, of a chauvinistic nationalism in Germany, a promoter of the ideal of a pure and autochthonous Volk, and an implacable opponent of reason, are thereby continuing, one assumes unwittingly, an interpretive tradition that achieved its logical culmination and fullest expression during the Nazi reign.

By placing Herder in the service of an ideology that in fact represented the very opposite of what he believed, his latter-day advocates did him and his cause—the promotion and, he hoped, the eventual achievement of universal *Humanität*—grave and perhaps irreparable harm. But it was they and not Herder who rejected the principles of the Enlightenment, who wanted to submerge the individual within the collective identity of the Volk, and who urged the abandonment of reason in order to embrace a new concept of "life" that, in fact, served only death.

Ironically enough, it was Mephistopheles himself who had warned of the dangers of disparaging our rational faculties and surrendering to seductive chimeras that only mask the unknown. In a revealing aside, he mocks Faust for his readiness to renounce his best possession, which Mephistopheles sneeringly warns will merely hasten an even greater sacrifice:

> Go ahead, hold reason and knowledge in contempt,
> That human power most sublime,
> Let yourself be emboldened by the spirit of lies
> Through magic and illusion,
> Then you will be mine absolutely—
>
> (Verachte nur Vernunft und Wissenschaft,
> Des Menschen allerhöchste Kraft
> Laß nur in Blend- und Zauberwerken
> Dich vom dem Lügengeist bestärken,
> So hab' ich dich schon unbedingt—)[42]

In turning Herder into Faust, his modern interpreters succeeded, at least for a time, in putting him in league with the devil. Let us hope that, in the end, like Faust Herder will also manage to escape his clutches.

NOTES

1. Rudolf Haym, *Herder nach seinem Leben und seinen Werken dargestellt* (Berlin: Rudolph Gaertner, 1877), 1:347.

2. Haym, *Herder nach seinem Leben und seinen Werken dargestellt*, 317.

3. Hermann August Korff, *Sturm und Drang*, vol. 1, *Geist der Goethezeit. Versuch einer ideellen Entwicklung der klassisch-romantischen Literaturgeschichte* (Leipzig: J. J. Weber, 1923), 75.

4. Oskar Walzel, "Goethe und das Problem der faustischen Natur," in *Vom Geistesleben des 18. und 19. Jahrhunderts* (Leipzig: Insel, 1911), 143. This essay first appeared in *Internationale Wochenschrift für Wissenschaft, Kunst und Technik* (August 29, 1908).

5. Max Kommerell, *Der Dichter als Führer in der deutschen Klassik* (Berlin: Georg Bondi, 1928), 109.

6. Nicholas Boyle, *The Poetry of Desire (1749–1790)*, vol. 1, *Goethe: The Poet and the Age* (Oxford: Oxford University Press, 1991), 219.

7. Günther Jacoby, *Herder als Faust. Eine Untersuchung* (Leipzig: Felix Meiner, 1911),

8. Eugen Kühnemann, *Herders Leben* (Munich: C. H. Beck, 1895), iii.

9. Hans-Georg Gadamer, *Volk und Geschichte im Denken Herders* (Frankfurt: Vittorio Klostermann, 1942). The text is based on a lecture Gadamer gave on May 29, 1941, at the German Institute in occupied Paris.

10. Wilhelm Dilthey, "Die dichterische und philosophische Bewegung in Deutschland 1770–1800," in *Gesammelte Schriften* (Stuttgart: B. G. Teubner, 1957), 5:16.

11. Dilthey, "Die dichterische und philosophische Bewegung in Deutschland," 20.

12. Dilthey, "Die dichterische und philosophische Bewegung in Deutschland," 17.

13. Dilthey, "Die dichterische und philosophische Bewegung in Deutschland," 20.

14. Walzel, "Goethe und das Problem der faustischen Natur," 141–42.

15. Rudolf Unger, "Zur neueren Herderforschung," *Germanisch-Romanische Monatsschrift* 1 (1909): 145.

16. Unger, "Zur neueren Herderforschung," 145.

17. Unger, "Zur neueren Herderforschung," 147.

18. Unger, "Zur neueren Herderforschung," 147.

19. Korff, *Sturm und Drang*, 32.

20. Korff, *Sturm und Drang*, 23.

21. Korff, *Sturm und Drang*, 47.

22. Korff, *Sturm und Drang*, 75.

23. Josef Nadler, "Goethe oder Herder?" *Hochland* 22, no. 1 (1924): 1.

24. Nadler, "Goethe oder Herder?" 5.

25. Nadler, "Goethe oder Herder?" 13.

26. Nadler, "Goethe oder Herder?" 7–8.

27. Nadler, "Goethe oder Herder?" 5.

28. Nadler, "Goethe oder Herder?" 7.

29. Nadler, "Goethe oder Herder?" 8.

30. Nadler, "Goethe oder Herder?" 8.

31. Nadler, "Goethe oder Herder?" 9.

32. Nadler, "Goethe oder Herder?" 11.

33. Nadler, "Goethe oder Herder?" 11.

34. Walther Kieser, *Die Gestalt des Volkes im nationalsozialistischen Weltbild. Ein Versuch ihrer staatswissenschaftlichen Erfassung* (Würzburg: Triltsch, 1936), 1. Quoted in Bernhard Becker, "Herder in der nationalsozialistischen Germanistik," in *Herder im "Dritten Reich,"* ed. Jost Schneider (Bielefeld: Aisthesis, 1994), 145.

35. Heinz Kindermann, "Einführung," *Von Deutscher Art und Kunst*, ed. Heinz Kindermann (Leipzig: Philipp Reclam, 1935), 5.

36. Kindermann, "Einführung," 6.

37. Wolfdietrich Rasch, *Sein Leben und Werk im Umriss* (Halle: Niemeyer, 1938), v.

38. Hans Dahmen, *Die nationale Idee von Herder bis Hitler* (Cologne: H. Schaffstein, 1934).

39. Jost Schneider, "Was bleibt von Herder? Eine Einleitung," in *Herder im "Dritten Reich,"* 7.

40. Wolfgang Pross, "Naturalism, Anthropology, and Culture," in *The Cambridge History of Eighteenth-Century Political Thought*, ed. Mark Goldie and Robert Wokler (Cambridge: Cambridge University Press, 2006), 218, 219.

41. Pross, "Naturalism, Anthropology, and Culture," 221.

42. Johann Wolfgang von Goethe, *Faust: Texte*, vol. 7, pt. 1, *Sämtliche Werke. Briefe, Tagebücher und Gespräche*, ed. Albrecht Schöne (Frankfurt: Deutscher Klassiker Verlag, 1994), 1851–55.

BIBLIOGRAPHY

Boyle, Nicholas. *The Poetry of Desire (1749–1790)*. Vol. 1, *Goethe: The Poet and the Age*. Oxford: Oxford University Press, 1991.

Dahmen, Hans. *Die nationale Idee von Herder bis Hitler*. Cologne: H. Schaffstein, 1934.

Dilthey, Wilhelm."Die dichterische und philosophische Bewegung in Deutschland 1770–1800." In *Gesammelte Schriften*, 5:12–27. Stuttgart: B. G. Teubner, 1957.

Gadamer, Hans-Georg. *Volk und Geschichte im Denken Herders*. Frankfurt: Vittorio Klostermann, 1942.

Goethe, Johann Wolfgang von. *Faust: Texte*. Vol. 7, pt.1, *Sämtliche Werke. Briefe, Tagebücher und Gespräche*. Edited by Albrecht Schöne. Frankfurt: Deutscher Klassiker Verlag, 1994.

Haym, Rudolf. *Herder nach seinem Leben und seinen Werken dargestellt*, vol. 5. Berlin: Rudolph Gaertner, 1877.

Jacoby, Günther. *Herder als Faust. Eine Untersuchung*. Leipzig: Felix Meiner, 1911.

Kieser, Walther. *Die Gestalt des Volkes im nationalsozialistischen Weltbild. Ein Versuch ihrer staatswissenschaftlichen Erfassung*. Würzburg: Triltsch, 1936.

Kindermann, Heinz, ed. *Von Deutscher Art und Kunst*. Leipzig: Philipp Reclam, 1935.

Kommerell, Max. *Der Dichter als Führer in der deutschen Klassik*. Berlin: Georg Bondi, 1928.

Korff, Hermann August. *Sturm und Drang*. Vol. 1, *Geist der Goethezeit. Versuch einer ideellen Entwicklung der klassisch-romantischen Literaturgeschichte*. Leipzig: J. J. Weber, 1923.

Kühnemann, Eugen. *Herders Leben*. Munich: C. H. Beck, 1895.

Nadler, Josef. "Goethe oder Herder?" *Hochland* 22, no. 1 (1924): 1–15.

Pross, Wolfgang. "Naturalism, Anthropology, and Culture." In *The Cambridge History of Eighteenth-Century Political Thought*, edited by Mark Goldie and Robert Wokler, 218–49. Cambridge: Cambridge University Press, 2006.

Rasch, Wolfdietrich. *Sein Leben und Werk im Umriss*. Halle: Niemeyer, 1938.

Schneider, Jost, ed. *Herder im "Dritten Reich."* Bielefeld: Aisthesis, 1994.

Unger, Rudolf. "Zur neueren Herderforschung." *Germanisch-Romanische Monatsschrift* 1 (1909): 145–68.

Walzel, Oskar. "Goethe und das Problem der faustischen Natur." In *Vom Geistesleben des 18. und 19. Jahrhunderts*, 135–65. Leipzig: Insel, 1911.

4

Coleridge's Critique of Goethe's *Faust*

Frederick Burwick

Coleridge may have known Goethe's *Faust. Ein Fragment* (1790) while attending the University of Göttingen. If so, it would certainly have been remembered during the two occasions (May and June 1799) when Coleridge and his student friends ascended the Brocken, site of Goethe's "Walpurgisnacht." The Faustian significance of that experience was certainly in Coleridge's memory when he retold his narrative of the Brocken on later occasions (1809, 1817, 1819). When Goethe's *Faust, Part I* (1808) first appeared, Coleridge was among those who expressed his concern for the apparent immorality. When Crabb Robinson read "a number of scenes" to him in 1812, Coleridge expressed further objections to aspects of character and motivation. In spite of his long-nurtured antipathy to *Faust,* he briefly entertained a proposal in 1814 to translate the work; he returned to and completed the task in 1820–1821. Although Goethe's posthumous *Faust, Part II* (1832) was published two years before Coleridge's death (July 25, 1834), he is not known to have mentioned it. In his final years, however, Coleridge reasserted his interest in writing his own Faust-story. As he had earlier explained to Crabb Robinson, the life and horrible death of Michael Scott (ca. 1160–1235), a legendary necromancer, was perfectly suited to a Faustian narrative of a pact with the devil.

This chapter will review Coleridge's appraisal of Goethe's *Faust* and examine its significance in relation to his criticism of other dramatic expositions of the necromancer, witches, and demons, and to his own projected Faustian tale. That Coleridge was familiar with Goethe's *Faust. Ein Fragment* (1790) was affirmed by Crabb Robinson in August 1812. Upon reading and discussing "a number of scenes out of the new *Faust* [1808]," Coleridge acknowledged that he now had a greater appreciation of "the genius of

Goethe." Nevertheless, he judged Goethe's "want of religion and enthusiasm" as "an irreparable defect." To Coleridge's objection that Mephistopheles is not a "character," Crabb Robinson proposed that he ought to be read as an abstraction rather than as a character, to which Coleridge could offer no satisfactory opposition. But Coleridge did introduce his argument about "ventriloquism"[1] interfering with, or completely usurping, the proper development of character. The author is constrained by dramatizing a consciousness too closely akin to his own. Mephistopheles, that is, was not a character but merely the negative side of Goethe himself. Coleridge admired the "Dedication" ("Zueignung"), but was not pleased with the "Prologue in Heaven" ("Prolog im Himmel"). He was less offended by Goethe's parody of the book of Job than Crabb Robinson had anticipated. Avoiding the widespread insistence upon "the patience of Job," Goethe was closer to the biblical text both in representing God's sanctioning Satan's intervention (Job 1:7–12) and in dramatizing Faust's Joblike impatience. Coleridge held, Crabb Robinson recorded, that Job "was the most impatient of men, and he was rewarded for his impatience: his integrity and sincerity had their recompense, because he was superior to the hypocrisy of his friends." The argument conforms well to Goethe's own affirmation of activity ("*Tätigkeit*"), his representation of Faust's restless quest, and his depiction of Mephistopheles as the spirit that always negates ("der Geist der stets verneint") (*F*, 1338).[2]

A week later, visiting Captain James Burney (brother of Fanny Burney), Coleridge provided "a very spirited sketch of *Faust*," again with his own critique: "He thinks the character of Faust himself not *motiviert.* He would have it explained how he was thrown into a state of mind which led to the catastrophe." Crabb Robinson protested that this was no "powerful objection," for the simple reason that Goethe turned directly to "the last stage of the process," not Faust's long career, but his frustrated self-appraisal in old age: "We see Faust wretched— he has acquired the utmost that finite powers can obtain, and he languishes for infinity. Rather than be finitely good he would be infinitely miserable."[3] Coleridge on this occasion was already formulating his plans for "writing a new *Faust*," one that would elaborate character motivations.

Two years later, Crabb Robinson encouraged John Murray to solicit Coleridge as the poet best suited to translate *Faust*. In his response of August 23, 1814, Coleridge declared that "among the many volumes of praiseworthy German Poems the Louisa of Voss and the Faust of Goethe are the two, if not the only ones, that are emphatically *original* in conception, & characteristic of a new & peculiar sort of Thinking and Imagining." Assuming that Murray will offer reasonable recompense, Coleridge affirmed that he "should like to attempt the Translation." His major misgiving was how it might be received by the public. In any case, it would need to be accompanied by a critical essay which Coleridge promised to provide. "Men of Genius will admire it, of necessity; those most, who think deepliest & most imaginatively—The Louisa would delight *all* of Good Hearts."[4] Although the literary prestige of Johann Heinrich Voss declined even as Goethe's reputation continued to rise, Coleridge's comparison of the literary merits of *Luise* (1795) and *Faust* (1808) was by no means invidious. He sincerely admired the poem and had proposed translating it several years earlier.[5] The point of his comparison is clear: Voss is sure of a warm public reception; Goethe is more apt to find his admirers exclusively among the dilettanti and intellectual elite.

Nowhere in Crabb Robinson's account of 1812 does he mention Coleridge's objections to the fantastic and supernatural scenes. Those concerns were apparently aroused by Charles Lamb, who knew Goethe's work only through Madame de Staël's excerpts. In response to the news of Murray's commission, Lamb cautioned Coleridge to avoid the project: "if 'Faust' be no better than in her [Madame de Staël's] abstract of it, I counsel thee to let it alone. How canst thou translate the language of cat monkeys? Fie on such fantasies!"[6] Lamb refers to the scene in "Witch's Kitchen" ("Hexenküche") but Coleridge, in a subsequent letter to Murray, extends it to "Walpurgis Night" ("Walpurgisnacht") as well:

> I think the 'Faust' a work of genius, of genuine and original Genius. The Scenes in the Cathedral and the Prison must delight and affect all Readers not predetermined to dislike. But the Scenes of Witchery and that astonishing Witch-Gallop up the Brocken will be denounced as *fantastic* and absurd. Fantastic they are, and were meant to be; but I need not tell you, how many will detect the supposed fault for one, who can enter into the philosophy of that imaginative Superstition, which justifies it.[7]

On repeated occasions Coleridge had already undertaken the effort to instruct the public in the "philosophy of that imaginative Superstition." In his lectures on Shakespeare he provided a well-reasoned defense of the witches and ghost in *Macbeth*,[8] and, as he reminded Murray,

> I have shewn to the full conviction of no small number of first-rate men that every one of the Faults so wildly charged on the Hamlet by the Decriers of Shakespear, and palliated even by his admirers only on the score of their being overbalanced by its Beauties, forms an essential part of the essential Excellence of that marvellous *Plenum* of the myriad-minded man.[9]

Coleridge repeated his praise of "myriad-minded" Shakespeare in the *Biographia Literaria*,[10] and in his lectures provided a powerful rationale for the dramatic appearance of the ghost of Hamlet's father.[11] As Coleridge must have realized, the haunting supernaturalism of his own poetry was one of the major reasons that he was considered by Murray and others as preeminently suited for the task of translating Goethe's work.

He stayed with the task for less than two months before giving it up. Remarking that Murray "treated me in a strange way," Coleridge lamented that in the task of translating *Faust* he had "employed some weeks unprofitably—when it was of more than usual necessity that I should have done otherwise."[12]

Up to this point, there is still no mention of the immorality or obscenity of *Faust* in Coleridge's comments. In a letter to Lord Byron, written six months after he had abandoned the effort at translation, Coleridge repeated his admiration of the work and reconfirmed his readiness "to undertake the translation," but added that he worried that the public response would be negative, not simply because of "the fantastic character of its Witcheries," but also because "the general tone of the morals and religious opinions would be highly obnoxious to the taste and Principles of the present righteous English public."[13] Coleridge asked Byron to review his collection of poetry in two volumes and to "recommend them to some respectable publisher." Affirming that "it will give me great pleasure to comply with your request," Byron also urged Coleridge to submit another play to Drury Lane. Byron had previously exerted his influence in securing the production of Coleridge's *Remorse* (Drury Lane, January 23, 1813; revived April 14, 1817).

> We have had nothing to be mentioned in the same breath with "Remorse" for very many years; and I should think that the reception of that play was sufficient to encourage the highest hopes of an author and audience. It is to be hoped that you are proceeding in a career which could not but be successful.[14]

In his negotiations with Murray, Coleridge agreed that he would render *Faust* "in a style of versification equal to 'Remorse.'" Coleridge stressed that "a large proportion of the work cannot be rendered in blank verse, but must be in wild *lyrical* metres." But he insisted that he, and not Murray, would control the rights to adapt it for the stage. In "My Advice and Scheme," the plan for translating *Faust* that he submitted to Thomas Boosey and Sons on May 12, 1820, Coleridge emphasized that the work must be "translated in the manner & metre of the original."[15] No doubt resurrecting whatever portion of the poem that he had managed to complete during the weeks he had spent "employed . . . unprofitably" in translating for Murray, Coleridge completed sixteen months later a version for Boosey that omitted the introductory scenes in the theater and in heaven, as well as the scenes of witchery.

Coleridge did not need Byron's encouragement to turn again to the drama. After the success of *Remorse*, however, his efforts profited others, not himself. *Zapolya*, written expressly for performance at Drury Lane, was rejected at that theater. Following difficulties between Murray and Rest Fenner, a revised version, *Zapolya: A Christmas Tale* (1817) was belatedly published by the latter. When Thomas Dibdin moved from Drury Lane to the Surrey Theatre, he adapted Coleridge's play for performance as melodrama. Opening on February 9, 1818, *Zapolya; or, The War Wolf* was announced on the playbill as "founded on Mr. Coleridge's favorite dramatic Poem." In spite of the successful run of the play, Coleridge had no claim to copyright nor to any share of the box office revenue under the existing copyright laws. The staging of Coleridge's translation of Goethe was similarly adapted as melodrama by Henry Milner. Opening at the Royal Coburg Theatre, London, on Monday, June 7, 1824, "Goethe's Terrific Drama of *Faustus*" was Milner's reworking of Coleridge's translation, anonymously published in 1821 and just released in its third edition in 1824.[16] For the crucial "Walpurgis Night," omitted from Coleridge's translation, Milner inserted the translation of this scene by Percy Bysshe Shelley.[17] The production was further indebted to the edition with Coleridge's translation because it was accompanied by the illustrations which Henry Moses copied from Moritz von Retzsch, and which were copied, in turn, in the set designs, scenery, and costumes for the Coburg production.[18] Although he must have resented the brazen appropriation of his work, Coleridge never mentioned in writing Dibdin's *Zapolya* nor Milner's *Faustus*.

Coleridge's comments on Goethe's *Faust* are not easily reconciled with his critique of other works of demonic magic such as Christopher Marlowe's *The Tragical History of Doctor Faustus*, Robert Greene's *Friar Bacon and Friar Bungay*, or Pedro Calderón de La Barca's *El Mágico Prodigioso*. Clearly for Coleridge, the problem lay not in the "Witcheries" per se, but in the immorality of those "Witcheries." In spite of Lamb's dismay at "the language of cat monkeys," a more challenging problem was the language of Mephistopheles, who speaks, as the devil might well be supposed to speak, a language sometimes eloquent, sometimes lewd and crude, as when he summarizes male anatomy as "hands and feet, / And head and testicles" ("Händ' und Füße / Und Kopf und H[oden]") (*F*, 1820–21).[19] In "Witch's Kitchen" Mephistopheles declares his nobility and as proof, with a thrust of his hips, presents his codpiece-clad genitals to the Witch. The stage direction states that "He makes a crude gesture" ("Er macht eine unanständige Gebärde"): "Look here, this is the Coat of Arms that I bear!" ("Sieh her, das ist das Wappen, das ich führe!") (*F*, 2513). The Witch, of course, finds his lewdness highly amusing. "That's your way! / You are a rogue and always have been" ("Das ist in euer Art! / Ihr seid ein Schelm, wie Ihr nur immer war't!") (*F*, 2514–15). One need only to turn to Mephistopheles' banter with Martha in the garden, or with the old Witch at the Walpurgis orgy for other instances of dubious "morals" that, as Coleridge told Byron,[20] would be judged "highly obnoxious" by the English public. Even Shelley, who boldly undertook a translation of the "Walpurgis Night" episode avoided by Coleridge, chose to omit Mephistopheles' obscene exchange with the old witch (*F*, 4136–43), and he left out such lines as "the witch farts and the ram stinks" ("Es furzt die Hexe, es stinkt der Bock") (*F*, 3961). As Shelley wrote to Jefferson Hogg, *Faust* "has passages of surpassing excellence, though there are some scenes—which the fastidiousness of our taste would wish erased."[21]

Because Mephistopheles' vulgarities were blatant, the task of selecting only the "inoffensive passages" was far easier for Coleridge than it was for Harriet Bowdler in editing *The Family Shakespeare* (1807). Her purpose was made more explicit in the title of her second edition, *The Family Shakespeare, in Ten Volumes; in Which Nothing Is Added to the Original Text; But Those Words and Expressions Are Omitted Which Cannot with Propriety Be Read Aloud in a Family* (1818).[22] The expurgated edition was published under her brother's name, Thomas Bowdler, to avoid the impression that a woman should possess such a comprehensive knowledge of sexually improper allusions. But as subsequent critics have shown, a lot of naughtiness escaped her notice.[23] Fully aware of Shakespeare's dramatization of rape and adultery, Coleridge was especially intrigued with the way in which Shakespeare imposed a moral corrective on potentially wayward infractions. Coleridge expressed an admiration for Caliban as a "creature of the earth," part man and part brute. Son of the witch Sycorax, supposedly sired by the devil, Caliban possesses "mere understanding without moral reason," and is without "the instincts which belong to mere animals." In Coleridge's account, or rather in John Payne Collier's notes,

> Caliban is a noble being: a man in the sense of the imagination, all the images he utters are drawn from nature & are all highly poetical; they fit in with the images of Ariel: Caliban gives you images from the Earth – Ariel images from the air. Caliban talks of the difficulty of finding fresh water, the situation of the Morasses & other circumstances which the brute instinct not possessing reason could comprehend. No mean image is brought forward and no mean passion but animal passions & the sense of repugnance at being commanded.[24]

Granting that Collier occasionally twisted Coleridge's words, it seems likely that Coleridge did indeed praise Shakespeare for not having Caliban's language debased with crude words or "mean images." The argument that he is driven by "no mean passions but animal passions" is true only in the sense that his rutting sexual desire is an "animal passion" and not motivated by the "mean passion" to hurt or dominate. His attempt to rape Miranda was thus merely the procreative urge to produce a litter of Calibans.

> PROSPERO. I have used thee,
> Filth as thou art, with human care, and lodged thee
> In mine own cell, till thou didst seek to violate
> The honour of my child.

> CALIBAN. O ho, O ho! Would't had been done!
> Thou didst prevent me; I had peopled else
> This isle with Calibans.[25]

In spite of similarities to other magicians and sorcerers of the stage from Marlowe to Goethe, Shakespeare's Prospero stands apart as untainted by the Black Arts and free of any bargaining with the Dark Powers. The bawdy elements are also associated with Caliban and his drunken raptures in the company of Stephano and Trinculo. As Coleridge observes, Prospero has endeavored to initiate Miranda and Ferdinand into a love uncorrupted by the baser brutish passions represented in Caliban.[26]

In addition to Shakespeare's *The Tempest*, Coleridge recognized other antecedents to Goethe's use of the magical and marvelous, including Shakespeare's *A Midsummer Night's Dream* and Calderón's *La Vida es Sueño*.[27] Francis Beaumont and John Fletcher, in Coleridge's appraisal, had been seduced by Calderón into "romantic Loyalty to the greatest Monsters."[28] Although Gordon MacMullan referred to the Delphia, the titular character of *The Prophetess* (1647) by Fletcher and Philip Massinger, "as a kind of a curiously feminized Prospero,"[29] Coleridge complained that she was thoroughly "Anti-Shakespearean," her supernatural and demonic powers lacking all motivation and rationale. The comparison holds only because, like Prospero directing Ferdinand's courtship of Miranda, Delphia uses her powers to secure the marriage of Diocles to her niece Drusilla. How she has acquired her powers is unexplained. Even with her repeated demonic conjurings, Coleridge declared, the plot had

> no *Interest* (for a vulgar curiosity about—not what is to *happen* next—but about what the Witch will *do* next, whether Thunder or a Brimstone She Devil, or an Earthquake cannot be called *Interest* —)—Miserable parodies & thefts of fine Lines in Shakespeare—and the compound, a senseless Day-dream, with all the wildness without any of the terror of a Nightmair—in short, Stupidity from malice (of self-conceit) prepense aping Madness.[30]

Coleridge denounced the "Witcheries" of *The Prophetess* because they failed to contribute to the exposition of plot and character. He had the opposite reason for objecting to the "Witcheries" of Goethe's *Faust*. The scenes in "Auerbach's Cellar" ("Auerbachs Keller in Leipzig"), "Witch's Kitchen," and atop the Brocken played out the supernatural action as thoroughly "in character" for a devil whose modus operandi was the lechery he assumed would ultimately ensnare the soul of Faust. Thoroughly integrated into the character and actions of Mephistopheles, the "Witcheries" were aptly obscene.

Among the many reasons that Coleridge never acknowledged his translation, certainly not the least were his qualms about the obscenities and blasphemies of Mephistopheles. Yet even in denying that he ever "put pen to paper as translator of Faust,"[31] he delineated the attraction and repulsion he felt for Goethe's text. When "pressed—many years ago—to translate the Faust . . . I so far entertained the proposal as to read the work through with great attention."[32] His major reservation, he repeated once again, was "whether it became my moral character to render into English—and so far, certainly, lend my countenance to language—much of which I thought vulgar, licentious, and blasphemous." Whatever it may be morally, it nevertheless possessed poetically a language that is "very pure and fine."

> The intended theme of the Faust is the consequences of a misology, or hatred and depreciation of knowledge caused by an originally intense thirst for knowledge baffled. But a love of knowledge for itself, and for pure ends, would never produce such a misology, but only a love of it for base and unworthy purposes. There is neither causation nor progression in the Faust; he is a ready-made conjuror from the very beginning; the *incredulus odi* is felt from the first line. The sensuality and the thirst after knowledge are unconnected with each other. Mephistopheles and Margaret are excellent; but Faust himself is dull and meaningless. The scene in Auerbach's cellar is one of the best, perhaps the very best; that on the Brocken is also fine; and all the songs are beautiful.[33]

Although he disapproved of the coarse language, Coleridge readily granted that the bantering and pranks with the four revelers in Auerbach's Cellar and the dancing with the witches on Walpurgis Night were dramatically effective. He tended to see the play much as Retzsch had depicted it in his engraved plates: a series of striking scenes, yet not comprising a whole. "The scenes," he declared, "are mere magic-lantern pictures, and a large part of the work is to me very flat."[34] In Coleridge's critical vocabulary "flatness" expressed a want of dramatic development and effect.[35]

Rather than translate from Goethe, how much easier it would have been, Coleridge said, to write his own Faustian tale. He claimed that he had conceived this plan even before Goethe's *Faust* was published in 1808.[36] As early as August 20, 1812, the idea of creating his own version of the fatal pact with the devil had been a part of his engagement with Goethe's version. I have argued that Coleridge's criticism of *Faust* must be understood in relation to his criticism of other dramatic expositions of the necromancer, witches, and demons. I now extend that argument to include his own projected Faustian tale. In spite of the early appropriation in Marlowe's tragedy of the chapbooks on the adventures and damnation of Doctor Johannes Faustus, that material had its own separate development within German culture, so that in Goethe's hands it could be transformed into a thoroughly German national drama. As Coleridge surmised, the boundaries of tolerable obscenities may have been more relaxed and liberal in German society, but the challenge in translating also resided in Goethe's representation of the hypocrisy that pervaded the conservative religious communities, whether those of the Lutheran north or the Catholic south. Of course a similar religious history might inform a more exclusively British narrative.[37] Byron's *Manfred* provides a reminder that the Faustian character had emerged, alongside Don Juan and Prometheus, as a major archetype of the age.[38]

Coleridge planned to base his Faustian narrative on the life of Michael Scott (ca. 1175–ca. 1235), astrologer and alchemist, whom Dante named in his *Inferno* as one singularly skilled in magical arts.[39] Familiar with Henry Francis Cary's dual language edition, Coleridge may have been intrigued by the description of Scott as one "who truly knew the game of magic frauds."[40] Boccaccio, too, referred to Scott in the *Decameron* as among the greatest masters of necromancy.[41] The exploits of Michael Scott had also been introduced to contemporary readers by Sir Walter Scott in *The Lay of the Last Minstrel*.[42] He was also the subject of a novel by Allan Cunningham, *Sir Michael Scott, a Romance*.[43] Indeed, it may have been the reception of Cunningham's novel that ultimately discouraged Coleridge from further pursuing the possibility.

That Goethe ought to have developed the character of Faust in terms of "misology" was an anticipation based not only on Faust's opening monologue, but on a well-established tradition of abjuration and conjuration. The disillusioned scholar abjures the traditional disciplines of knowledge, and begins to conjure the dark powers. Marlowe's Faustus delivers a model version of abjuration and conjuration in the speech that begins, "Settle thy studies Faustus, and beginne / To sound the deapth of that thou wilt professe" (1604 text; I.i.31–93).[44] Goethe's Faust utters his version of such a speech with the lines, "Here I now stand, a poor fool, / Just as clever as I was before" ("Da steh' ich nun, ich armer Tor, / Und bin so klug als wie zuvor") (*F*, 354–85). In *The Tempest*, Shakespeare has inverted the model, for he shows Prospero not abjuring traditional knowledge, but rather, at the very end of the play, abjuring his magic:

> PROSPERO. I'll break my staff,
> Bury it certain fathoms in the earth,
> And deeper than did ever plummet sound
> I'll drown my book. (V.i.33–57)

Byron's Manfred conforms to the traditional model when, in his opening soliloquy, he rehearses those endeavors of learning which he now resigns because "they avail not" (I.i.14–24).

The problem that Coleridge confronted in Goethe's text was that, in spite of his opening speech, Faust did not abandon knowledge in pursuit of the power to be gained by black magic. If Coleridge wanted a character succumbing to misology, then Michael Scott was indeed a much better protagonist for such a drama. He commenced his career as a successful scholar, first at Oxford and then the Sorbonne where he took his degree in mathematics. From Paris he moved to the venerable university of Bologna, and then on to Palermo. At every institution he continued to explore new fields of learning. In Toledo he mastered the Arabic language. He next went to Sicily, where he became attached to the court of Ferdinand II. He then served as astrologer and physician at the court of Holy Roman Emperor Frederick II, and joined with other scholars in translating Aristotle and Averroës into Latin. In spite of the high esteem he enjoyed at the Vatican under Pope Gregory IX, rumors of his practices in the black arts commenced in Rome before his return to England in 1230. He brought with him the works of Aristotle, and his achievement as commentator on the philosopher secured him a place of admiration but also of envy and of suspicion. Sir Walter Scott stated that throughout the south of Scotland, "any great work of great labour or antiquity is ascribed either to Auld Michael, Sir William Wallace, or the Devil."

Twice in his notebook entries of 1820, Coleridge speculated about writing on Michael Scott, a "Homo Agonistes," whose story has "the advantage of Dr. Faustus"; it could be set in Cumberland in the time of John Wyclif (ca. 1330–1384). He described a "Prelude" to the drama which would provide an "Interpretation of the Bible" in "the Language of the Senses," adapting, too, the Parable of the Garden (Isaiah 5:1–7).[45] In the subsequent entry, Coleridge correctly set the period back a century: "Magic – Michael Scott (Edward I time [1239–1307])." On the history of magic, Coleridge's note went on to trace the lore from "Zoroaster Disc[iples]."[46] In the *Table Talk*, Coleridge again asserted that the very labor of translation made it seem more worthwhile to attempt an original composition:

> To revive in my mind my own former plan of Michael Scott. But then I considered with myself whether the time taken up in executing the translation might not more worthily be devoted to the composition of a work which, even if parallel in some points to the Faust, should be truly original in motive and execution, and therefore more interesting and valuable than any version which I could make.[47]

According to Henry Crabb Robinson, Coleridge was reluctant to continue with his translation of Goethe's *Faust* because he was convinced that he could write a better Faust-story based on the wizardly deeds of Michael Scott.

Crabb Robinson had been the mediator in Coleridge's negotiations with Murray. When a retrospect on Coleridge's career appeared in the *Quarterly Review* (November 1834)[48] a few months after Coleridge's death (July 25, 1834), Crabb Robinson was prompted to respond to the author's denigration of Goethe's *Faust* and his misunderstanding of Coleridge's involvement in the translation:

> I read . . . the greater part of the admirable article in the *Quarterly*—one of the finest articles that I have read in a long time. It comes from a personal friend, from one well acquainted with the German. . . . His praise of Coleridge is most affectionate—his praise perhaps overstrained. His details on metric are beyond my reach. I do not think he is duly aware of Goethe's pre-eminence; least of all can assent to his judgment concerning *Faust.* He alludes to a fact known principally to me, for I was commissioned by Murray to propose to Coleridge the translation of *Faust.* Coleridge answered me after a considerable time that he could not execute his purpose; it was burthensome. "I felt I could make a better!" This reviewer did not relate; perhaps did not know the fact. But to prove that Coleridge could have made a better *Faust,* he gives an analysis of a *Michael Scott,* projected by Coleridge.[49]

Crabb Robinson, who learned that John Gibson Lockhart was the author before penning the above note, need not have been surprised that Lockhart would know about Coleridge aborting the translation commissioned by Murray—Murray, after all, was the owner and publisher of the *Quarterly Review* and Lockhart was his editor.[50]

Lockhart's account of Coleridge's Faustian "Michael Scott" was taken directly from the *Table Talk,* edited by Henry Nelson Coleridge and published by Murray with the imprint of 1835.[51] In his account in the *Table Talk,* Coleridge delineated the course of misology through five stages. The Prologue would introduce Michael Scott gathering the laurels of learning that comes easily to his brilliant mind, so easily that jealous rivals accuse him of dabbling in the occult. The first act commences five years later, embittered by his unjust imprisonment:

> He appeared in the midst of his college of devoted disciples, enthusiastic, ebullient, shedding around him bright surmises of discoveries fully perfected in after-times, and inculcating the study of nature and its secrets as the pathway to the acquisition of power. He did not love knowledge for itself— for its own exceeding great reward— but in order to be powerful. This poison-speck infected his mind from the beginning. The priests suspect him, circumvent him, accuse him; he is condemned, and thrown into solitary confinement: this constituted the *prologus* of the drama. A pause of four or five years takes place, at the end of which Michael escapes from prison, a soured, gloomy, miserable man. He will not, cannot study; of what avail had all his study been to him? His knowledge, great as it was, had failed to preserve him from the cruel fangs of the persecutors; he could not command the lightning or the storm to wreak their furies upon the heads of those whom he hated and contemned, and yet feared.

Even in his youthful success, the seeds of misology had already germinated. He thrilled at his triumph and sense of superiority rather than at the expansion of knowledge. In his imprisonment he nurtured schemes of vengeance, so that upon his escape he abjured his former studies, and turned to witchcraft:

> Away with learning! away with study! to the winds with all pretences to knowledge! We *know* nothing; we are fools, wretches, mere beasts. Anon I began to tempt him. I made him dream, gave him wine, and passed the most exquisite of women before him, but out of his reach. Is there, then, no knowledge by which these pleasures can be commanded? *That way* lay witchcraft, and accordingly to witchcraft Michael turns with all his soul. He has many failures and some successes; he learns the chemistry of exciting drugs and exploding powders, and some of the properties of transmitted and reflected light: his appetites and his curiosity are both stimulated, and his old craving for power and mental domination over others revives. At last Michael tries to raise the Devil, and the Devil comes at his call. My Devil was to be, like Goethe's, the universal humorist, who should make all things vain and nothing worth, by a perpetual collation of the great with the little in the presence of the infinite. I had many a trick for him to play, some better, I think, than any in the Faust.

The second act thus shows the perversion of knowledge as it is turned to the service of base and unworthy purposes. As Coleridge made clear, this act is filled with strange laboratory experiments, the curious and hallucinatory effects of drugs, the pyrotechnics of explosive powders, and the tormenting pranks of the devil. In the third act, events begin to take a darker turn:

> In the mean time, Michael is miserable; he has power, but no peace, and he every day more keenly feels the tyranny of hell surrounding him. In vain he seems to himself to assert the most absolute empire over the Devil by imposing the most extravagant tasks: one thing is as easy as another to the Devil. "What next, Michael?" is repeated every day with more imperious servility. Michael groans in spirit; his power is a curse: he commands women and wine! But the women seem fictitious and devilish, and the wine does not make him drunk. He now begins to hate the Devil, and tries to cheat him. He studies again, and explores the darkest depths of sorcery for a receipt to cozen hell; but all in vain. Sometimes the Devil's finger turns over the page for him, and points out an experiment, and Michael hears a whisper—"Try *that*, Michael!" The horror increases; and Michael feels that he is a slave and a condemned criminal.

Having imagined himself empowered by the devil whose aid he had enlisted, Michael is increasingly aware that he has become instead the Devil's puppet. In the fourth act, he seeks to obliterate the futility of his predicament by spending his days and nights indulging mindlessly in erotic delights.

> Lost to hope, he throws himself into every sensual excess.—in the mid career of which he sees Agatha, my Margaret, and immediately endeavours to seduce

> her. Agatha loves him; and the Devil facilitates their meetings; but she resists Michael's attempts to ruin her, and implores him not to act so as to forfeit her esteem. Long struggles of passion ensue, in the result of which his affections are called forth against his appetites, and, love-born, the idea of a redemption of the lost will dawns upon his mind.

Amidst the lustful pleasures, Michael discovers true love. Agatha's pure and unsullied devotion enables him to seek salvation. In the fifth act, Coleridge was on familiar ground in the dramatic exposition of guilt, the psychological torment that informed such poems as "Christabel," "Dejection: An Ode," and "The Pains of Sleep." In this final act, Coleridge's intention was to lead Michael Scott from guilt to grace, from despair to redemption. The Devil, however, has recognized the change in his slave and consequently redoubles his efforts to keep him ensnared in eternal damnation:

> This is instantaneously perceived by the Devil; and for the first time the humorist becomes severe and menacing. A fearful succession of conflicts between Michael and the Devil takes place, in which Agatha helps and suffers. In the end, after subjecting him to every imaginable horror and agony, I made him triumphant, and poured peace into his soul in the conviction of a salvation for sinners through God's grace.[52]

Goethe had presented Margaret as fully victimized by her seducer. Her mother dies from the sleeping potion she has given her so that she might enjoy the guilty tryst with her lover. Her brother dies in trying to drive off the villain who has made a whore of his sister. Falling into madness, she kills her newborn infant. Coleridge has replaced her with Agatha, who resists the lustful seduction and offers redemptive love. Lockhart readily declared that Coleridge's projected drama would have been far superior to Goethe's *Faust.* Crabb Robinson remained skeptical: "It certainly would have been more moral and more religious, but it would have had little in common with Goethe's *Faust.*"[53]

Following the debacle of Coleridge's abandoning his translation for Murray, Crabb Robinson again found an opportunity for discussing *Faust* with Coleridge on the occasion of Ludwig Tieck's visit to London in 1817. The first meeting, on June 13, inspired no brilliant conversation: Tieck "was not the greatest talker to-day"; "Coleridge was not in his element. . . . His German was not good and his English was not free." Eleven days later, when Crabb Robinson escorted Tieck to Highgate, the conversation improved:

> Coleridge read some of his own poems and he and Ludwig Tieck philosophized. Coleridge talked the most. Tieck is a good listener and is an unobtrusive man. . . . [Tieck] spoke with great love of Goethe, yet censured his impious prologue to *Faust* and wishes an English translation might be from the earlier edition written in Goethe's youth.[54]

Crabb Robinson was apparently unaware of Coleridge's work with Boosey when he recorded reading "the English Faustus" in November 1821. In his letter to Goethe, January 31, 1829, he mentions "the disgrace of such publications . . . as Lord Leveson Gower's Faustus [1823]," and he laments that Coleridge had not followed through with his endeavor:

> Coleridge, too, the only living poet of acknowledged genius who is also a good German scholar attempted Faust, but shrunk from it in despair. Such an abandonment, and such a performance as we have had force to one's recollection the line, "For fools rush in where angels fear to tread."[55]

From his correspondence with both Boosey and Bohte, Goethe had been informed, as Crabb Robinson had not, that "the English Faustus" of 1821 was the work of Coleridge.[56]

During the last years of his life, Coleridge's reply to queries about his translating *Faust* varied to some degree from the account recorded in the *Table Talk* for February 16, 1833. John Hookham Frere, who was to publish his own translation of a scene from *Faust*,[57] asked Coleridge, "Had you ever thought of translating the 'Faust'?" Coleridge's explanation of why he was "prevented" turned into a critique:

> I was prevented by the consideration that though there are some exquisite passages, the opening chorus, the chapel and the prison scenes for instance, to say nothing of the Brocken scene where he has shown peculiar strength in keeping clear of Shakespear, he has not taken that wonderful admixture of Witch Fate and Fairy but has kept to the real original witch, and this suits his purpose much better.

Thus far Coleridge's appraisal was positive. Turning to the negative, he declared that "the conception of Wagner" was bad. But the real fault lay in the character of Faust himself. Again Coleridge reasserted to his criticism that Faust's misology was untenable:

> Whoever heard of a man who had gained such wonderful proficiency in learning as to call up spirits &c. being discontented. No, it is not having the power of knowledge that would make a man discontented—neither would such a man have suddenly become a sensualist.

Coleridge also answered Frere's question about Shelley's translation of *Faust*, saying that he admired it very much but lamented Shelley's atheism.[58] Coleridge's evasive replies about translating *Faust* were doubtlessly rooted in the very grounds that he declared— both moral and aesthetic. The latter are given more weight after 1821, when he began to stress his frustration at the impossibility of capturing both tone and sense of *Faust* in English, accompanied by the conviction that translation cost him more effort than he would need to create an original Faustian tale on Michael Scott.

In June 1820, at the very time he had recommenced his efforts in translating *Faust,* Coleridge confided to Maria Gisborne that Goethe's great tragedy "could not be endured in English and by the English, and he did not like to attempt it with the necessity of the smallest mutilation!"[59] Coleridge's translation was published anonymously by Thomas Boosey and Sons in September 1821. Two years later he complained with the authority of one who spoke from sad experience:

> I would have attempted to translate . . . "Faustus," but I must give it up in despair. To translate it so as to make the English readers acquainted with the plot, is a foolish task. The beauty of this work consists in the fine colour of the style and in the tints, which are lost to one who is not thoroughly *au fait* with German life, German philosophy, and the whole literature of that country. The antithesis between the slang of Mephistopheles, the over-refined language of Faustus, and the pastoral simplicity of the Child of Nature, Margaret, requires a man's whole life to be made evident in our language.[60]

Here Coleridge's critique of *Faust,* written after he had given the task his best effort, reflects upon why he despaired at completing a full translation. Among the scenes that he avoided entirely were the "Prologue in Heaven," the "Prelude in the Theatre" ("Vorspiel auf dem Theater"), "Auerbach's Cellar," the "Witch's Kitchen," most of the "Walpurgis Night," and all of the "Walpurgis Night's Dream" ("Walpurgisnachtstraum"). Even the scenes that he did translate failed to measure up to his own standards.[61]

Precisely because Goethe had crafted such a preeminently national work, it was thoroughly imbued with nuances of German culture that remain inaccessible "to one who is not thoroughly *au fait* with German life, German philosophy, and the whole literature of that country." Coleridge met these criteria far more adequately than other contemporaries who made the attempt,[62] but he knew his own limits in selecting scenes for translation. In his numerous recollections and reflections on *Faust,* his critique persistently acknowledged the poetic genius and imagination of Goethe, lamented the lewd innuendos and gestures of Mephistopheles, and objected to the misconceived misology of Faust. He was haunted by Goethe's accomplishment both for the translation that he failed to complete, and for his own Faustian drama that he failed to write.

NOTES

1. Samuel Taylor Coleridge, *Biographia Literaria,* 2 vols., ed. James Engell and Walter Jackson Bate, vol. 7, *The Collected Works of Samuel Taylor Coleridge*

(Princeton: Princeton University Press; London: Routledge and Kegan Paul, 1983), 2:135 [hereafter *BL*].

2. Henry Crabb Robinson, *On Books and Their Writers*, 3 vols., ed. Edith J. Morley (London: J. M. Dent and Sons, 1938), 1:107 (August 13, 1812). See also Crabb Robinson, *Diary, Reminiscences, and Correspondence*, 3 vols., ed. Thomas Sadler (London: Macmillan, 1869), 1:305, 388, 407. Johann Wolfgang von Goethe, *Goethes Faust. Der Tragödie erster und zweiter Teil. Urfaust*, ed. Erich Trunz (Hamburg: Christian Wegner Verlag, 1963), [*F*].

3. Crabb Robinson, *On Books and Their Writers*, 1:108 (August 20, 1812).

4. To John Murray (August 23, 1814), in *Collected Letters of Samuel Taylor Coleridge*, 6 vols., ed. Earl Leslie Griggs (Oxford: Clarendon, 1956–1971), 3:521–23 [hereafter *CL*].

5. In a letter to William Sotheby, August 26, 1802, Coleridge had described a plan to translate Voss' *Luise, ein ländliches Gedicht in drei Idyllen* (1795), *CL*, 3:856–57. The translation which Thomas De Quincey prepared for *Blackwood's* in 1821 was published posthumously, *The Works of Thomas De Quincey*, 21 vols., ed. Grevel Lindop et al. (London: Pickering and Chatto, 2000–2003), 3:366–73.

6. To Coleridge (August 26, 1814), in *The Letters of Charles and Mary Lamb*, 3 vols., ed. E. V. Lucas (London: J. M. Dent and Sons, 1935), 2:134–35.

7. To John Murray (September 10, 1814), *CL*, 3:528.

8. Samuel Taylor Coleridge, *Lectures 1808–1819: On Literature*, 2 vols., ed. Reginald A. Foakes, vol. 5, *The Collected Works of Samuel Taylor Coleridge* (Princeton: Princeton University Press; London: Routledge and Kegan Paul, 1987), 1:531; 2:114, 120, 248, 305 [hereafter *LL*].

9. To John Murray (September 10, 1814), *CL*, 3:528.

10. Coleridge, *BL*, 2:19.

11. Coleridge, *LL*, 1:380, 387–90, 540–45; 2:295–99, 456–57, 537–38.

12. To Daniel Stuart (October 16, 1814), *CL*, 3:536.

13. To Byron (March 30, 1815), *CL*, 4:562.

14. To Coleridge (March 31, 1815), *Byron's Letters and Journals*, 12 vols., ed. Leslie A. Marchand (Cambridge, MA: Belknap Press of Harvard University Press, 1973–1982), 4:285–86.

15. To Thomas Boosey and Sons (May 10, 1820), *CL*, 5:42–44. Carl F. Schreiber, "Coleridge to Boosey—Boosey to Coleridge," *Yale University Library Gazette* 20 (1947): 8–9. "My Advice & Scheme / S. T. Coleridge," single sheet dated May 12, 1820. Huntington Library MS accession number 131334.

16. *Faustus: from the German of Goethe* [trans. Samuel Taylor Coleridge] (London: Thomas Boosey and Sons, 4 Broad-Street, Exchange, and Rodwell and Martin, New Bond-Street, 1821). *Faustus. From the German of Goethe. Embellished with Retzsch' Series of 27 Outlines, Ill. of the Tragedy Engraved by Henry Moses. With Portr. of the Author*, 3rd ed. (London: Thomas Boosey and Sons, 1824).

17. Percy Bysshe Shelley, "Scenes from the Faust of Goethe" ["Prologue in Heaven" and "Walpurgisnacht"], *The Liberal*, 1 (October 26, 1822); complete transcription in *Posthumous Poems of Percy Bysshe Shelley*, ed. Mary Wollstonecraft Shelley (London: John and Henry L. Hunt 1824).

18. Frederick Burwick, "The Faust Translations of Coleridge and Shelley on the London Stage," *Keats-Shelley Journal* 59 (2010): 86–98. Scenery by Jones, Phillips, Danson, and W. Stanfield; costumes by Smythers and Mrs. Follet.

19. Walter Arndt translates "H- -" as "Arse," an anatomical substitution that avoids the sexual reference. Goethe, *Faust*, trans. Walter Arndt, ed. Cyrus Hamlin (New York: W. W. Norton, 1976).

20. To Byron (March 30, 1815), *CL*, 4:562.

21. To Jefferson Hogg (October 22, 1821), *Letters of Percy Bysshe Shelley*, 2 vols., ed. Frederick Jones (Oxford: Clarendon, 1964), 2:361.

22. *The Family Shakespeare*, 4 vols. (London: J. Hatchard, 1807); *The Family Shakespeare, in Ten Volumes; in Which Nothing Is Added to the Original Text; But Those Words and Expressions Are Omitted Which Cannot with Propriety Be Read Aloud in a Family* (2nd ed., 1818; rev. 1820; facsimile repr., Kyoto: Eureka Press, 2009).

23. Eric Partridge, *Shakespeare's Bawdy: A Literary and Psychological Essay and a Comprehensive Glossary* (London: Routledge and Kegan Paul, 1968).

24. Coleridge, *LL*, 1:364–65.

25. Shakespeare, *The Tempest* (I.ii.345–51), *The Complete Works of Shakespeare*, ed. Hardin Craig (Chicago: Scott, Foresman, 1951), 1254.

26. Steffanie Anne Levinson, "Revealing Shakespeare's Bawdy: A Bakhtinian Analysis of the Grotesque in *The Tempest*" (M.A. thesis, San Francisco State University, 1996).

27. Samuel Taylor Coleridge, *The Friend*, 2 vols., ed. Barbara Rooke, vol. 4, *The Collected Works of Samuel Taylor Coleridge* (Princeton: Princeton University Press; London: Routledge and Kegan Paul, 1969), 1:420n.

28. Samuel Taylor Coleridge, *Marginalia*, 2 vols., ed. George Whalley et al., vol. 12, *The Collected Works of Samuel Taylor Coleridge* (Princeton: Princeton University Press; London: Routledge and Kegan Paul, 1980–2001), 1:369–70, 380, 389, 398 [hereafter *M*].

29. Gordon MacMullan, *The Politics of Unease in the Plays of John Fletcher* (Amherst: University of Massachusetts Press, 1994), 183.

30. Coleridge, *M*, 1:369–70.

31. Coleridge, "Faust. – Michael Scott, Goethe, Schiller, and Wordsworth" (February 16, 1833), *Table Talk*, 2 vols., ed. Carl Woodring, vol. 14, *The Collected Works of Samuel Taylor Coleridge* (Princeton: Princeton University Press; London: Routledge, 1990), 1:343; 2:200 [hereafter *TT*].

32. To Daniel Stuart (September 12, 1814), *CL*, 3:533. In addition to reading *Faust* "with great attention," Coleridge described his daily schedule while translating for John Murray as including six hours of writing, four in the morning and two in the evening. Part of this time was devoted to writing "Principles of Genial Criticism."

33. "Faust. – Michael Scott, Goethe, Schiller, and Wordsworth" (February 16, 1833), *TT*, 1:338–39; 2:199.

34. "Faust. – Michael Scott, Goethe, Schiller, and Wordsworth," *TT*, 1:339; 2:199.

35. On *The Queen of Corinth* by Beaumont and Fletcher, Coleridge underlined the Queen's supposed outrage at "a Lady wronged in my Court" (II.iii.198), and commented, "O flat! Flat! Flat! Sole! Flounder! Plaice! All stinking! Stinking flat!" *M*, 1:371.

36. Coleridge, February 16, 1833, *TT*, 1:336–37, and 1:336 n. 1.

37. Surveys of the Faust tradition in literature: Paul Bates, *Faust: Sources, Works, Criticism* (New York: Harcourt, 1969); E. M. Butler, *The Fortunes of Faust* (London: Cambridge University Press, 1952); Philip Mason Palmer and Robert Pattison More,

The Sources of the Faust Tradition from Simon Magus to Lessing (New York: Octagon Books, 1966).

38. In the Aarne-Thompson typological catalogue, "The devil's contract" is in category AT 756B. Hans-Jörg Uther, *The Types of International Folktales: A Classification and Bibliography Based on the System of Antti Aarne and Stith Thompson*, vols. 1–3 (Helsinki: Academia Scientiarum Fennica, 2004).

39. Dante Alighieri, *The Divine Comedy*, 3 vols. Text; 3 vols. Commentary (Princeton: Princeton University Press, 1970); *Inferno*, cnt. 20, l. 116. Among the Sinners with their Heads on Backwards are the Astrologers, sorcerers, and magicians; represented by Michael Scott, Asdante, and Guy Bonatti.

40. Dante Alighieri, *Inferno*, 2 vols., trans. Henry Francis Cary (London: 1805–1806), cnt. 20, l. 117: "Michele Scotto . . . , che veramente/ de le magiche frodo seppe 'l gioco." Dante Alighieri, *The Vision; nor Hell, Purgatory, and Paradise*, 3 vols., trans. Henry Francis Cary (London: 1819). Coleridge's annotations, *M*, 2:133–38.

41. Giovanni Boccaccio, *The Decameron*, trans. James Macmullen Rigg (London: G. Routledge and Sons; New York: E. P. Dutton [192–?]), vol. 2, pt. 5, nvl. IX. "Bruno and Buffalmacco prevail upon Master Simone, a physician, to betake him by night to a certain place, there to be enrolled in a company that go the course. Buffalmacco throws him into a foul ditch, and there they leave him. 'You are then to know,' quoth Bruno, 'sweet my Master, that 'tis not long since there was in this city a great master in necromancy, hight Michael Scott, for that he was of Scotland, and great indeed was the honour in which he was held by not a few gentlemen.'"

42. Emile Grillot de Givry, *Le musée des sorciers, mages et alchimistes* (Paris, 1929); *Witchcraft, Magic, and Alchemy*, trans. J. Courtney Locke (Boston: Houghton and Mifflin, 1931), 92. See also Sir Walter Scott, *The Lay of the Last Minstrel* (London: Printed for Longman, Hurst, Rees, and Orme; Edinburgh: A. Constable by James Ballantyne, 1805), cnt. II, vv. 13–19; in this account, Michael Scott "cleft the Eildon hills in three and bridled the river Tweed with a curb of stone," and was buried with his book of magic "on a night of woe and dread" in Melrose Abbey.

43. Allan Cunningham, *Sir Michael Scott, a Romance*, 3 vols. (London: H. Colburn, 1828). The reviewer for the *Monthly Review*, 7 (January to April 1828), 129–30, declared that the author was "very injudicious in the choise of his materials," incapable of sorting out fiction and fact, and ultimately losing "all controil over his reason." Cunningham "breaks forth in impassioned apostrophes, and utters such denunciations as could be exceeded only in a certain asylum which we forbear to name." A more tolerant review, apparently by Thomas De Quincey, appeared in the *Edinburgh Saturday Post*, December 1827. Evidence for this conjectural attribution is presented in Stuart Tave, "De Quincey, Allan Cunningham, and the *Edinburgh Saturday Post*," *Review of English Studies* 41, no. 162 (1990): 230–32.

44. *Marlowe's Doctor Faustus, 1604–1616. Parallel Texts*, ed. W. W. Greg (Oxford: Clarendon Press, 1950).

45. Samuel Taylor Coleridge, *The Notebooks of Samuel Taylor Coleridge*, 5 vols. Text; 5 vols. Notes, ed. Kathleen Coburn, vol. 5 with Anthony John Harding (New York: Pantheon, 1957, 1961; Princeton: Princeton University Press, 1973, 1990, 2002), 4642 [hereafter *CN*]. Although she dates this entry as early as February–March 1820, Kathleen Coburn states that "it may be relevant to notice that the first

article in the *London Magazine* for August 1820 (ii 124–42) was 'Goethe and his Faustus'; it tells the story of the 16th-century Dr. John Faustus."

46. *CN*, 4690; this undated entry was apparently written shortly after the previous entry, dated "June 30th, 1820."

47. "Faust. – Michael Scott, Goethe, Schiller, and Wordsworth" (February 16, 1833), *TT*, 1:337–38; 2:197–99.

48. John Gibson Lockhart, "Samuel Taylor Coleridge," *Quarterly Review* (November 1834).

49. Crabb Robinson, *On Books and Their Writers*, 1:447–48 (October 7, 1834).

50. John Murray founded the *Quarterly Review* in 1809; William Gifford was the first editor, succeeded by Lockhart, who held the post from 1825 until 1853.

51. *Specimens of the Table Talk of Samuel Taylor Coleridge*, 2 vols., ed. Henry Nelson Coleridge (London: John Murray, 1835).

52. "Faust. – Michael Scott, Goethe, Schiller, and Wordsworth" (February 16, 1833), *TT*, 1:337–38; 2:197–99.

53. Crabb Robinson, *On Books and Their Writers*, 1:448 (October 7, 1834).

54. Crabb Robinson, *On Books and Their Writers*, 1:207–8 (June 13 and 24, 1817).

55. Crabb Robinson to Goethe (January 1829), *Briefe an Goethe*, 2 vols., ed. Karl Robert Mandelkow (Hamburg: Christian Wegner Verlag, 1969), 2:496. Crabb Robinson also visited Goethe in August 1829; *On Books and Their Writers*, 1:367–74 (August 2–18, 1829).

56. Burwick, "'An orphic tale': Goethe's *Faust* Translated by Coleridge," *International Faust Studies: Adaptation, Reception, Translation*, ed. Lorna Fitzsimmons (London and New York: Continuum, 2008), 124–45.

57. John Hookham Frere, *Works*, 3 vols., ed. W. E. Frere (London: Basil Montegu Pickering, 1872; rev. 2nd ed., 1874), 2:402–3: act III, sc. vii ["Der Nachbarin Haus," lines 2901–31] (December 1835).

58. *TT*, 1:573–74.

59. Maria Gisborne's Journal, June 25, 1820. *Maria Gisborne and Edward E. Williams*, ed. F. L. Jones (Norman: University of Oklahoma Press, 1951), 37.

60. Gioacchino de'Prati (1790–1863), "An Autobiography (The Medical Advisor's Life and Adventures)," pt. II, chap. 13, *Penny Satirist* (October 13, 1838), in *TT*, 2:490–91. M. H. Fisch, "The Coleridges, Dr. Prati, and Vico," *Modern Philology* 41 (1943): 121.

61. Frederick Burwick, "Coleridge as Translator," *The Oxford Handbook of Coleridge*, ed. Frederick Burwick (Oxford: Oxford University Press, 2009), 412–32.

62. *Extracts from Göthe's Tragedy of Faustus, Explanatory of the Plates by Retsch, Intended to Illustrate That Work; Translated by George Soane A.B. Author of 'The Innkeeper's Daughter' – 'Falls of Clyde' – 'The Bohemian', &c. &c. &c* (London: printed for J. H. Bohte, 4 York Street, Covent Garden; by G. Schulze, 13 Poland Street, Oxford Street, 1820); *Faust: A Drama by Goethe; and, Schiller's Song of the Bell*, trans. Lord Francis Leveson Gower (London: John Murray, 1823); *Faust: A Dramatic Poem*, trans. Abraham Hayward (London: E. Moxon, 1833); *Faustus, A Dramatic Mystery; The Bride of Corinth; The First Walpurgis Night*, trans. John Anster (London: Printed for Longman, Rees, Orme, Brown, Green, and Longman, 1835).

BIBLIOGRAPHY

Anonymous. Review of *Sir Michael Scott, a Romance*. *Monthly Review* 7 (January to April 1828): 129–30.

Bates, Paul. *Faust: Sources, Works, Criticism*. New York: Harcourt, 1969.

Boccaccio, Giovanni. *The Decameron*. Translated by James Macmullen Rigg. 2 vols. London: G. Routledge and Sons; New York: E. P. Dutton, [192–?].

Burwick, Frederick. "Coleridge as Translator." In *The Oxford Handbook of Coleridge*, edited by Frederick Burwick, 412–32. Oxford: Oxford University Press, 2009.

——. "The Faust Translations of Coleridge and Shelley on the London Stage." *Keats-Shelley Journal* 59 (2010): 86–98.

——. "'An orphic tale': Goethe's *Faust* Translated by Coleridge." In *International Faust Studies: Adaptation, Reception, Translation*, edited by Lorna Fitzsimmons, 24–45. London and New York: Continuum, 2008.

Butler, E. M. *The Fortunes of Faust*. London: Cambridge University Press, 1952.

Byron, George Gordon, Lord. *Byron's Letters and Journals*. Edited by Leslie A. Marchand. 12 vols. Cambridge, MA: Belknap Press of Harvard University Press, 1973–1982.

Coleridge, Samuel Taylor. *Biographia Literaria*. Edited by James Engell and Walter Jackson Bate. 2 vols. Vol. 7, *The Collected Works of Samuel Taylor Coleridge*. Princeton: Princeton University Press; London: Routledge and Kegan Paul, 1983.

——. *Collected Letters of Samuel Taylor Coleridge*. Edited by Earl Leslie Griggs, 6 vols. Oxford: Clarendon, 1956–1971.

——. *The Friend*. Edited by Barbara Rooke, 2 vols. Vol. 4, *The Collected Works of Samuel Taylor Coleridge*. Princeton: Princeton University Press; London: Routledge and Kegan Paul, 1969.

——. *Lectures 1808–1819: On Literature*. Edited by Reginald A. Foakes. 2 vols. Vol. 5, *The Collected Works of Samuel Taylor Coleridge*. Princeton: Princeton University Press; London: Routledge and Kegan Paul, 1987.

——. *Marginalia*. Edited by George Whalley et al. 2 vols. Vol. 12, *The Collected Works of Samuel Taylor Coleridge*. Princeton: Princeton University Press; London: Routledge and Kegan Paul, 1980–2001.

——. "My Advice & Scheme/ S. T. Coleridge." Single sheet dated May 12, 1820. Huntington Library MS accession number 131334.

——. *The Notebooks of Samuel Taylor Coleridge*. Edited by Kathleen Coburn, vol. 5 with Anthony John Harding. 5 vols. Text; 5 vols. Notes. New York: Pantheon, 1957, 1961; Princeton: Princeton University Press, 1973, 1990, 2002.

——. *Specimens of the Table Talk of Samuel Taylor Coleridge*. Edited by Henry Nelson Coleridge. 2 vols. London: John Murray, 1835.

——. *Table Talk*. Edited by Carl Woodring. 2 vols. Vol. 14, *The Collected Works of Samuel Taylor Coleridge*. Princeton: Princeton University Press; London: Routledge, 1990.

Cunningham, Allan. *Sir Michael Scott, a Romance*. 3 vols. London: H. Colburn, 1828.

Dante Alighieri. *The Divine Comedy*. 3 vols. Text; 3 vols. Commentary. Princeton: Princeton University Press, 1970.

——. *Inferno*. Translated by Henry Francis Cary. 2 vols. London: Printed for James Carpenter, 1805–1806.

——. *The Vision; or Hell, Purgatory, and Paradise.* Translated by Henry Francis Cary. 3 vols. London: Printed for Taylor and Hessey, 1819.

De Quincey, Thomas. Review of *Sir Michael Scott, a Romance. Edinburgh Saturday Post* (December 1827).

——. *The Works of Thomas De Quincey.* Edited by Grevel Lindop et al. 21 vols. London: Pickering and Chatto, 2000–2003.

Fisch, M. H. "The Coleridges, Dr. Prati, and Vico." *Modern Philology* 41 (1943): 121.

Frere, John Hookham. *Works.* Edited by W. E. Frere. 3 vols. London: Basil Montegu Pickering, 1872; rev. 2nd ed., 1874.

Gisborne, Maria. *Maria Gisborne and Edward E. Williams, Shelley's Friends: Their Journals and Letters.* Edited by Frederick L. Jones. Norman: University of Oklahoma Press, 1951.

Givry, Emile Grillot de. *Le musée des sorciers, mages et alchimistes.* Paris: Librairie de France, 1929. Translated by J. Courtney Locke as *Witchcraft, Magic, and Alchemy.* (Boston: Houghton and Mifflin, 1931).

Goethe, Johann Wolfgang von. *Extracts from Göthe's Tragedy of Faustus, Explanatory of the Plates by Retsch, Intended to Illustrate That Work; Translated by George Soane A.B. Author of 'The Innkeeper's Daughter' – 'Falls of Clyde' – 'The Bohemian', &c. &c. &c.* London: printed for J. H. Bohte, 4 York Street, Covent Garden; by G. Schulze, 13 Poland Street, Oxford Street, 1820.

——. *Faust.* Translated by Walter Arndt. Edited by Cyrus Hamlin. New York: W. W. Norton, 1976.

——. *Faust: A Drama by Goethe; and, Schiller's Song of the Bell.* Translated by Lord Francis Leveson Gower. London: John Murray, 1823.

——. *Faust: A Dramatic Poem.* Translated by Abraham Hayward. London: E. Moxon, 1833.

——. *Faustus, A Dramatic Mystery; The Bride of Corinth; The First Walpurgis Night.* Translated by John Anster. London: Printed for Longman, Rees, Orme, Brown, Green, and Longman, 1835.

——. *Faustus: From the German of Goethe.* [Translated by Samuel Taylor Coleridge]. London: Thomas Boosey and Sons, 4 Broad-Street, Exchange, and Rodwell and Martin, New Bond-Street, 1821.

——. *Faustus. From the German of Goethe. Embellished with Retzsch' Series of 27 Outlines, Ill. of the Tragedy Engraved by Henry Moses. With Portr. of the Author* [Translated by Samuel Taylor Coleridge]. 3rd ed. London: Thomas Boosey and Sons, 1824.

——. *Goethes Faust. Der Tragödie erster und zweiter Teil. Urfaust.* Edited by Erich Trunz. Hamburg: Christian Wegner Verlag, 1963.

Lamb, Charles and Mary. *The Letters of Charles and Mary Lamb.* Edited by E. V. Lucas. 3 vols. London: J. M. Dent and Sons, 1935.

Levinson, Steffanie Anne. "Revealing Shakespeare's Bawdy: A Bakhtinian Analysis of the Grotesque in *The Tempest.*" M.A. thesis, San Francisco State University, 1996.

Lockhart, John Gibson. "Samuel Taylor Coleridge." *Quarterly Review* (November, 1834).

MacMullan, Gordon. *The Politics of Unease in the Plays of John Fletcher.* Amherst: University of Massachusetts Press, 1994.

Mandelkow, Karl Robert, ed. *Briefe an Goethe*. 2 vols. Hamburg: Christian Wegner Verlag, 1969.
Marlowe, Christopher. *Marlowe's Doctor Faustus, 1604–1616. Parallel Texts*. Edited by W. W. Greg. Oxford: Clarendon Press, 1950.
Palmer, Philip Mason, and Robert Pattison More. *The Sources of the Faust Tradition from Simon Magus to Lessing*. New York: Octagon Books, 1966.
Partridge, Eric. *Shakespeare's Bawdy: A Literary and Psychological Essay and a Comprehensive Glossary*. London: Routledge and Kegan Paul, 1968.
Prati, Gioacchino de. "An Autobiography (The Medical Advisor's Life and Adventures)." Pt. II, chap. 13. *Penny Satirist* (October 13, 1838). In Coleridge, *Table Talk*, 2:490–91.
Robinson, Henry Crabb. *On Books and Their Writers*. Edited by Edith J. Morley. 3 vols. London: J. M. Dent and Sons, 1938.
———. *Diary, Reminiscences, and Correspondence*. Edited by Thomas Sadler. 3 vols. London: Macmillan, 1869.
Schreiber, Carl F. "Coleridge to Boosey—Boosey to Coleridge." *Yale University Library Gazette* 20 (1947): 8–9.
Scott, Walter, Sir. *The Lay of the Last Minstrel*. London: Printed for Longman, Hurst, Rees, and Orme; Edinburgh: A. Constable and Co. by James Ballantyne, 1805.
Shakespeare, William. *The Complete Works of Shakespeare*. Edited by Hardin Craig. Chicago: Scott, Foresman, 1951.
———. *The Family Shakespeare*. Edited by Thomas Bowdler. 4 vols. London: J. Hatchard, 1807.
———. *The Family Shakespeare, in Ten Volumes; in Which Nothing Is Added to the Original Text; But Those Words and Expressions Are Omitted Which Cannot with Propriety Be Read Aloud in a Family*. Edited by Thomas Bowdler. 10 vols. London, Printed for Longman, Hurst, Rees, Orme, and Brown, 2nd ed., 1818; rev. 1820; facsimile reprint, Kyoto: Eureka Press, 2009.
Shelley, Percy Bysshe. *Letters of Percy Bysshe Shelley*. Edited by Frederick Jones. 2 vols. Oxford: Clarendon, 1964.
———. *Posthumous Poems of Percy Bysshe Shelley*. Edited by Mary Wollstonecraft Shelley. London: John and Henry L. Hunt [1824].
———. "Scenes from the Faust of Goethe" ["Prologue in Heaven" and "Walpurgisnacht"]. *The Liberal* 1 (October 26, 1822).
Tave, Stuart. "De Quincey, Allan Cunningham, and the *Edinburgh Saturday Post*." *Review of English Studies* 41, no. 162 (1990): 230–32.
Uther, Hans-Jörg. *The Types of International Folktales: A Classification and Bibliography Based on the System of Antti Aarne and Stith Thompson*. 3 vols. Helsinki: Academia Scientiarum Fennica, 2004.
Voss, Johann Heinrich. *Luise, ein ländliches Gedicht in drei Idyllen*. 1795; 3rd ed. Königsberg: F. Nicolovius, 1800.

5

Remembering *Faust* in Argentina

Andrew Bush

When *Faust* settled on Broadway in 1955 as the long-running musical *Damn Yankees,* the grand ambitions at stake in the Goethean model were reduced to the populist dream of a fervent baseball fan to topple the perennial champions. In a deal with the devilish Mr. Applegate, the aging Joe Boyd was transformed for the space of a single season into the young slugger Joe Hardy, carrying his team to triumph. It was a big victory for the national imaginary. Opening just ten years after World War II, the musical reminded its audience that America was always only apparently consigned to the comfortable sidelines, when in fact it was concealing its superpowers, which might always be brought into play to combat the injustice of any one team claiming to hang all the pennants in its own clubhouse. In this Americanization of the Faust theme, Joe's strength was represented as a concomitant of his innocence. The temptress whom he would ultimately resist, then, was not only little Lola, but beyond her, a vision of the corrupting force of knowledge, sophistication, and high culture, in a word, of Europe, for which *Faust* itself was the ready exemplar. Goethe was invoked in order to be overturned—the very stuff of parody.

I recall that familiar story to set the stage for another parody, another Americanization (in another America), a highly unfamiliar adaptation of the Faust story by Argentine poet Estanislao del Campo (1834–1880), occasioned by the performance of Charles Gounod's *Faust,* opening in Buenos Aires on August 24, 1866. Local literary legend has it that while still in his theater box at the Teatro Colón, though no doubt having examined the Italian libretto published previously in the press, Del Campo extemporized some verses on the Faust theme before his fellow poet Ricardo Gutiérrez, who enthusiastically encouraged him to continue. Del Campo, the story proceeds, returned home to a long night of poetic composition, and his wife found him at his desk the following morning with a substantial draft of his "Fausto" in hand. What is certain is that his text appeared under the pseudonym of "Anastasio el Pollo" (Anastasio the Chick) in the periodical press in Buenos Aires a month later, on September 30; again, with some corrections, in a different paper on October 3 and 4; and the following month, in a separate pamphlet sold as a benefit for the military hospitals just then receiving Argentine casualties from the ongoing war with Paraguay.[1]

An operatic *Faust* may have been a novelty in Buenos Aires in that late summer and fall, but the allusion in Del Campo's pseudonym would have stirred the memory of readers of the River Plate papers. Anastasio el Pollo recalled the name under which Hilario Ascasubi (1807–1875), writing from exile in Uruguay in 1854, published his polemics against the Argentine dictator Manuel Rosas: *Aniceto el Gallo o gacetero prosista y gauchipoeta argentino* (Aniceto the Cock or prose-writing gazetteer and Argentine gaucho-poet), to cite the title as it appeared when Ascasubi later republished the work in Paris in 1872. The latter epithet, moreover, situates both Ascasubi's poetry and that of Del Campo's "Fausto" in the sui generis River Plate literary tradition of the *gauchesca,* a city-born poetry written in a stylized language meant to capture the voice of the gauchos, that is, nomadic rural laborers of the pampas, reflecting on events of national significance in a defamiliarizing mode and from the limited point of view of personal circumstance. Even at its acme in the two-part epic by José Hernández (1834–1886)—*El Gaucho Martín Fierro* (1872) and *La Vuelta de Martín Fierro* (1879)—the gauchesca has resisted translation and transmigration. The gauchesca in general has thus been largely left off the map of a Goethean "world literature" and, more particularly, Del Campo's "Fausto" has been neglected in the conversation of otherwise assiduous readers of the *Faust* legacy.[2]

Del Campo deploys the chief elements of the gauchesca—the gaucho perspective, the stylized idiom, the conversation between friends—but against the grain. His gaucho protagonist had been swept up by a crowd into the Teatro Colón, where he attended the performance of Gounod's *Faust,* and upon leaving the city, he chanced upon a friend to whom he recounted the story as he understood, or more precisely, misunderstood it. The comic incident seems to be at the farthest remove from the grounding of the genre in political debate. Thus, on first reading, and in fact in many subsequent readings, Del Campo's "Fausto" has been taken as a double parody: on the one hand, a burlesque version of the Faust theme, and on the other, a playful deflation of the political ambitions of the gauchesca genre. But it is in this respect that the seemingly anodyne example of *Damn Yankees* offers a useful preface, for in the shift to a popularizing and above all a local mode of expression, the national imaginary is at stake in Del

Campo's book-length poem. Here too, the Faust theme, along with the operatic form of Gounod's adaptation, stands for a European culture in opposition to which a process of Americanization is construed. The politics of that process will be my concern.

The frame tale of "Fausto" may be summarized as follows: a certain Don Laguna, having come into Buenos Aires from the countryside for commercial purposes and suffering some misadventures there, comes upon an old friend, Anastasio el Pollo, on the outskirts of the city. They recognize one another and embrace, and then fall into easy conversation, in the course of which Don Laguna mentions the Devil. Anastasio el Pollo interrupts:

> "Shut it,
> friend! Don' ya know,
> just t'other night I saw
> the demon?"
> "Jesus Christ!"
> "You do good to cross yourself."
>
> (—¡Callesé
> amigo! ¿No sabe usté
> que la otra noche lo he visto
> al demonio?
> —¡Jesucristo!
> —Hace bien, santigüesé.)[3]

Thereupon he recounts how he was carried along by a crowd into the Teatro Colón where he heard the performance of Gounod's opera. But having no prior experience of theatrical representation, he makes no ontological distinctions, and so relates what he saw as real.

Don Laguna is incredulous at first, but becomes absorbed in the tale, which the two friends intersperse with commentary. Thus, for example, Gounod's librettists Jules Barbier and Michel Carré limit Faust's initial responses to Méphistophélès to a laconic exchange:

> *MÉPHISTOPHÉLÈS.* Are you afraid of me?
>
> *FAUST.* No.
>
> *MÉPHISTOPHÉLÈS.* Do you doubt my power?
>
> *FAUST.* Perhaps.
>
> *MÉPHISTOPHÉLÈS.* Put it to the test, then.
>
> *FAUST.* Begone!
>
> (*MÉPHISTOPHÉLÈS.* Te fais-je peur?
>
> *FAUST.* Non.

MÉPHISTOPHÉLÈS. Doutes-tu ma puissance?

FAUST. Peut-être!

MÉPHISTOPHÉLÈS. Mets-la donc à l'épreuve!

FAUST. Va-t'en!)[4]

Thereupon, Méphistophélès expands into an ironic retort:

MÉPHISTOPHÉLÈS. Fie! Fie! Is this your courtesy!
But learn, my friend, that with Satan
One should behave in a different way.
I've entered your door with infinite trouble.
Would you kick me out the very same day?

(*MÉPHISTOPHÉLÈS.* Fi!—c'est là ta reconnaissance!
Apprends de moi qu'avec Satan
L'on en doit user d'autre sorte,
Et qu'il n'était pas besoin
De l'appeler de si loin
Pour le mettre ensuite à la porte!)[5]

At the corresponding point in del Campo's poem, Anastasio el Pollo first delivers the Devil's lines as reported speech: "My Doctor, don't let yourself be frightened" ("Mi Dotor, no se me asuste").[6] Faust's rejoinder, however, is set at the distance of indirect discourse with an interpretive introduction concerning his state of mind, and followed by an evaluative assessment by the gaucho interlocutors:

The Doctor, more than a bit afraid,
told him to hit the road . . .
"He did good, wouldn't you say?"
"I'd say absolutely, bro."

(El Dotor, medio asustao
le contestó que se juese . . .
—Hizo bien: ¿no le parece?
—Dejuramente, cuñao.)[7]

And then the irony of the libretto representing supernatural apparition as a question of etiquette is condensed into a new figure: "But the Devil started in / alleging transportation costs . . . " ("Pero el Diablo comenzó / A alegar gastos de viaje . . .").[8] Rhetorical reduction to the colloquial is the general mechanism of the gauchesca, but here there is a sudden shift of register, and an unmasking. The libretto had already practiced a shift from an ironized discourse of learning (both the learning and the irony signaled by a change in language from German to Latin) in Goethe's scene:

> *FAUST.* So that is what was hidden in the poodle:
> a wandering scholar! The *casus* is amusing.
>
> *MEPHISTOPHELES.* My compliments to your learning, sir!
> you made me sweat profusely.
>
> (*FAUST.* Das also war des Pudels Kern!
> Ein fahrender Scolast? Der Casus macht mich lachen.
>
> *MEPHISTOPHELES.* Ich salutiere den gelehrten Herrn!
> Ihr habt mich weidlich schwitzen machen.)[9]

But upon arrival in Buenos Aires, the discursive field of courtesy to which scholarship had been reduced—the one mocked as the other is mocked—is transformed into the discourse of commerce, in which the value of European imports, cultural or otherwise, is to be articulated. When the retelling of the opera comes to an end, del Campo quickly closes the frame tale as well, sending the two friends on from the riverside, where they had bathed and rested their horses, to an inn, where Don Laguna completes his transaction: he uses the money he made in his commercial dealings to repay Anastasio el Pollo's storytelling by inviting him to dinner.

The principal theoretician of the genre Josefina Ludmer argues that "Fausto" plays a pivotal role as both a transformative culmination of the motif of gaucho-goes-to-city that had been a mainstay of the gauchesca from the time of its first major practitioner, Bartolomé Hidalgo (1788–1822), and also an anticipation of some of the key features of Hernández' *Martín Fierro*.[10] Prior to "Fausto," the gaucho, that is, the real and suffering body of the rural laborer, was incorporated into the new nation-state by induction into the military; and at the same time, the voice of the gaucho was incorporated into the national literature through the formation of the stylized poetry of the gauchesca. Or, as Ludmer suggests, the two forms of incorporation were one; the public space entered by the gaucho-goes-to-city motif was at once political and literary. For del Campo, she avers, the public space identified as the city, where national ambitions are conceived, is rather defined as the place of economic exchange. And in that economy, literature is split off from politics and assigned to the autonomous field of culture. In the poems of Hidalgo, the gaucho was an autochthonous figure, who, like the unfenced lands he crossed, was a trope for liberty, reconstructed in the national image by the gauchesca as a plain-spoken patriot, that is, one who cedes the freedom of the pampa life to become a defender of his country's freedom. The gauchos of "Fausto" are ex-soldiers, whose business in town is not civic celebration, as was the case for Hidalgo's characters, but private enterprise and private entertainment. It is not the gauchos, but the gauchesca that contributes to the war effort—a matter of book sales. Throughout her penetrating discussion of "Fausto," Ludmer emphasizes the startling innovation of what she reads as the depoliticization of the genre in the mode of parody.

And critics were indeed startled in the early reception of del Campo's poem. Most notably, a generation of readers distracted themselves with a debate over whether a certain type of horse and a certain feature of horsemanship were apt for gauchos. (One might imagine theater reviewers in the New York papers, having no more contact with baseball than reading the sports columns, arguing about the batting stance adopted on stage by Joe Hardy.) The initial conventions of the gauchesca, above all, the stylized language of the poetry, founded a claim to heightened verisimilitude, and hence, a transparent means of access to the *realia* of national life embodied by the gauchos—even if that pretended transparency rather veiled the ideological construction of the trope of liberty, that is, the gaucho-as-patriot. Del Campo's literary commerce, on the contrary, was altogether explicitly a matter of intertextuality, which, Ludmer explains, "questions the referentiality of the representation and carries it to literature itself."[11] To miss this point and with it the ontological distinction between representation and reality is to place literary criticism of del Campo's "Fausto" in the same position as his gauchos occupied in relation to the opera. And when Argentine critics turned their attention to the intertextual mode of "Fausto," it was often to register offense; if there is parody, then its object must be the gauchos. Since the gauchos, as they came to be known through the gauchesca, offered a voice for constructing the nation in opposition to colonial rule (Hidalgo) to the dictatorship of Manuel de Rosas in the poetry of del Campo's immediate and openly acknowledged model, Hilario Ascasubi, alias Aniceto el Gallo, and to the subsequent self-proclaimed civilizing mission of Sarmiento's republicanism (Hernández), then opposition to the gauchos through parody was very nearly anti-patriotic. Yet the barb of the parody could be said to have landed elsewhere. Anastasio el Pollo takes the place of del Campo himself at the opera, in more than one sense. His unsophisticated reaction to the representation may also be read as a stand-in for the rising, commercial bourgeoisie of Buenos Aires who made up the real audience, people eager to attend an operatic performance that they could not appreciate.

Examination of a curious defense of "Fausto" by Argentine folklorist Augusto Raúl Cortázar may help to illuminate the underlying issues.[12] Cortázar concedes that the gaucho elements in the frame tale are inauthentic, but he asserts, on the other hand, that del Campo finds his most authentic voice where the poem departs most decidedly from the generic markers of the gauchesca and also from the Goethean pretext, namely in the lyrical descriptions that have been likened to interludes in opera. For there, according to Cortázar, the poem is "a perfect 'projection'" of the "traditional, popular, anonymous and oral poetry" of a folklore transplanted from the Iberian Peninsula to the Americas with the Conquest.[13] In displacing the burden of authenticity from the gaucho as the national voice of the Argentine land to the gaucho as popular voice of a Pan-Hispanic folk, Cortázar concludes that the poem's achievement resides precisely in that "Fausto" is "free of political contaminations and social and ideological implications."[14] But not so, and for the same reason, Cortázar's critical assessment: his reading is grounded in a certain Pan-Hispanism that grew in Spain and its former colonies in reaction to U.S. expansion in the nineteenth century, including the war with Mexico, and culminating in the defeat of Spain in the Caribbean in 1898. As early as 1900, Uruguayan Enrique Rodó, in his highly influential essay *Ariel*, warned against the threat of those damned Yankees to the north, and urged that the autonomous field of culture might make for a bulwark against neo-colonialism, if only the continent would understand itself as Latin, rather than Anglo-Saxon, America.[15] Rodó focused more on the French connection, but intellectuals in Spain, including Cortázar's teacher, the medievalist Ramón Menéndez Pidal, saw similar grounds for a post-colonial alliance.

"When writers turn to popular roots as subject matter for fiction, they expose the flows of darkened meaning that underlie official discourse," argues Francine Masiello with respect to postmodern literature in the Southern Cone. She continues: "The impulse allows us to reflect on the different languages of civil society, to expand the basis for common experience, and to rethink the place where art and literature invent their spectators and readers. Although often accused of brokering the interests of elites . . . , literature that returns to popular beginnings exposes the mutilations of the social corpus."[16] One ought to beware of anachronism, of course, though Ludmer has made clear that against the grain of its predominant patriotism, the gauchesca also gave voice to the mutilated social and physical body in the lament of gaucho war casualties.[17] More generally, just as the inauguration of British neocolonialism in the River Plate hardly awaited the demise of the old Spanish colonialism, so there is but a small gap between the liberal crisis of the founding and foundering of nation-states in nineteenth-century Latin America and the neoliberal crisis of our own times. Rather than as a wholesale depoliticization, then, the relationship between popular and high culture in "Fausto" may be read in a geopolitical light.

To recuperate the political dimension of opera, I take a detour from del Campo's poem to Werner Herzog's film *Fitzcarraldo* (1982).[18] A page from

Eduardo Galeano's *Las venas abiertas de América Latina* will suffice to set the historical stage:

> Manaus had five thousand inhabitants in 1849; it had seventy thousand in little more than half a century. There rubber magnates built their extravagantly designed and sumptuously decorated mansions with precious Oriental woods, Portuguese majolicas, columns of Carrara marble, and furniture by French master cabinetmakers. The nouveau riche of the jungle had the most costly foods brought from Rio de Janeiro; Europe's top couturiers cut their dresses and outfits; they sent their sons to study at British schools. The Amazonas theater, a baroque monument in triumphantly poor taste, is the chief symbol of that vertigo of wealth at the beginning of our century. Caruso navigated the river through the jungle to sing to Manaus' inhabitants for a kingly fee on opening night; Pavlova, who was supposed to dance there, could not get beyond Belem but sent her apologies.[19]

Based on the life of Carlos Fermín Fitzcarrald, the film pushes the story farther upriver, where the protagonist Brian Fitzgerald conceives the same ambition for the Peruvian outpost of Iquitos, namely, to build an opera house and bring Caruso to sing on opening night. To achieve this goal, Fitzcarraldo will need cash, and would therefore make himself a rubber baron; but with all the accessible lands already bought up, he is forced to undertake an extraordinary plan: he will steam upriver, have his boat dragged over a hill to a parallel tributary, and make his way to exploit an untapped forest, thus avoiding some impassable white water. The missing ingredient is a sufficient labor force. But for this, from the beginnings of Conquest up to the present, including the making of the film, there are indigenous peoples.

Fitzcarraldo and his crew steam along through the jungle to a region known to be inhabited by "bare-asses," that is, a people unconquered and unconverted—though quite well clothed. While remaining undiscovered on the forested banks of the river, they receive the intruders with drumming, which is understood on board as a precursor to armed resistance. Fitzcarraldo is informed that the Jivaros, as they are called in the film, have a belief that a white god will come to them on a ship. A latter-day Cortés who had gained advantage for the conquest of the Aztecs from the prophecies of the return of Quetzalcoatl from the east, Fitzcarraldo sees his chance. Lacking military power with which to engage in combat, he sets up his gramophone. This god, he declares, comes not with cannons: "He comes with the voice of Caruso" ("Er kommt mit der Stimme von Caruso"). Fitzcarraldo plays an aria and strikes a triumphant pose reminiscent, for the film audience, of Il Duce. The drumming falls silent. Far from an autonomous, depoliticized field, opera constitutes the voice of political economy in the film: conquest and colonization, exploitation of indigenous labor and natural resources. Or as Marcia Landy writes of Luchino Visconti's film *Il gattopardo* (*The Leopard,* 1963), so too one might say of Herzog's *Fitzcarraldo*: "the self-conscious use of history in collusion with operatic themes and techniques contributes to a critical—not monumental or antiquarian—engagement with questions of politics and power, particularly with the failure of popular struggle."[20]

Failure is ambivalent in *Fitzcarraldo.* On the one hand, the silence of the Jivaros—in fact, no more than the decision not to provide subtitles for their dialogue—proves more potent than the divine voice of Caruso. After contact, when the Jivaros board the ship, Fitzcarraldo quickly realizes that the people scrutinizing him as he eats are not fooled. They make an ontological distinction. They know he is no god. What he does not understand is that all the while that he believes that he is exploiting their labor en route to exploiting their land, they are exploiting him and his technological resources, for they need and eventually will use his ship, setting it adrift as a sacrifice to the spirit of the falls. But despite this misadventure, Fitzcarraldo succeeds in bringing his battered ship back to port in Iquitos, with a boatload of Jivaros, if not of rubber. And selling the vessel back to the same sporting rubber baron who was betting against his enterprise, he spends the proceeds on the arts, as we would say. He funds the transport of Caruso, his diva, and the accompanying orchestra upriver upon his hobbled steamship, where they perform at the riverside in the final scene of the film. The popular struggle of an outsider (Fitzcarraldo is an Irishman) against the rubber barons is lost in the field of political economy, but won in the autonomous field of art. He has brought the voice of his secularized divinity to Iquitos after all. One hardly notices that the warriors who had taken command of his ship in the service of their own gods are summarily dismissed from the film before that denouement—although they are offered a champagne toast, more evidence of colonial good sportsmanship.

In a powerful, sweeping interpretation of Spanish colonial discourse as the "polemics of possession," Rolena Adorno argues that "the native—colonized or indomitable—stands always at the heart of colonial writings, even when not explicitly mentioned."[21] But as Fitzcarraldo both depicts and reenacts, colonialism is not terminated, but quite the contrary, reinforced when polemics concerning possession of such lands and resources as the Amazonian jungle are disputed between criollos and recent European immigrants, competing to supply European and North American markets, while the dispossessed indigenous peoples are ushered silently from the stage. Recalling Landy's analysis of the operatic as history, once again, and her observation that Garibaldi constitutes a "structuring absence" in *The Leopard,* one might say that the indigenous peoples of the Americas are likewise a structuring absence, particularly in the nation-building discourses of the nineteenth century. The gauchos, pressed into military service in the campaigns to exterminate the native population of the pampas, are made to take their place, in the gauchesca, as the native voice. In Herzog's film, the drums are silenced, and the voice of Caruso, the voice of the God of Conquest, sings for Fitzcarraldo and his rubber baron rivals alike, resolving economic competition under the aegis of a neocolonial, globalized market in the embrace of a "world culture," which is always, and only, the culture of Europe. In del Campo's "Fausto," the unempowered strike back, raising their voice in a critical—not monumental or antiquarian—engagement with questions of geopolitical power upon the structuring absence of the native music of the pampa. To parody opera is to question the framing dichotomy of civilization and barbarism in both literary and political discourse, as delineated at their intersection in Argentine letters, *Facundo, o, civilización y barbarie* (1845), by Domingo Faustino Sarmiento, who, after staunch opposition to Rosas and exile, would rise to power as the president of Argentina in 1868, two years after Gounod's opening and del Campo's response.[22] More particularly, it is to contest foreign hegemony by challenging the equation of civilization with Europe and barbarism with America.

Under the aegis of a trope borrowed from Rodó's *Ariel,* "voz magistral," but translated by way of RCA-Victor, as "the voice of the Master," Roberto González Echevarría has argued that "the concept of culture has served as an ideology that gives meaning to Latin American literature, whereas modern Latin American literature emerges as it labors to unsettle that relationship."[23] The observation may be glossed by remarking that in the foundational discourses of modern Latin America, culture, both as a concept and as a set of productions, was European. But in serving to map an autonomous discursive field, separate from political economy, the concept of culture provided the grounds upon which to imagine a literature that would speak for Latin America. Ludmer's highly condensed formula for the gauchesca—"defining the word [*palabra*] 'gaucho' in the voice [*voz*] of the gaucho: voice/word [voz] (of the) 'gaucho'"[24]—may be extended to the whole of Latin American literature in its contest with (European) culture. Latin American literature would define "Latin America" in "Latin American," the words and voice of "Latin Americans," that is a figure in quotation marks, because it is itself the invention of that literature. Ludmer's deliberate tautology is an irony directed at Latin American literary criticism, but it touches Latin American literature as well, in that the autonomous or autochthonous literature reflexively defining itself as emancipation is nevertheless listening to the voice of its European master enunciating the concept of culture—perhaps no more than a spotted dog silenced by a gramophone.[25]

Rodó's narrator in *Ariel,* whose title indicates overtly its European (i.e., Shakespearean) pretext, does not himself pretend to speak "Latin American," that is, to produce a definitive Latin American literature, so much as he seeks to teach the ideology of the concept of culture. A generation earlier, del Campo's "Fausto" had already been engaged in unsettling that relationship much in the terms that Gonzalez Echevarría extrapolates from his reading of *Ariel*: "Literature issues from that hell where the dark figures of negation and transformation deface concepts predicated on authority and tradition."[26] In del Campo's poem, opera speaks for Culture, singing out the voice of the Master; and the gauchesca form takes the part of literature, defacing culture's authority by constructing an alternative, local knowledge. Like the Jivaros of Herzog's film, del Campo's Mandinga, a local name for the devil, slips away before the brandished sword of the archangel, "lo mesmito que un *peludo* / bajo la tierra ganó" (emphasis added to underline the local zoological term, to be rendered, perhaps, "jus' like brer armadillo / he made his underground getaway," so as to allude to his character as a folkloric shifter).[27] To see the disappearance of the Jivaros at the end of *Fitzcarraldo* as their own triumph would be wishful thinking, recalling that their return as the indigenous extras on the film set meant that they were made to drag a real steamship up a real hill. Yet the Mandinga of "Fausto" has not simply been defeated by a Higher Authority, for he has entered the land in the form of the (voz) peludo, and the land will retain his voice in much of the literature speaking "Latin American" in the nineteenth and twentieth centuries.

If Gounod's opera in Buenos Aires may have provided a contingent occasion for the enactment of the duel with culture, the *Faust* legacy offers an especially apt background from which to imagine a literature issuing from hell in a contest with its own ideological project—apt and enduring. Reviewing the trajectory of that project as it has reached contemporary Latin American letters a century later, González Echevarría notes: "What this postmodern literature is attempting to dismantle is nothing less than the central romantic trope, irony, and it does so by abolishing the individual self, whose quest for absolute knowledge is thwarted by the infinity of knowledge. What emerges out of the abolition of that self is the correlative figure of a Super Negator."[28] The postmodern superconsciousness, deconstructing irony, is also a belated arrival. Goethe had already imagined his Mephistopheles as "the Spirit of Eternal Negation" ("Ich bin der Geist der stets verneint!") (*F*, 1338).

That spirit travels through Gounod to del Campo and on to a contemporary play by Argentine Edgar Brau, who enters the conversation of "world literature" along the bias of our current form of globalization. Brau has sought an exit from the political economy of both the nineteenth-century crisis of liberalism figured as the city in del Campo's poem and the neoliberal crisis of the recent Argentine crash and its aftermath, by publishing his *Fausto* online where it is available free of charge: a renewed quest for access to infinite knowledge.[29] Moreover, his protagonist, also called

Fausto, is a transnational living in the northeastern United States, though an Argentine by origin, as indicated by the local dialect of the River Plate in his prose speech. In this context it has become possible for the author to imagine and for the new Faust to achieve absolute knowledge, represented as a formula that will overcome death, once and for all. Leaping over del Campo and Gounod to their origin, his intertext lies in plain view: a copy of Goethe's *Faust* upon the table at center stage. However, unlike Goethe's Faust, who has attained the limits of human knowledge, but requires the intervention of Mephistopheles to take a step beyond aging, forerunner of death, to realize his abiding desire, Brau's Fausto has already succeeded without Mefistófeles' help. He has found the secret of immortality, yet having crossed the former boundaries of knowledge and reached the tree of life, this Faust lacks resolve to eat, mass produce, and globalize delivery of its fruit. He fears that in negating death he will also be negating life. Brau's Fausto has the power to become the Super Negator, which he declines, while Mefistófeles argues, paradoxically, on behalf of mankind for Fausto to affirm the negator's role and to disseminate eternal life.

In Brau's drama, Mefistófeles applauds irony whenever he finds it in Fausto—"Bravo Doctor, your irony puts me at ease" ("Bravo, Doctor; a mi me tranquiliza tu ironía")[30]—as an initial alternative to credulity, including Fausto's resistance to believing that the devil he seems to see is real. But another peculiarity: it is also Mefistófeles who would undo Fausto's ironies in order to reach, of all things, an authentic voice, which speaks in the play in verse declaimed—an ironic authenticity—in the King's Castilian, rather than an Argentine *voseo*. Mefistófeles urges not only that knowledge is power but also that power is progress toward the fulfillment of mankind's deepest desire to be as the gods. He sees any step forward and says, "it is good"—a veritable, modern (and precisely not postmodern) industrial revolutionary. Faust is then the name for whosoever takes a decisive step, beginning with the engineer of the first wheel, or even the eating of the fruit in the biblical Garden, up to the scientist on stage with his new elixir.

This Fausto neither overturns nor yet admits Mefistófeles' argument that to be born to die is hardly a wise decision. And yet, Fausto reasons, "Nobody can decide for another" ("Nadie puede decider por otro"), eliciting the vituperation of Mefistófeles:

> That's all we needed! Democracy added on to metaphysics, to philosophy! Spermatozoids of the world: unite to vote! Ay, I saw it coming. But Doctor, dear little doctor; did you decide? Were you perchance able to choose? Those little dictators chose, Doc, your parents. And one could say not even they; the Great Dictator chose, when giving a start to life with his despotic will. Life and democracy are not meant for one another, Doc.

(¡Faltaba eso nada más! ¡La democracia agregada a la metafísica, a la filosofía! . . . ¡Espermatozoides del mundo: uníos para votar! . . . Ay, lo veía venir. Pero Doctor, *doctorcillo*; ¿qué decidiste tú? ¿Acaso pudiste elegir? . . . Eligieron los pequeños dictadores, Doc; tus padres. Y puede decirse que ni siquiera ellos; eligió el Gran Dictador, al dar con su voluntad despótica inicio a la vida. Vida y democracia no congenian, Doc.)[31]

Here is the devil's own work, the return of Mandinga from his Argentine burrow with corrosive irony: to cast life, in the wake of the Dirty War, on the side of dictatorship.

The voice of those masters may yet be rejected in Brau's *Fausto* by listening instead to the music of the celestial spheres. "There was music. And then the poet appeared" ("Había música. Y entonces apareció el poeta"), admits Mefistófeles:[32] a beginning, to recall Goethe's *Faust*, before the word that was nonetheless neither Mind, nor Power, nor Act ("*Sinn*," "*Kraft*," "*Tat*") (*F*, 1229, 1233, 1237). "Who, how, why?" ("¿Quién, cómo, por qué?"), Fausto asks, but Mefistófeles rejoins that the secret is not to be revealed: "not even I can gain access to the mystery" ("ni siquiera yo puedo acceder al misterio").[33] So neither the knowledge of Fausto nor Mefistófeles is absolute. The ultimate end cannot be attained, because the beginning remains a mystery, outside of the logos, that is, of reason and its instrumentality, of mastery as a trope for progress. The alternative mystery of music is presented as evidence of a limitation of divinity, a "Dios ciego" ("blind God") who may compose its harmony, but without a providential plan.

Odd that Anastasio el Pollo never mentions to Don Laguna that the Devil he saw and all the figures in the Teatro Colón were singing. Perhaps the memory of that music returns, too, in Brau's *Fausto*, as the figure for the small margin of liberty that a super-negator might achieve, not in defeating, but at least in resisting dictatorship. The stage directions call for a violin. A different, dispossessed collective memory might call for drumming.

NOTES

1. The slightly augmented text of the pamphlet of November 1866 would be the basis of the many editions to follow to the present day. Citations here refer to the widely available text: Estanislao del Campo, "Fausto, impresiones del gaucho Anastasio el Pollo en la representación de esta ópera," in *Poesía gauchesca*, ed. Jorge B. Rivera (Caracas: Biblioteca Ayacucho, 1977), 145–87. Translations of this and other texts, unless otherwise noted, are mine.

2. Even a more standard Castilian remained at the margins of the narrow canon that grew in place of Goethe's expansive view, at least until the late-twentieth-century dissemination of the work of Jorge Luis Borges and, subsequently, of his

heirs in the Latin American Boom. Hence, Juan Valera's novel *Las ilusiones del doctor Faustino* (1874–1875 in its initial publication as a serial), which engages Goethe intermittently, but explicitly, is little read outside of his native Spain. See Valera, *Las ilusiones del doctor Faustino*, ed. Cyrus C. De Coster (Madrid: Clásicos Castelia, 1970).

3. Del Campo, "Fausto," 151, ll. 157–60.

4. Both the French text and the English translation are cited from *Faust: A Lyric Drama in Five Acts*, Libretto, Jules Barbier and Michel Carré; Music, Charles Gounod (Boston: Oliver Ditson, 1906), 7; the translator is unnamed. I have modified the translation. For an Italian text, such as del Campo would have heard in performance in Buenos Aires, see *Gounod's Faust, A Lyric Opera in Five Acts. In Italian and English. Contains the Music of the Favourite Melodies* (New York: Samuel French, 1879), 4; again the translators are not named.

5. Barbier and Carré, *Faust: A Lyric Drama*, 7.

6. Del Campo, "Fausto," 155, l. 317.

7. Del Campo, "Fausto," 155–56, ll. 321–24.

8. Del Campo, "Fausto," 156, ll. 325–26.

9. Johann Wolfgang von Goethe, *Faust I & II*, ed. and trans. Stuart Atkins, vol. 2, *Goethe's Collected Works* (Cambridge, MA: Suhrkamp/Insel, 1984), 35, ll. 1323–26. Johann Wolfgang von Goethe, *Faust: Texte*, ed. Albrecht Schöne, vol. 7, pt. 1, *Sämtliche Werke. Briefe, Tagebücher und Gespräche* (Frankfurt: Deutscher Klassiker, 1994), 64, ll. 1323–26 [hereafter *F*].

10. Josefina Ludmer, *El género gauchesco: Un tratado sobre la patria* (Buenos Aires: Sudamericana, 1988). See especially the third chapter, "En el paraíso del infierno / El *Fausto* argentine / Un pastiche de crítica literaria," 241–75. For a diacritical reading of Ludmer's theoretical contribution, see Andrew Bush, "Feet Notes: The Fancy Foot Work of Josefina Ludmer on the *Gauchesca*," *Romance Studies* 23, no. 1 (2005): 55–69.

11. Ludmer, *El género gauchesco*, 260.

12. Augusto Raúl Cortázar, *Poesía gauchesca argentina, interpretada con el aporte de la teoría folklórica* (Buenos Aires: Editorial Gaudalupe, 1969), 55–73.

13. Cortázar, *Poesía gauchesca*, 72.

14. Cortázar, *Poesía gauchesca*, 73.

15. Enrique Rodó, *Ariel, Obras completas*, ed. Emir Rodríguez Monegal (Madrid: Aguilar, 1967), also available in English translation under the title *Ariel*, trans. F. J. Stimson (Boston: Houghton Mifflin, 1922). See also, Walter D. Mignolo, *The Idea of Latin America* (Malden, MA: Blackwell, 2005), 59, where he remarks, for instance, that "'*Latin*' America is not so much a subcontinent as it is the political project of Creole-Mestizo/a elites."

16. Francine Masiello, *The Art of Transition: Latin American Culture and Neoliberal Crisis* (Durham, NC: Duke University Press, 2001), 182–83.

17. See, especially, Ludmer, *El género gauchesco*, 169–201.

18. *Fitzcarraldo*, directed by Werner Herzog (Werner Herzog Filmproduktion, 1982).

19. Eduardo Galeano, *Open Veins of Latin America: Five Centuries of the Pillage of a Continent*, trans. Cedric Belfrage (New York: Monthly Review Press, 1973), 102.

20. Marcia Landy, *Cinematic Uses of the Past* (Minneapolis: University of Minnesota Press, 1996), 150.

21. Rolena Adorno, *The Polemics of Possession in Spanish American Narrative* (New Haven: Yale University Press, 2007), 4–5. As she indicates, the observation was first articulated in her "New Perspectives in Colonial Spanish American Literary Studies," *Journal of the Southwest* 32 (1990): 173–90.

22. See Domingo Faustino Sarmiento, *Facundo o civilización y barbarie,* ed. Nora Dottori and Silvia Zanetti (Caracas: Biblioteca Ayacucho, 1985), available in English as *Facundo: Civilization and Barbarism,* trans. Kathleen Ross (Berkeley: University of California Press, 2003). It is tempting to identify the author Domingo *Faustino* Sarmiento as an implied referent of the pact with the devil in del Campo's poem (recall Valera's *Faustino*). But before rushing to that convenient conclusion, it is necessary to register an explicit historical reference in the text. When Anastasio el Pollo first names the protagonist of the opera as a Doctor Fausto, Don Laguna interjects what he takes to be a correction: "—¿Dotor dice? Coronel / de la otra Banda, amigaso" ("Doctor, you say? Colonel / from the other side, dear friend"), by which he means a certain officer from the *Banda Oriental,* that is, Uruguay, Col. Fausto Aguilar. See del Campo, "Fausto," 154, ll. 257–58.

23. Roberto González Echevarría, *The Voice of the Masters: Writing and Authority in Modern Latin American Literature* (Austin: University of Texas Press, 1985), 8; for the quotation and translation of Rodó, see González Echevarría, 25. For an alternative approach to the "Voice of the Master" closely related to my discussion, see also the critical history of RCA's exploitation of industrial labor in Jefferson R. Cowie, *Capital Moves: RCA's Seventy-Year Quest for Cheap Labor* (Ithaca, NY: Cornell University Press, 1999).

24. Ludmer, *El género gauchesco,* 31.

25. Caruso's arrival in Iquitos is played as Fitzcarraldo's triumph over rude commercialism, but it is simultaneously a defeat of the original artistic project, that is, the project of artistic originality. The singer's presence is derivative; he follows on the heels of his own recording. The round about river tour was always already superfluous in the age of mechanical reproduction.

26. González Echevarría, *The Voice of the Masters,* 13–14.

27. Del Campo, "Fausto," 182, ll. 1255, 1245, and 1256, respectively.

28. González Echevarría, *The Voice of the Masters,* 4–5.

29. Edgar Brau, *Fausto* (Buenos Aires: Cimbelino Ediciones Online, 2009), cimbelino@fullzero.com.ar (accessed May 7, 2009).

30. Brau, *Fausto,* 9.

31. Brau, *Fausto,* 26.

32. Brau, *Fausto,* 50.

33. Brau, *Fausto,* 50.

BIBLIOGRAPHY

Adorno, Rolena. "New Perspectives in Colonial Spanish American Literary Studies." *Journal of the Southwest* 32 (1990): 173–90.

———. *The Polemics of Possession in Spanish American Narrative.* New Haven: Yale University Press, 2007.

Brau, Edgar. *Fausto*. Buenos Aires: Cimbelino Ediciones Online, 2009. cimbelino@fullzero.com.ar (accessed May 7, 2009).
Bush, Andrew. "Feet Notes: The Fancy Foot Work of Josefina Ludmer on the Gauchesca." *Romance Studies* 23, no. 1 (2005): 55–69.
Cortázar, Augusto Raúl. *Poesía gauchesca argentina, interpretada con el aporte de la teoría folklórica*. Buenos Aires: Editorial Gaudalupe, 1969.
Del Campo, Estanislao. "Fausto, impresiones del gaucho Anastasio el Pollo en la representación de esta ópera." In *Poesía gauchesca*, edited by Jorge B. Rivera, 145–87. Caracas: Biblioteca Ayacucho, 1977.
Faust: A Lyric Drama in Five Acts. Libretto, Jules Barbier and Michel Carré. Music, Charles Gounod. Boston: Oliver Ditson, 1906.
Galeano, Eduardo. *Las venas abiertas de América Latina*. Rev. ed. Mexico: Siglo XXI, 2007.
Goethe, Johann Wolfgang von. *Faust I & II*. Translated and edited by Stuart Atkins. Vol. 2, *Goethe's Collected Works*. Cambridge, MA: Suhrkamp/Insel, 1984.
———. *Faust: Texte*. Edited by Albrecht Schöne. Vol. 7, pt. 1, *Sämtliche Werke. Briefe, Tagebücher und Gespräche*. Frankfurt: Deutscher Klassiker, 1994.
González Echevarría, Roberto. *The Voice of the Masters: Writing and Authority in Modern Latin American Literature*. Austin: University of Texas Press, 1985.
Gounod's Faust, A Lyric Opera in Five Acts. In Italian and English. Contains the Music of the Favourite Melodies. New York: Samuel French, 1879.
Herzog, Werner, dir. *Fitzcarraldo*. Werner Herzog Filmproduktion, 1982.
Landy, Marcia. *Cinematic Uses of the Past*. Minneapolis: University of Minnesota Press, 1996.
Ludmer, Josefina. *El género gauchesco: Un tratado sobre la patria*. Buenos Aires: Sudamericana, 1988.
Masiello, Francine. *The Art of Transition: Latin American Culture and Neoliberal Crisis*. Durham, NC: Duke University Press, 2001.
Mignolo, Walter D. *The Idea of Latin America*. Malden, MA: Blackwell, 2005.
Rodó, Enrique. *Ariel*. In *Obras completas*. Edited by Emir Rodríguez Monegal. Madrid: Aguilar, 1967.
———. *Ariel*. Translated by F. J. Stimson. Boston: Houghton Mifflin, 1922.
Sarmiento, Domingo Faustino. *Facundo o civilización y barbarie*. Edited by Nora Dottori and Silvia Zanetti. Caracas: Biblioteca Ayacucho, 1985.
———. *Facundo: Civilization and Barbarism*. Translated by Kathleen Ross. Berkeley: University of California Press, 2003.
Valera, Juan. *Las ilusiones del doctor Faustino*. Edited by Cyrus C. De Coster. Madrid: Clásicos Castelia, 1970.

6

The Complete *Faust* on Stage: Peter Stein and the Goetheanum

David G. John

The illustrious director Peter Stein claimed that his production of Goethe's *Faust I* and *II* for Expo 2000, the Hanover World's Fair, with subsequent runs in Berlin and Vienna, was "the first professional performance of the complete tragedy."[1] This declaration suppresses cultural memory of the Goetheanum's *Fausts,* which had been staged approximately every five years since 1938 in Dornach, Switzerland, the world center for anthroposophy, a socio-philosophical movement founded in 1923–1924 by Rudolf Steiner (1861–1925).[2] There are many anecdotes and some recordings of complete *Faust* readings, but none of a complete performance before the Goetheanum's and Stein's, so these are unique. I witnessed the most recent Goetheanum production, directed by Wilfried Hammacher, eighteen hours in length, over three days in May 2004, after having seen Stein's production, which ran thirteen hours, in Vienna in 2001. Stein in fact has himself been to Dornach and viewed at least some of the *Faust* scenes performed there, but from his claim about his own production it is clear that he does not recognize the Goetheanum's as a comparable accomplishment, at least in terms of its completeness and the qualifications of its actors. Let me deal quickly with the two factual errors of Stein's claim. First, the Goetheanum *Faust* of 2004, like his, included every single one of Goethe's 12,111 lines (like many audience members, I followed along with my Reclam edition open on my lap). Second, the Goetheanum actors, most of them members of the company for years, are also highly trained paid professionals. This I determined by personal interviews with the actor of Faust, Christian Peter, the director of the section for fine arts of the Anthroposophical Society, Martina Maria Sam, and the project director and business manager of the production, Thomas Didden. An extensive website listed all participants and included a great deal of background information on the production as well as a detailed final report.[3] But it is hardly worth spending time on such trivial points. What counts is the quality of these productions and what they did with Goethe's tragedy as well as for its audiences. In the following I shall compare the two with a view to assessing them as contributions to the stage history of this work. Following the broad approach of performance theorists Richard Schechner and Marvin Carlson, I shall structure my analysis into six parts by focusing on the elements that I find most significant in this case: the business of production, the place of performance and audience, the cast, the underlying philosophy, the language, the lighting, and color. Since I have already largely made my case in praise of Stein's production,[4] I shall keep my references to it minimal, and concentrate for the most part on the Goetheanum version.

THE BUSINESS OF PRODUCTION

It may seem strange to begin analyzing a work of art as a business enterprise, but in this case it is fitting since unlike most major European stagings, which occur within the framework of a permanent company's repertoire and enjoy significant public subsidy, that was not the case with either of these. We might also recall that Goethe himself, as intendant of the Weimar court theater, was highly conscious of the balance sheet. The organizers of the Hanover World's Fair initially dismissed Stein's project because it seemed to them fiscally unwise; in order to address their concern, he took personal responsibility, rallying backers from the public, private, and corporate worlds to meet his estimated costs of 25 million DM.[5] The major sponsors he attracted included numerous corporations as well as hundreds of small business and private donors. He also secured revenues from the television media which bought the rights to film and distribute the production on their networks. Roswitha Schieb's *Programmbuch* on Stein's production begins with a brief introduction written by the director, "Zur Entstehungsgeschichte unserer Faust-Aufführung" (History of the genesis of our *Faust* production),[6] in which the word "our" stands out, pointing to Stein's sense of communal effort and valuing of cooperation between private and public sectors and the arts. The production was a resounding commercial success.[7]

The international Anthroposophical Society is in part a huge business whose every activity must be supported fiscally by its members, with rarely much subsidy from public coffers. The regular mounting of *Faust* is just one of their major enterprises, and the 2004 version was preceded by an extensive fundraising effort which paralleled Stein's. Dornach's budget was set at 12 million Swiss francs, and the final report of October 2004 reports total expenditures of 11.75 million SF and an income of 11.61 million, hence a small loss of just .14 million, or virtually a balanced budget. The Anthroposophical Society first made a major internal commitment of 3 million SF to mount the event, using funds derived from society activities such as the sale of publications and membership fees. Approximately 3 million SF were expected from ticket sales, and the rest was to be sought through public donations in cash and in kind from numerous partners, and indeed with success, finally including funding from the Region of Basel Lottery, Swiss cantons Aargau and Solthurn, the city of Basel, the Swiss University of Continuing Education, Swiss Air, RailAway, Basel Culture, and the *Basler Zeitung*. These sponsors were listed on the Goetheanum website, as were a supportive network of interested members internationally and thousands who traveled to Dornach to see the production, let alone buy related books, products, and souvenirs, just as Stein's audiences did. The critical importance of this fiscal dimension to the Goetheanum *Faust* was underscored to me during my interviews with members of the administration, and their admirably open final report on the website contains the details.

THE PLACE OF PERFORMANCE AND AUDIENCE

Stein's performance took place in three different cities, yet in a sense in a common space and with a common audience. By using a variety of screens, backdrops, and movable bleachers, he converted a large empty space of warehouse proportions—his rehearsal space in Hanover and the rehearsal and performance spaces in Berlin and Vienna were in fact disused factories or warehouses—into eighteen different stage and seating arrangements, all illustrated in Schieb's *Programmbuch*.[8] The effect was to integrate the audience into the play, and in some scenes such as the "Hall of Knights" ("Kaiserliche Pfalz Rittersaal") to close the first act of part two, the audience became part of the action themselves, sitting at banquet tables and dining on bread, cheese, and wine along with the performers.[9] The audience's frequent change of location and unreserved seats encouraged mixing and interchange, which extended the performance space at intermissions to refreshment and communal dining areas, as was the case in the Goetheanum. Both audiences became a family of theatergoers who not only saw *Faust* but were literally *in* it and lived it for most of three days. Because of this commitment of time and resources by each member of the audience, the vast majority of them Goethe and *Faust* admirers, the journey to the place of performance, be it Hanover, Berlin, Vienna, or Dornach, took on the air of a pilgrimage.

The Goetheanum in Dornach is not merely the administrative center for world anthroposophy; the structure's architecture itself represents some of the movement's fundamental principles. Inside, one is surrounded by symbols of anthroposophic thought, from the images in elaborate stained glass windows in the theater, depicting the movement's mythology, to sculptures, paintings, and interior architecture.[10] Inside and out, the basic trapezoid shape, rounded corners and curves, reject the logocentricity of traditional Western architecture in favor of socio-humanistic fluidity and reflect the anthroposophists' belief that there is a metaphysical dimension beneath all that we perceive. These characteristics are also evident in structures far beyond the central place of performance. In other parts of the town many dwellings are constructed in the same architectural style, as they are far beyond its borders, indeed in many areas of the world. The massive Goetheanum theater itself, accommodating a thousand spectators, is like the heart of an organism that pulses into an international community of believers. Moreover, since most in the audience had come from afar and were accommodated close to the theater, we virtually lived together and shared the Goetheanum complex as a focus of daily activity where we experienced *Faust*, interacted during intermissions, and ate vegetarian food in a rustic communal dining hall before sharing accommodations for the night.

The atmosphere in the Goetheanum was that of a grand family gathering, a communion of believers. Yet it was certainly not without sophisticated intellectual and critical dimensions. There was much debate about the effectiveness of the production in representing an anthroposophic interpretation of *Faust*, as in, for example, the final scenes of part two, which for many contained too much Christian imagery, contradicting anthroposophy's disavowal of being a religious sect. Founder Rudolf Steiner himself was not a Christian, being born and raised in a non-religious household, and in his lifetime he did not support attempts to make Christianity a part of anthroposophic thought. On the founding of a "society of Christians" by anthroposophists Friedrich Rittelmeyer and Emil Bock he commented, "this movement toward a Christian conversion did not grow from the principles of anthroposophy. Its origin lies in the personalities of individuals who were seeking a new religious path from their experience of Christianity, not of anthroposophy."[11]

I was impressed by the deep knowledge of Goethe's text that many audience members possessed, and not just the older set, for I sat for some time with teenagers from the Stuttgart Waldorf School who were well versed in the work and showed a delightfully critical appreciation. I was also taken by the presence in the audience of some two dozen physically and mentally handicapped young and middle-aged people, some of them severely so. Into this grand space they walked, shuffled, limped, or were wheeled, with the help of numerous caregivers, finding their places not on the periphery but among the best seats in the house. There was considerable clatter as they did, during the frequent exits and entries for intermissions, and occasionally even during the performance itself when some reacted to events on stage with shouts of surprise, elation, dismay, or revulsion. One had to smile and think of the eighteenth-century marketplace performances of itinerant companies where Goethe was weaned on his first *Faust* by puppet players, and where audiences were anything but respectfully silent. I expected their presence to be temporary but was surprised to learn that they would be with us for the entire eighteen hours. This for me was one of the most remarkable aspects of the Goetheanum *Faust*, for it drove home emphatically the movement's holistic commitment to a blend of medical science, psychology, and metaphysics to support their central belief that every human is enlivened by a soul that is healthy and intact and can be—must be—nourished and developed. As most anthroposophical principles, this commitment to the physically disadvantaged in society was introduced by Rudolf Steiner, who worked with the handicapped to develop useful pedagogical techniques and demonstrated a personal commitment to them, believing that they are as teachable as any others. Steiner already began to develop this view during his employment for the Ladislaus Specht family in Vienna in 1884. His caritative commitment showed itself in other ways at that time as well, as, for example, in his advocacy of social, political, and economic structures based on justice and respect, and his support of public medical services. The Waldorf school system, which he also founded, teaches such principles.[12] The anthroposophic movement's devotion to socio-humanism and its holistic combination of medical science, psychology, and metaphysics can be likened readily to the seasoned Faust's wide-ranging interests as they are described in the "Night" ("Nacht") and "Before the Gate" ("Vor dem Tor") scenes of part one.

The producers of the Goetheanum *Faust* conducted research on the nature of their audiences and published the results in their final report. These show 11,000 attendees, 66 percent of capacity, double the number that saw the 1999 production, and the largest combined audience to have seen any Goetheanum *Faust* production since the practice began in 1938. Among them were 1,500 schoolchildren and youths, and another 29 percent of the remaining audience, or 2,755 individuals, were under the age of fifty. In all then, 38.68 percent of the entire audience of 11,000 could be called "young," a claim that neither Stein's nor many other *Faust* productions could or still can make. Of course this demographic statistical gathering had its practical role in providing information for the Anthroposophical Society in its future marketing and proselytizing intentions, but the accomplishment of attracting youth, and providing them with such a learning experience, is no less admirable because of it.

THE CAST

Stein's self-confidence and commitment led him to cast the show well before the finances were secure, and he demonstrated a remarkable ability to build a co-operative team. Schieb's volume includes a lengthy rehearsal diary (*Probentagebuch*), a valuable chronicle of the pre-production period and at the same time a record of growing co-operation, trust, and solidarity among the cast and its director. Stein asked his team to commit in advance two and a half years to the project, a year to rehearse and eighteen months to perform, a commitment virtually unheard of in the fluid acting profession. He carefully selected his cast, a balanced mix of beginners, young, middle-aged, and senior actors. Stein's claim about using only professional actors should be understood in terms of the kinds of actors he was using. Indeed his production attracted some of the best, such as Bruno Ganz, his elder Faust, and Corinna Kirchhoff, his Helena, but it also had a large contingent of proficient unknowns, and the Goetheanum's cast was much the same.[13] The loyalty of this cast was different than Stein's, however; it was a commitment first to the work and its author, then to the principles of anthroposophy, and only thereafter to director Hammacher. Many of them had also performed in previous Goetheanum *Fausts*, including major roles. Over the years they had developed personal preferences for staging and acting the work, and Christian Peter had even directed the previous version in 1999, but they were prepared to re-focus and adapt to Hammacher's conception. Not all of them agreed with his interpretation and emphasis, especially his mounting of the final act, but they nevertheless carried out their responsibilities professionally. Their esprit de corps was no less evident than that of Stein's troupe, for their loyalty to the idea of performing *Faust* as an expression of the anthroposophical worldview, hence their loyalty to the founder of anthroposophy, was akin to, in fact probably deeper than, that of Stein's actors to him.

THE UNDERLYING PHILOSOPHY

A lifetime admirer of Goethe and *Faust*, Stein had wanted to stage the full tragedy for years but was wary of its length and complexity. He was attracted to the modern relevance of its themes, such as world population, uncertainty about the future, dealing with the virtual economy, the creation of artificial intelligence, the expropriation of Nature, ecological abuse, the acceleration of daily life, the ephemeral nature of meaningful experiences, and the inexorable and inevitable failure of human striving.[14] If there is a consistent philosophy here, it is a fundamentally negative, pessimistic stance to the Faust saga and human lot; but it was dramatic performance, excitement about the theatrical potential of Goethe's text, rather than philosophy, that dominated Stein's thoughts. In fact he rejected the use of the play as a tool to illustrate any philosophy or worldview, which is precisely what the Goetheanum *Fausts* do, and I would suggest that it was principally for this reason that he utterly rejected and refused to recognize the anthroposophists' production. Stein's deep antipathy in fact had nothing to do with whether the Goetheanum in Dornach performed Goethe's entire text, and used professional actors, or not. Although Stein does not set his adoration of Goethe's work into the framework of a specific metaphysical or philosophical system, one could argue nevertheless that his motivation was fundamentally akin to the anthroposophists' who shared his devotion to Goethe and *Faust* as an exemplary work, except that they framed it with a worldview which they define, disseminate, and advocate as an organization.

To try to understand this view and how it applies to *Faust,* one must read the works of their founder. Much maligned by non-anthroposophists, Rudolf Steiner at least deserves their respect as a Goethe scholar and expert. His co-editorship with Bernhard Suphan and Karl von Bardeleben of seven volumes of the Weimar Edition (Weimarer Ausgabe) of Goethe's complete works, specifically the volumes of Goethe's scientific writings on morphology, natural science, mineralogy, geology, and climatology,[15] has guaranteed him this academic recognition. Beyond that contribution to critical editing, the volume of Steiner's own publications dwarfs even Goethe's, with some four hundred titles to his credit.[16] Here lies the definitive collected wisdom of the anthroposophical movement, its foundation laid by the writings in Steiner's *Wo und wie findet man den Geist?* (Where and how does one find spirituality?) (1908–1909).[17] Many of Steiner's subsequent works focus on Goethe and *Faust,* foremost his *Geisteswissenschaftliche Erläuterungen zu Goethes Faust* (Humanistic commentaries on Goethe's *Faust*).[18] An extensive list of Steiner's thirty-five lectures and writings on Goethe's *Faust* is provided by Heinrich Proskauer in his critical edition, *Goethes Faust,*[19] and most of them can be found in Steiner's *Geisteswissenschaftliche Erläuterungen zu Goethes Faust* as well. *Wo und wie findet man den Geist?* contains eighteen lectures that Steiner held in Berlin between October 1908 and May 1909 on an eclectic range of topics from revelation to biblical wisdom, superstition, physical nourishment, health, Tolstoy and Carnegie, thought training, human nature and temperament, the riddles in Goethe's *Faust,* Nietzsche, Isis and Madonna, clairvoyance, and European mysteries. There are many references throughout to Goethe generally and to *Faust.* Four of the essays are of particular interest to us now.

"Goethes geheime Offenbarung - exoterisch" (Goethe's secret revelation -exoteric)[20] contains as its central object of interpretation the "Märchen von der grünen Schlange und der schönen Lilie" which Goethe published at the end of the *Unterhaltungen deutscher Ausgewanderter*.[21] Steiner also wrote a simplified version of this interpretation in an essay to which many of his followers turn for understanding.[22] Goethe's extensive planning notes to the tale, which stemmed from both himself and his circle of friends, themselves suggest many possibilities for explaining it, but they certainly define no clear line of interpretation.[23] The tale, long an enigma to Goethe readers and scholars, relates the story of a supernatural snake who sacrifices herself for a beautiful lily and the well-being of others. The main symbol, the snake, is seen by anthroposophists as representing a person who is prepared to sacrifice her or his life and personality to create of the self an ideal form. As Steiner wrote, "He who cannot free himself from his own little ego, whoever is incapable of creating the higher ego in himself, cannot realize Goethe's vision in its entirety" ("Wer nicht loskommen kann von seinem eigenen kleinen Ich, wer nicht imstande ist, das höhere Ich in sich auszubilden, der kann nach Goethes Ansicht nicht zur Vollkommenheit gelangen").[24] The tale reveals Steiner's interest in the question of whether or not a human can encourage and fashion his own development consciously, after nature and society have dealt him his genetic and social cards. For many anthroposophists this tale is the central and most accessible portion of Steiner's writings dealing with Goethe's *Faust*. The fact that it is housed in a fairy tale, a literary form anchored in the fantastic and surreal, demonstrates that their, and Steiner's, understanding and explanation of the tragedy is not based on logical, but rather supra-rational, even metaphysical thinking. This I have found to be the case in all of Steiner's writings on the subject. The tale itself is enigmatic, and Steiner's self-confident interpretation of it is confusing. In Vienna in the nineties he studied all nineteen of Goethe's fairy tales, and claimed that they showed what forms self-development could take.[25] The other three essays in *Wo und wie findet man den Geist?* that are of interest to us, "Goethes geheime Offenbarung-esoterisch" (Goethe's secret revelation-esoteric)[26] and the two on the riddles in *Faust*,[27] are, in the first case, an even more metaphysical explanation of the fairy tale, and in the second and third, first general, then metaphysical, overviews of the individual topics on *Faust* treated in *Geisteswissenschaftliche Erläuterungen zu Goethes Faust*. The third essay draws the conclusion that the final words of *Faust II* and the fairy tale of the green snake and the lily contain the same message. Let us look now at the individual topics on *Faust* treated by Steiner in the first volume of *Geisteswissenschaftliche Erläuterungen zu Goethes Faust, Faust, der strebende Mensch* (Faust, the striving man).

This volume contains essays based on lectures, one given in Berlin in 1910, and fifteen in Dornach in 1915–1916. They reflect an optimistic, holistic adherence to the nineteenth-century German concept *Geisteswissenschaft*, or humanistic studies, as opposed to those of natural science, which were dominated by the nineteenth-century positivistic approach, though Steiner makes no reference to its theoretical founders,[28] nor does he quote specifically from any other critical sources on *Faust*. This confident exegetical position and the exposition of it in the essays have remained as the accepted and prescriptive interpretation of *Faust* for many, if not most, anthroposophic readers and audiences despite the horrors of two world wars in between and the deep questioning of life's meaning which is the twentieth century's legacy. The lectures on which they are based speak in a voice removed from the theater of war and the central problems of European society at the time. In his fifties when the war began, Steiner was not called up directly into the fighting, and so continued his lecturing and writing wherever it was possible. He designated the war years as "a difficult time," explaining, "It isn't good to regard this difficulty as a sickness, as we so often call it, for sickness is often a process of healing: the true sickness has preceded the physically evident one. This is the case with what we refer to currently as the sad events in the world. Something unhealthy preceded it, but on a much deeper level. We should see much deeper into it than we humans customarily look at things."[29] There is here no direct intellectual involvement in the reality of war itself.

It is striking that when one talks with dedicated anthroposophists about *Faust* today, their primary reference is still to Steiner, whose major writings on the subject were all conceived in that period and frame of mind. The titles of the sixteen lectures in the *Geisteswissenschaftliche Erläuterungen zu Goethes Faust* address what Steiner considered to be key parts or dimensions of *Faust*, and these remain as his signposts for interpreting the tragedy in the context of Goethe's work:

1. Goethe's *Faust* from a humanistic point of view.
2. Faust's struggle to find the source of life which is drenched in Christ's spirit.
3. Faust's penetration into the world of the spirit. The meditation of the Earth Spirit, of the elemental world.
4. Pentecost atmosphere. The transformation of guilt to a higher level of perception. Faust's initiation with the spirits of the earth.
5. The Faust mood.
6. *Faust,* the world's greatest poem of striving. The classical phantasmagoria.
7. Faust's ascension.
8. Mystical recognition and spiritual revelation of nature. Perception of the spirits.
9. The realm of the mothers. The Mater Gloriosa.
10. The questions of necessity and chance in life.
11. Wisdom—beauty—goodness. Michael—Gabriel—Raphael.
12. The historical meaning of *Faust*.

13. The burial. The nature of the lemurs and the thick and dry-headed devils.
14. Goethe's insights into the mysteries of human existence.
15. View of the true realities Goethe sought.
16. Goethe's quest for the depths of life's creative force and the secrets of the world in his *Faust*. The luciferian and ahrimanic seduction.

Two observations spring immediately to mind. Several of these titles, and indeed the contents of the essays, justify the assumption that Steiner's thinking and the movement he founded are essentially Christian, even if he insisted the contrary. Then, oddly, although a number of the essays obviously deal directly with themes and parts of *Faust*, this list excludes the Gretchen figure, the social issues surrounding her death, and indeed the greater socio-economic and historical problems that surface in part two, the questions that attract the attention of most modern *Faust* theater directors, audiences, and scholars. The volume's editors, Edwin Froböse and Hans Erhard Lauer, supplied no footnotes or critical apparatus that could connect it with these aspects.

The second volume concentrates on *Faust II* and contains the texts of twelve Steiner lectures given in Dornach between September 1916 and January 1919, with one more in Prague, June 1918. As was the case with the first volume, the dating and location are striking. It was the height of the war, yet removed from the field of battle. The volume is marked by the same escapism that allowed the author to continue his thoroughly optimistic worldview and interpretation of *Faust*, and the overall approach continues to be consistent with the tenets of the late nineteenth- and early twentieth-century humanistic view of the world. The editors, Lauer and Froböse, included eight pages of notes, but the scholarly apparatus is sparse.[30] The notes cite two scholars, Adolf von Harnack (1851–1930), with whom Steiner feuded, and Karl Julius Schröer (1825–1900), whose scholarship became the basis of the critical notes to Proskauer's anthroposophically sanctioned edition of Goethe's primary text. Schröer, a dialect researcher, cultural historian, idealist, and professor at the Technical University of Vienna, greatly influenced Steiner when he studied there between October 1879 and August 1883, albeit without completing final examinations in any discipline. Schröer in fact had suggested the young Steiner as co-editor for the Goethe volumes in the Weimar Edition[31] and was later acknowledged by his protegé as responsible for bringing him to see Goethe's *Faust* as the highest expression of optimism in mankind, a belief Steiner would nurture for life. Later, Steiner recognized him thus: "I thank God and good fortune that here in Vienna I met a man who—after Goethe, of course—can call himself the world's best *Faust* expert, a man whom I regard highly and respect as a teacher, scholar, poet, and human being" ("Ich danke es Gott und einem guten Geschicke, daß ich hier in Wien einen Mann kennenlernte, der – nach Goethe selbstverständlich – sich als der beste Faustkenner rühmen darf, einen Mann, den ich hochschätze und verehre als Lehrer, als Gelehrten, als Dichter, als Menschen").[32] Contact with Schröer convinced Steiner that Goethe represented a high point of German culture which the German people no longer enjoyed. Yet he shared none of the fin-de-siècle pessimism of the time and carried Schröer's idealism into Goetheanum productions to this very day. The experience also biased him forever in his interpretation. Scholarship from a different point of view is not represented in these volumes. Indeed, the elementary inclusion of line references to the primary work, so that readers may check the accuracy of Steiner's many citations and paraphrases from it, is also missing. One recalls the fact that Steiner never completed his studies in any discipline at the University of Vienna, although he delved into an astounding variety of subjects.[33] This scholarly eclecticism, some more severe in their judgment might call it dilettantism, left its mark on all of his writings. Despite the fact that he had earned a reputation through his editorial involvement in the Weimar Edition of Goethe's complete works, which is a long-respected example of accomplished positivistic scholarship, he abandoned that approach almost completely in his later writings, denouncing the "Rationalists and those bound by reason" as incapable of true understanding.[34]

THE LANGUAGE AND ACTING

Although concentrating foremost on the theatricality of *Faust*, Stein insisted from the start that he would privilege Goethe's text above all, paying scrupulous attention to its detail and the clues it offers for stage presentation. This position ignited an explosion of criticism.[35] The rehearsal of each scene began with a communal reading of the text and discussion about its conversion to the stage, then proceeded to the first tentative run-through and the development of a concept. The text acted as the springboard for the entire range of theater semiotics.[36] In this regard, Schieb highlights quotations from Stein during rehearsals, including these:

> One of the goals when we recite the lines is musicality. The actors must know how the next sentence sounds so that they can, so to say, anticipate the direction of the intonation and the tone clearly. . . . Gestures, mimicry, and text should all complement each other together. It does not work well to set these elements in parallel simultaneously. It is much more exciting if gestures are prepared early and then enacted so that they occur ahead of the spoken text or, by contrast, just follow briefly after it.
>
> When the musical accompaniment begins, then the actors must always speak against it. The music orients itself to whatever is in the text; it is a matter

of translating the language into music, so to speak. The spoken language, on the one hand, should either reinforce what the music has to say, and on the other, stand in contrast to it, but never allow itself to be overwhelmed by it.[37]

Such statements reflect principles of Stein's directing technique and his concept of the relationship between text and performance.[38] It might come as a surprise to him, but some of his concepts could well be applied to the Dornach production, in some ways perhaps even with his approval, in others definitely not. His emphasis on the text's "musicality . . . the direction of the intonation and the tone," and his point that the "gestures, mimicry, and text should all complement each other together" direct us to think of the interplay between the spoken text and its parallel representation in the Dornach *Faust,* which was expressed strikingly through the eurythmics of that performance.

The extensive press information package for the Dornach production, presented on the Goetheanum *Faust* website and for the most part still accessible there, contained among other instructive articles the text of an interview with the Faust actor Christian Peter, in which he says the following about the language of the play and the relation of the Goetheanum actors to it:

The training in our school for rhetoric and drama is designed so that every actor also learns to speak in chorus. The art of speaking in chorus consists of remaining an individual person and at the same time finding one's way simultaneously into the same impulse field as the others. . . . Goethe's "Faust" . . . plays in various "locations of consciousness." These could be interpreted in various ways: as dreams or day-dreams, or as journeys of the soul. . . . But how can that be shown to the audience? Should one demonstrate it through physical action, or try to show that the activity takes place on another level of consciousness? This has always been attempted in the history of the theater, and is still attempted again and again; and there are various possibilities for doing so. The advantage of eurythmy is that it is an unnatural medium. When the eurythmics begin, not just one figure appears, but the language itself becomes visible. As an audience member I see what I would otherwise just hear. To some degree I enter a virtual space.

(Die Ausbildung an unserer Schule für Sprachgestaltung und Schauspiel ist so ausgerichtet, dass jeder Schauspieler auch das Sprechen im Sprechchor lernt. Die Kunst des Sprechens im Chor besteht darin, als Persönlichkeit bestehen zu bleiben und gleichzeitig mit den anderen in einen Impuls hineinzufinden. . . . Goethes "Faust" . . . spielt an verschiedenen "Bewusstseins-Orten." Diese könnte man nun verschieden interpretieren: als Träume oder Wachträume, oder als Seelenreisen. . . . Doch wie lässt sich das für den Zuschauer darstellen?! Zeigt man einen physischen Handlungsstrang auf, oder versucht man zu zeigen, dass sich das Geschehen auf einer anderen Bewusstseins-Ebene abspielt?! Dies wurde in der Theatergeschichte ja übrigens immer wieder versucht; und hierfür gibt es ja auch verschiedene Möglichkeiten. Der Vorteil der Eurythmie ist nun, dass sie ein unnaturalistisches Mittel ist. Wenn Eurythmie eingesetzt wird, tritt nicht etwa eine Figur auf, sondern die Sprache wird sichtbar gemacht. Als Zuschauer sehe ich demnach etwas, was ich sonst nur höre. Ich betrete gewissermassen einen virtuellen Raum.)[39]

Eurythmy was invented by Rudolf Steiner in 1912 with the work *Eurythmie als sichtbare Sprache* (Eurythmy as Visible Speech) and first introduced to Dornach productions of some *Faust* scenes during the First World War. Steiner's wife as of 1914, Marie von Sievers, led eurythmic instruction and the development of eurythmic practice as an art form, assisted by the Russian dancer Tatiana Kisseleff.[40] Anthroposophic teachers and scholars such as Steiner himself, Werner Barfod, Hedwig Greiner-Vogel, Marjorie Raffé (with Cecil Harwood and Marguerite Lundgren), and Magdalene Siegloch, have expounded on the sophisticated connections between eurythmy and the physical and spiritual worlds, poetic language, movement, subconscious association, and astrology. There is no question in my mind that the presence of eurythmy in the Goetheanum's *Faust*, which is not a director's choice but a requirement for any anthroposophical staging of the work, is the most important difference between Stein's production and the Goetheanum's. This is immediately evident to even the most naïve observer, for it is the main reason why the latter ran eighteen hours instead of Stein's thirteen. Although the eurythmic activity sometimes occurred simultaneously with spoken scenes, for the most part it was an extension of them, understandably so in light of the belief that the eurythmic artists are "speaking" on a different level. Christian Peter explained:

In the best case the audience hears the voice of the speaker and simultaneously has language made visible through movement, that is to say, the eurythmists themselves "speak." The sole intention of what they wish to express is incorporated in motion. As an actor, I work differently: I speak, and I communicate part of the meaning or message with my hands. Thereby I divide the message into language gestures or mime.—All of us know what this is: when we try to express something in a language in which we are not so conversant, we "speak" more with our hands.—If a eurythmist were also speaking audibly in conjunction with their movement, their "visible language," then they would in a sense be communicating on a double level.

(Im besten Falle ist es so, dass der Zuschauer die Stimme des Sprechers hört und gleichzeitig den Eindruck hat, der Eurythmist würde selbst sprechen. Eurythmie ist die durch Bewegung sichtbar gemachte Sprache, das heisst, dass der Eurythmist selbst "spricht." Die ganze Intention des Ausdrucks geht in die Bewegung. Als Schauspieler arbeite ich anders: Ich spreche, und einen Teil der Mitteilung oder Botschaft kommuniziere ich mit der Hand. Damit teile ich die Mitteilung in Sprache und Gebärde oder Mimik auf.—Wir kennen das alle:

> Wenn wir in einer Sprache, die uns nicht so geläufig ist, etwas ausdrücken wollen, "sprechen" wir mehr mit den Händen.—Wenn der Eurythmist zu seiner Bewegung, der "sichtbaren Sprache," auch noch hörbar sprechen würde, dann würde er gewissermassen doppelt kommunizieren.)[41]

Steiner's relentless search for "spirituality," the realm of the human soul, the essence of the human spirit, and his central teaching that it is our responsibility to explore and expand its dimensions, rest on the belief that a spiritual dimension does in fact exist beyond the physical (*"sinnliche"*) realm. He further divided this spiritual dimension into two parts, the "super-" and "sub-spiritual" realms (*"übersinnlich"* and *"untersinnlich"*), the former associated with the desired elevation of human experience toward increased awareness of the spiritual and hope, the latter the sinking of human experience into darkness and despair. In the battle of the Lord and Mephistopheles for Faust's soul, Goethe's tragedy depicts a constant vacillation among the three realms. Most scenes and the characters that inhabit them clearly belong to one of the three. For example, the entire Gretchen tragedy of part one and the historical scenes of part two belong generally to the "physical realm," and scenes dominated by Mephistopheles, such as the "Witch's Kitchen" ("Hexenküche") and the two "Walpurgis night" scenes, to the "sub-spiritual realm," while scenes or parts of scenes in which the Lord and his representatives are dominant, such as the "Prologue in Heaven" ("Prolog im Himmel") of part one and the Chorus Mysticus which concludes part two, belong to the "super-spiritual realm." In sections in which the "super-" or "sub-spiritual realms" prevail, eurythmists usually provided a parallel or complementary commentary in gestural and kinetic form, either as individuals, or as small or large choral groups, sometimes as many as two dozen of them at once in lengthy, elaborate balletic scenes accompanied by the orchestra. Hence, they are a constant visual reminder of the text's oscillation between physical and metaphysical realms and a bridge from the physical world to that beyond.

For approximately five hours, then, the Dornach audience witnessed dimensions of *Faust* that according to anthroposophic belief could not be experienced through the spoken language and mimetic acting. They helped the audience to understand the parts of the work in which sub-sensual and supra-sensual worlds are visited and explored. One could conclude that this is an extraordinary enrichment of Goethe's play. It is at the very least an interesting one for audiences and scholars alike. It is also a further comment on Stein's remark about professional actors, for the eurythmists in the *Faust* production, like the actors, were highly trained professionals, some of them among the most experienced and accomplished in their field, and their presence effectively doubled the number of players on stage, making the cast about twice the size of Stein's. Added to these were the forty musicians of the orchestra, located in the balcony at the rear of the hall, whence they performed an accompanying musical score of sixty-two pieces which had been composed by Jan Stuten (1890–1948), the complete Dornach *Faust*'s first director, in consultation with Rudolf Steiner between 1915 and 1926, and traditionally used in all Goetheanum productions. By contrast, Stein's interest in music lay not so much in music per se but rather in what it represents. He emphasized not music but musicality, the structural elements of which music consists, measures, tones, and modulations, and hence his explanation: "The music orients itself exactly to what is in the text, it is, one could say, a translation of the spoken language into music."[42] This is an extension of his high regard for the language and rhetoric of the play, whose basic structure is a network of meters and rhymes. One of our abiding fascinations for Goethe's *Faust* rests on its dazzling variety of verse forms and the way in which these become identified with characters and scenes, such as the madrigal verse with Faust and Mephistopheles, or the rhymeless classical hexameters that first characterize Helena and lay the foundation for her poetic union with Faust in the interlocking rhymed pentameters thereafter (*F*, 8488–515, 9365–84).[43] This is the type of musicality for which Stein wished his actors to strive, a foundation that he admired and saw as one of the indicators of the excellence of the work. In similar terms, as the writings of Barfod, Greiner-Vogel, Siegloch, and other anthroposophic scholars demonstrate, the same metrical elements comprise the sub-structure of eurythmic art. Eurythmists' movements follow patterns conforming to metrical feet, some quite exotic, such as the amphibrach, strings of which are linked to provide templates for larger movements—meters in poetic terms—all of which parallel the metrics of the spoken text they enhance. Eurythmy, then, is not just the language, but the music of poetry, in visual form.[44]

I confess to having been skeptical at first that eurythmists can indeed communicate through gestures and movement the intricacies of Goethe's text, and particularly that an audience can understand what they are doing. I had felt the same during a visit to Southern India to investigate a production of *Faust* in the Kathakali dance form. In Kathakali, dancers in extraordinarily elaborate costumes and makeup can communicate a text word- for-word through intricate gestures and movements with the hands, fingers, eyes, and body. I tested the ability of experienced Kathakali audience members to "read" these signals, and became convinced of their ability to do just that.[45] I did the same in Dornach and became similarly convinced. Part of being an anthroposophist is to learn about and, to a degree, even to perform eurythmy, much to the chagrin of many Waldorf school pupils.

LIGHTING AND COLOR

Goethe is still recognized as one of the important figures in the history of color theory, credited by many as delivering the most significant advancement of that theory since Newton's *Opticks* of 1674. His extensive scientific experiments and empirical observations on the creation and effects of color stretched over two decades and are documented in two of the six volumes of his works on the subject of color in general, good summaries of which have been written by Rudolf Magnus and Bernd Witte.[46] The essential features that distinguished Goethe's color theory from Newton's were that Goethe's was physiologically founded, Newton's mathematically, and that Newton based his findings on the analysis of light, while Goethe's theory began with the dichotomy of light, which he considered an "elemental phenomenon" ("*Urphänomen*"), and darkness, which, in combination with light produced colors and shades. The entire tragedy of *Faust* revolves around the poles of darkness and light, Mephistopheles versus the Lord, negation versus hope, cynicism versus human dignity, ignorance versus enlightenment, desperation versus salvation. The symbolic meaning of various colors was also part of Goethe's theory, as described in the section of his works on color entitled "Sinnlich-sittliche Wirkung der Farbe" (Sensual and social effect of color).[47] Stein knew this, and in his direction of *Faust* used light, darkness, and color carefully to enhance the meaning and impact of many scenes. As a partner volume to Schieb's *Programmbuch*, the official photographer of Stein's production, Ruth Walz, published a spectacular collection of photographs illustrating the range of costumes and lighting the production contained.[48] Stein deliberately contrasted Mephistopheles and Faust in many scenes by the use of a dark red or black costume for Mephistopheles and a striking white one for Faust, each of which is enhanced by the presence or absence of light. There are also many instances of his effective use of other colors, brought about by combinations of costuming and lighting, for example his blending of green and gold, suggesting the juxtaposition of nourishing and destructive nature in "Night" ("Nacht") when the "Earth Spirit" ("Geist") appears; the gold of the setting sun at the conclusion of the Easter Sunday walk in "Before the City Gate," bringing a richness and warmth to the end of a day of rebirth, which changes in seconds to dark shadows and black as the spirit of Mephistopheles appears in poodle's form; the fecundity of nature's green in the "Forest and Cavern" ("Wald und Höhle") monologue; and most important, the climactic opening of part two, as the sun rises in the heavens, exposing the elemental phenomenon of light. Its intensity forces Faust to turn away and, with his back to its rays, experience instead light's refraction, its rainbow, its full range of colors, and thereby learn the most important lesson of the play: "Through colored refraction is life to us revealed" ("Am farbigen Abglanz haben wir das Leben") (*F*, 4727).[49]

Steiner's scholarly involvement in the Weimar Edition of Goethe's works, particularly because his association focused on the natural science section, brought him an understanding of Goethe's color theory, and at an early stage in his own studies he also became intrigued with the phenomena of light and color. At the same time he was influenced by Fichte's metaphysics, which he studied intensively in Vienna (1879–1890), and the two influences contributed to his concept of eurythmy.[50] Steiner's serious followers are also no strangers to Goethe's color theory, and in the Goetheanum production its principles were strongly in evidence through the lighting, sets, and costumes. Yet here the use of colors went much further that it did in Stein's production. Colors on the Goetheanum stage gained a powerful additional dimension through the costumes of the eurythmic artists. For the most part these consist of flowing gowns, representing the content and mood of the spoken word and situation, as well as the nature and feelings of characters. Their colors are linked to the spectrum of human moods illustrated by a zodiacal color wheel fundamental to the anthroposophical theory and understanding of color symbolism.[51] The eurythmists' movements engage the entire range of the spectrum and explore its endless variants, like a rainbow in motion, and in doing so expand their vocabulary from two dimensions, individual gestural and kinetic movement, and choral movement in conjunction with other eurythmists, to three, for color itself functions as a third language. In its physical essence, this display of color is a constantly changing representation of the phenomenon of light in its refracted form, which, with its counterpoint in darkness, forms the essential symbolic polarity of the tragedy. The central notion of life as a "colored refraction" is hence present in the Dornach production not only at the beginning of part two, but also throughout the work. Unfortunately, since the anthroposophists resist the duplication of eurythmic performance on film, one can normally only experience it firsthand, but there were some striking static examples of eurythmic scenes in the photo gallery of the 2004 *Faust* on the Goetheanum website.[52]

CONCLUSION

The Stein and Dornach *Fausts* share much, not least of which is the fact that together they hold the distinction of being the only productions in history to have performed Goethe's complete tragedy as a unified whole. Both were massive, independent commercial endeavors which set a standard for modern stagings of classical works and cooperation among the arts, business, and public sectors. The keys to their success were the passion and conviction of their producers, directors, actors, sponsors, and audiences about the intrinsic importance of their undertaking. The performance spaces in which the two productions occurred can be compared to shrines, constructed as places of gathering for believers, and comparisons can be struck between the nature of the qualifications of their casts and their devotion to the project. That said, in the end the Dornach *Faust* differed from Stein's in four important respects. First, the 2004 production was just the latest in a continuum which began almost seventy years earlier, and has been repeated regularly since, a remarkable record of longevity. These productions were always an exploration and expression of the anthroposophic worldview, a connection that many actors, directors, and audiences not sympathetic to that movement might find unacceptable. Second, because of its anthroposophic centering, the Goetheanum *Faust* offers more in terms of theatricality and the possibility of challenging contemporary interpretation than most productions. Unlike many innovative modern *Fausts* which emasculate Goethe's text by slashing it to a scrap of its original and emphasizing a narrow range of its thematics, the Goetheanum *Faust* honors the entire original and explores it again and again anew. Third, the eurythmic enhancement of Goethe's text allows Goetheanum productions to expand the text's metrical foundation into visual representation; and fourth, at the same time it absorbs the science and symbolism of Goethe's color theory and therewith highlights *Faust*'s central message that the meaning of life is communicated through a kaleidoscope of experience symbolized by refracted light. Eurythmy adds texture to the dichotomy between physical and metaphysical worlds, which is at the play's heart. Indeed, it is possible to appreciate and profit from this approach without accepting the anthroposophists' comprehensive philosophy.

NOTES

1. Peter Stein, "Zur Entstehungsgeschichte unserer Faust-Aufführung," in Roswitha Schieb, *Peter Stein inszeniert Faust von Johann Wolfgang Goethe*, ed. Roswitha Schieb with Anna Haas (Cologne: Dumont, 2000), 9. Translation from the German, as all others in this chapter, by the author, unless otherwise noted. Stein's statement also became part of a public interview with Pia Kleber and Hans Schulte which took place at an international conference on *Faust* at the University of Toronto, September 17–22, 2004.

2. Goetheanum Dornach, http://www.faust-goetheanum.ch/ then select Goetheanum/Goetheanum-Bühne/Faust. http://www.goetheanum.org/Goetheanum/Anthroposophische Gesellschaft/Geschichte (accessed October 18, 2009).

3. "Faust am Goetheanum 2004: Schlussbericht," Dornach, October 18, 2004, http://www.faust-goetheanum.ch/fileadmin/faust/download/Schlussbericht.pdf (accessed January 11, 2006). Goetheanum Dornach, http://www.faust-goetheanum.ch/ Goetheanum/Goetheanum-Bühne/Faust (accessed January 11, 2006). The information no longer appears on this site.

4. David G. John, "Co-operation and Partnership: Peter Stein's *Faust* 2000," in *Cultural Link: Kanada-Deutschland. Festschrift zum dreißgjährigen Bestehen eines akademischen Austauschs*, ed. Beate Henn-Memmesheimer and David G. John (St. Ingbert: Röhrig Universitätsverlag, 2003), 307–21.

5. Peter Stein, "'Das wird eine ganz fürchterlich strenge Übung . . .' Gespräch mit Peter Stein über sein 'Faust I & II'-Projekt," *Theater heute* 4 (1998): 1–2.

6. Stein, "Faust-Aufführung," 8–9.
7. John, "Co-operation and Partnership," 308–9.
8. Schieb, *Peter Stein*, 25–27.
9. John, "Co-operation and Partnership," 309.
10. Christoph Lindenberg, *Rudolf Steiner mit Selbstzeugnissen und Bilddokumenten*, 9th ed. (Reinbek bei Hamburg: Rowohlt Taschenbuch Verlag, 2004), 99. Hagen Biesantz and Arne Klingborg, Åke Fant, Hans Hermann, Rex Raab, and Nikolaus Ruff, *Das Goetheanum. Der Bau-Impuls Rudolf Steiners* (Dornach: Philosophisch-Anthroposophischer Verlag, 1978).
11. Rudolf Steiner, *Rudolf Steiner Gesamtausgabe*, ed. Hella Wiesberger, 436 vols. (Dornach: Rudolf Steiner-Nachlaßverwaltung, 1956ff.), 260a: 397 [hereafter *RSG*].
12. Lindenberg, *Rudolf Steiner*, 27–28, 119–23.
13. John, "Co-operation and Partnership," 310–11.
14. John, "Co-operation and Partnership," 308; Stein, "Faust-Aufführung," 8–9.
15. Johann Wolfgang von Goethe, *Werke*, "Weimarer or Sophienausgabe," 4 pts., 143 vols. (Weimar: Böhlau, 1887–1919), II, 6–12 [hereafter *WA*]. References to *Faust* are abbreviated as *F*.
16. *RSG* and Rudolf Steiner, *Katalog des Gesamtwerks* (Dornach: Rudolf Steiner Verlag, 2005).
17. Rudolf Steiner, *Wo und wie findet man den Geist?* 2nd ed. (Dornach: Rudolf Steiner Verlag, 1984); *RSG*, 57.
18. Rudolf Steiner, *Geisteswissenschaftliche Erläuterungen zu Goethes Faust*, ed. Hans Erhard Lauer and Edwin Froböse, vol. 1. *Faust, der strebende Mensch* (Dornach: Rudolf Steiner Verlag, 1955), vol. 2. *Das Faust-Problem. Die romantische und die klassische Walpurgisnacht* [1931], 4th ed. (Dornach: Rudolf Steiner Verlag, 1981); *RSG*, 272, 273.
19. Heinrich O. Proskauer, ed., *Goethes Faust*, 2 vols. (Basel: Zbinden, 1982), 1:11–14, repeated in 2:6–9.
20. Rudolf Steiner, "Goethes geheime Offenbarung - exoterisch," in *Wo und wie findet man den Geist? RSG*, 57:23–50.
21. Goethe, *Unterhaltungen deutscher Ausgewanderten*, *WA*, I, 18:225–73.
22. Rudolf Steiner, *Goethes Geistesart in ihrer Offenbarung durch seinen Faust und durch das Märchen "Von der Schlange und der Lilie"* (Dornach: Verlag der Rudolf Steiner-Nachlaßverwaltung, 1956), 65–84; *RSG*, 22.
23. Goethe, *Unterhaltungen deutscher Ausgewanderten*, *WA*, I, 42, pt. 2:444–46.
24. Steiner, *Gesammelte Aufsätze*, *RSG*, 30:94.
25. Lindenberg, *Rudolf Steiner*, 65.
26. Steiner, "Goethes geheime Offenbarung - esoterisch," *RSG*, 57:51–84.
27. Steiner, "Die Rätsel in Goethes 'Faust,'" *RSG*, 57:290–357.
28. Wilhelm Dilthey (1833–1911), Rudolf Unger (1876–1942), Hermann August Korff (1882–1963), Fritz Strich (1882–1963), and Paul Kluckhohn (1886–1957). Their thinking and writings represented an antipode to the nineteenth- and early-twentieth-century positivists who founded their work on the principles and methods of natural science.
29. Steiner, *Faust, der strebende Mensch*, *RSG*, 272:82–83.
30. Steiner, *Das Faust-Problem*, *RSG*, 273:269–76.
31. Lindenberg, *Rudolf Steiner*, 27.

32. Steiner, *Briefe Band I: 1881–1890*, *RSG*, 38, pt.1 [1985]:15.

33. Lindenberg, *Rudolf Steiner*, 22–27.

34. Steiner, *Faust, der strebende Mensch*, *RSG*, 272:84. A brief comment on the physical presentation of this volume and the next (v. 273, *Das Faust-Problem*) underscores my criticism. Officially part of the edition of Steiner's complete works, and thus carrying the sanction of the international Anthroposophical Society, the books have visually striking covers, with the titles presented diagonally in stunning gold script. The various academics to whom I have shown these books find that the covers connote a sense of "something romantic, in the sense of Romanticism as intellectual movement," and "a theater play for theater in the woods," "nothing scholarly," and "perhaps ghost- or horror stories." To modern readers, such covers seem to undermine any serious scholarly intentions their author and publishers may have had.

35. John, "Co-operation and Partnership," 311–16.

36. Schieb, *Peter Stein*, 99, 103, 153.

37. Schieb, *Peter Stein*, 103, 130.

38. John, "Co-operation and Partnership," 316–17.

39. Christian Peter, "Spielen – und Sprechen," Goetheanum Dornach, http://www.goetheanum.org. Unfortunately, at the time of writing (October 18, 2009), I can no longer find Peter's interview on the Goetheanum website. I read it in German on the site in 2006. Similar comments were conveyed to me by Mr. Peter during our interview in Dornach in 2004.

40. Lindenberg, *Rudolf Steiner*, 103.

41. Peter, "Spielen – und Sprechen."

42. Schieb, *Peter Stein*, 130.

43. Jochen Schmidt provides a good overview of such associations in *Goethes Faust Erster und Zweiter Teil. Grundlagen–Werk–Wirkung* (Munich: Beck, 1999), 334–37.

44. Hedwig Greiner-Vogel, *Die Widergeburt der Poetik aus dem Geiste der Eurythmie. Grundlinien einer goetheanistischen Poetik und Metrik* (Dornach: Verlag am Goetheanum, 1983), 90–95, 121.

45. David G. John, "Goethe's *Faust* in India: The Kathakali Adaptation," in *International Faust Studies: Adaptation, Reception, Translation*, ed. Lorna Fitzsimmons (London and New York: Continuum, 2008), 161–76.

46. Goethe, *Zur Farbenlehre*, *WA*, II, 1–5, pt. 1; Rudolf Magnus, trans. *Goethe as a Scientist* (New York: Schuman, 1949), 126–66; Bernd Witte, Theo Buck, Hans-Dietrich Dahnke, Regine Otto, and Peter Schmidt, *Goethe-Handbuch*, 4 vols. in 6 (Stuttgart, Weimar: Metzler, 1996–1999), 3:719–43.

47. Goethe, "Sinnlich-sittliche Wirkung der Farbe," *WA*, II, 1:310–31.

48. Ruth Walz, *Goethes Faust. Peter Steins Inszenierung in Bildern. Photographien von Ruth Walz* (Cologne: Dumont, 2001).

49. Goethe, *Zur Farbenlehre*, *WA*, II, 5, pt. 1:443–46.

50. Lindenberg, *Rudolf Steiner*, 19, 34.

51. Werner Barfod, *Tierkreisgesten und Menschenwesen. Ein Weg zu den Quellen der Eurythmie* (Dornach: Verlag am Goetheanum, 1998), 19–34.

52. Goetheanum Dornach, http://www.faust-goetheanum.ch/ then select Goetheanum/Bühne/Faust/Galerie (accessed January 11, 2006).

BIBLIOGRAPHY

Barfod, Werner. *Tierkreisgesten und Menschenwesen. Ein Weg zu den Quellen der Eurythmie*. Dornach: Verlag am Goetheanum, 1998.

Biesantz, Hagen, Arne Klingborg, Åke Fant, Hans Hermann, Rex Raab, and Nikolaus Ruff. *Das Goetheanum. Der Bau-Impuls Rudolf Steiners*. Dornach: Philosophisch-Anthroposophischer Verlag, 1978.

Carlson, Marvin. *Places of Performance. The Semiotics of Theatre Architecture*. Ithaca: Cornell University Press, 1993.

Goetheanum Dornach. "Faust am Goetheanum 2004: Schlussbericht." Dornach, October 18, 2004. http://www.faust-goetheanum.ch/fileadmin/faust/download/Schlussbericht.pdf (accessed January 11, 2006).

——. http://www.faust-goetheanum.ch/Goetheanum/Goetheanum-Bühne/Faust (accessed January 11, 2006).

——. http://www.goetheanum.org/Goetheanum/Anthroposophische Gesellschaft/Geschichte (accessed October 18, 2009).

Goethe, Johann Wolfgang von. *Werke*. Herausgegeben im Auftrage der Großherzogin Sophie von Sachsen. "Weimarer or Sophienausgabe." 4 pts., 143 vols. Weimar: Böhlau, 1887–1919.

Greiner-Vogel, Hedwig. *Die Widergeburt der Poetik aus dem Geiste der Eurythmie. Grundlinien einer goetheanistischen Poetik und Metrik*. Dornach: Verlag am Goetheanum, 1983.

John, David G. "Co-operation and Partnership: Peter Stein's *Faust* 2000." In *Cultural Link: Kanada-Deutschland. Festschrift zum dreißgjährigen Bestehen eines akademischen Austauschs*, edited by Beate Henn-Memmesheimer and David G. John, 307–21. St. Ingbert: Röhrig Universitätsverlag, 2003.

——. "Goethe's *Faust* in India: The Kathakali Adaptation." In *International Faust Studies: Adaptation, Reception, Translation*, edited by Lorna Fitzsimmons, 161–76. London and New York: Continuum, 2008.

Lindenberg, Christoph. *Rudolf Steiner mit Selbstzeugnissen und Bilddokumenten*. 9th ed. Reinbek bei Hamburg: Rowohlt Taschenbuch Verlag, 2004.

Magnus, Rudolf, trans. *Goethe as a Scientist*. New York: Schuman, 1949. Originally published as *Goethe als Naturforscher* (Leipzig: Johann Ambrosius Barth, 1906).

Peter, Christian."Spielen – und Sprechen." Goetheanum Dornach. http://www.goetheanum.org (accessed October 18, 2009).

Proskauer, Heinrich O., ed. *Goethes Faust*, 2 vols. Basel: Zbinden, 1982.

Raffé, Marjorie, Cecil Harwood, and Marguerite Lundgren. *Eurythmy and the Impulse of Dance*. [Dornach]: Rudolf Steiner Press, 1974.

Schechner, Richard. *Performance Theory*. Rev. ed. New York: Routledge, 1988.

Schieb, Roswitha, ed., with Anna Haas. *Peter Stein inszeniert Faust von Johann Wolfgang Goethe. Das Programmbuch Faust I und II*. Cologne: Dumont, 2000.

Schmidt, Jochen. *Goethes Faust Erster und Zweiter Teil. Grundlagen–Werk–Wirkung*. Munich: Beck, 1999.

Siegloch, Magdalene. *Eurythmie. Eine Einführung*. 1990. Stuttgart: Verlag Freies Geistesleben, 1997.

Stein, Peter."'Das wird eine ganz fürchterlich strenge Übung . . .' Gespräch mit Peter Stein über sein 'Faust I & II'-Projekt." *Theater heute* 4 (1998): 1–2.

———. "Zur Entstehungsgeschichte unserer Faust-Aufführung." In Schieb, *Peter Stein inszeniert Faust von Johann Wolfgang Goethe*, 8–9.

Steiner, Rudolf. *Eurythmie als sichtbare Sprache*. 1924. 5th ed. Dornach: Rudolf Steiner Verlag, 1990.

———. *Geisteswissenschaftliche Erläuterungen zu Goethes Faust*. Edited by Hans Erhard Lauer and Edwin Froböse. Vol. 1, *Faust, der strebende Mensch*. 1931. Dornach: Rudolf Steiner Verlag, 1955. Vol. 2, *Das Faust-Problem. Die romantische und die klassische Walpurgisnacht*. 1931. Dornach: Rudolf Steiner Verlag, 1981.

———. *Goethes Geistesart in ihrer Offenbarung durch seinen Faust und durch das Märchen "Von der Schlange und der Lilie."* Dornach: Verlag der Rudolf Steiner-Nachlaßverwaltung, 1956.

———. *An Introduction to Eurythmy*. Spring Valley, NY: Anthroposophic Press, 1984.

———. *Katalog des Gesamtwerks*. Dornach: Rudolf Steiner Verlag, 2005.

———. *Rudolf Steiner Gesamtausgabe*. Edited by Hella Wiesberger. Pt. A, vol. 1–45, Gesammelte Aufsätze, Veröffentlichungen aus dem Nachlaß. Pt. B, vol. 46–354, Vorträge. Pt. C, 82 vols. with irregular volume designation, Das künstlerische Werk. Reproduktionen und Veröffentichungen aus dem künstlerischen Nachlaß. Dornach: Rudolf Steiner-Nachlaßverwaltung, 1956–2005.

———. *Wo und wie findet man den Geist?* 2nd ed. Dornach: Rudolf Steiner Verlag, 1984.

Walz, Ruth. *Goethes Faust. Peter Steins Inszenierung in Bildern. Photographien von Ruth Walz*. Cologne: Dumont, 2001.

Witte, Bernd, Theo Buck, Hans-Dietrich Dahnke, Regine Otto, and Peter Schmidt, eds. *Goethe-Handbuch*. 4 vols. in 6. Stuttgart, Weimar: Metzler, 1996–1999.

7

Faustian Tesserae in the Cultural Mosaic

Contemporary Canadian Interplay with Goethe's *Faust*

Jörg Esleben

In the National Library of Canada in Ottawa, there is a glass panel created by John Dutton in 1967, depicting Johann Wolfgang von Goethe with diminutive figures of Faust and Mephistopheles at his side. In a library of national and international importance, this is a fitting commemoration of an author who contributed to shaping the idea of world literature as a global body of literary works with universal appeal beyond their own cultures of origin, and to his two-part drama *Faust* as probably the most globally recognized German contribution to world literature. Since Goethe's first readings from his drafts in the 1770s, the publication of a fragment of Part I in 1790, of the completed Part I in 1808, and finally of Part II shortly after his death in 1832, the drama has accumulated immense cultural "weight"—it has been the basis for a vast number of interpretations and appropriations, both in German-speaking cultures and around the world, including in Canada. As this chapter will show, collective memory of this reception history of the text and of the mythic stature of its author are an essential ingredient in contemporary Canadian responses to *Faust*. Canadian culture has engaged with the Faustian theme in a multitude of ways and media, and the two parts of Goethe's drama have played a prominent role in this. Canadian artists have responded to the themes and concerns of Goethe's text and to its reception history in works ranging from theatrical productions and other types of performances to fiction, visual art, and music. This Canadian interplay with Goethe's *Faust* has received very little scholarly attention.[1] The present chapter will begin to address this gap with a consideration of significant instances of contemporary Canadian artistic engagement with Goethe's *Faust*. The study is limited to the direct Canadian reception of Goethe's drama in artistic works and events as well as reviews of these. While other aspects such as the Canadian academic reception of *Faust* (e.g., in scholarly studies or university courses), and indirect influence through sources such as Charles Gounod's opera *Faust,* could yield valuable insights as well, they have been excluded here in the interest of maintaining a certain economy of material and a sharper focus in pursuing the questions guiding the inquiry: What does Goethe's *Faust* mean (what is it made to mean) in Canadian artistic responses? What functions and roles are given to the drama in such responses and the critical reactions to them? How are these functions and roles influenced by the origin and accumulated significance of Goethe's drama in a German cultural context, its universal qualities as world literature, and the specific Canadian historical and cultural context in which each instance of engagement was produced? What intercultural dimensions do these Canadian encounters with *Faust* have? The evidence presented by recent Canadian interplay with Goethe's text in narrative fiction, visual art and music, and drama and theatrical performance suggests that the success of this cross-cultural mediation, in terms of critical and audience response, depends on a judicious blending of the universal elements contained in the text, the specifically German mythic resonances of both Goethe and his *Faust* (what might be termed the foreign currency of author and text), and contemporary Canadian aesthetic and societal preoccupations. The chapter begins with a discussion of three instances of *Faust* reception that illustrate paradigmatically the challenges involved in achieving this blend, and then examines how a wide range of Canadian *Faust* events respond to these challenges.

FAUST AT THE CULTURAL CROSSROADS

The temporal starting point of the study is 1970, since this became a landmark year in Canadian *Faust* reception when University of Toronto professor Barker Fairley published his groundbreaking prose translation of both parts of the drama and had an adaptation of the translation produced at the newly established St. Lawrence Centre in Toronto in the same year. The critical and public reception of the St. Lawrence Centre production connected it to contemporary North American preoccupations (e.g., by reliance on the recent moon landing for comparisons and metaphors) and was marked by controversy over whether the production was successful in bridging the cross-cultural gap: on one end of the spectrum of opinion was the absolute position that Goethe's text is bound to German culture and essentially untranslatable, which was answered from the other end with a defense of Canadian *Faust* reception rooted in a pragmatic willingness to accept transformations in transposing a text from one cultural tradition to another.[2] Fairley himself acknowledged but refused to give in to the intercultural difficulties posed by the text in a 1969 essay about translating the drama: "*Faust* itself, the philosophical poem, the world-poem, still remains to the English mind a closed or half-closed book—a magnitude, no doubt, but also a mystery. Must it remain so? I don't believe it. And so we go on trying."[3] The case of Fairley's translation and its theatrical production, then, show that in *Faust* reception, the specifically German and the universal aspects of the text interact in not always predictable ways with the historical and cultural context in which reception takes place. Canadian artists and intellectuals have indeed heeded Fairley's call and gone on trying to bring Goethe's *Faust* closer to the Canadian public, in modes ranging from explicit didacticism to abstract citation, but conversely they have also brought aspects and questions of Canadian culture and identity to bear on the drama.

A brief discussion of two theatrical productions from the 1990s will illustrate the challenges and chances for success of this dual endeavor. The first of these was a professional production of *Faust I* in English under the direction of Hans Engel by Equity Showcase Theatre at Toronto's Harbourfront Centre in 1995. The reviewers for both the *Globe and Mail* and the *Toronto Star* found the production staid and boring,[4] with the latter arguing that "maybe it's that German Romanticism just doesn't play as well as it did in the early nineteenth century. In the end, Engel's artful interpretation of *Faust* does everything except the thing it needs to do most: make a case for the continuing relevance of Goethe's play."[5]

The same reviewer had a diametrically opposed reaction to another Toronto production of *Faust I* in 1999. Wagner found the production at the Tarragon Theatre, directed by Daniel Brooks with a cast of only five actors, "accessibly contemporary, without sacrificing thematic and dramatic scope" and "a deeply rewarding and exciting, if undeniably demanding, experience."[6] The review in the *National Post* was equally positive, with undertones of wonder that *Faust* can be staged so effectively.[7] In a *National Post* preview of the production, the director Daniel Brooks, who went on to become the first recipient of the Elinore and Lou Siminovitch Prize in Theatre for directing, was quoted as saying that "North American culture . . . is very influenced by German thought. *Faust* is about conflict, and the first part turns into a tragedy, which is quite accessible to audiences."[8]

As the critical reaction to these two productions show, success for the artists engaged in the cross-cultural mediation between *Faust* and Canadians depends on finding a well-balanced blend of the text's cultural origins, its universal mythic and philosophical qualities, and the concerns and horizons of the target culture. The remainder of the chapter is dedicated to examining how contemporary Canadian artists from various fields have attempted to achieve this blend.

NARRATIVE FICTION

Among works of fiction dedicated to the attempt, Eric Koch's *Icon in Love: A Novel about Goethe*, published in 1998, leans decidedly toward the didactic side.[9] The novel transposes Goethe into the twentieth century as the winner of the 1992 Nobel Prize for Literature. The plot of what Koch refers to as his "serious jest,"[10] thus echoing Goethe's characterization of *Faust II* in those same words, revolves around two focal points: Goethe's love for the also resuscitated Ulrike von Levetzow (the seventeen-year-old who was the last passionate love interest in the real Goethe's life) and a murder mystery among the laureates at the Nobel award ceremony. Among the myriad intertextual and historical references in Koch's erudite novel, the references to *Faust* are of central importance. They can be found on all diegetic levels. In an introductory biographical note on the real Goethe, Koch mentions the difficulty of staging and translating the drama. Quotations taken from Fairley's translation serve as mottos for chapters. Finishing Part II of the drama is constantly on the fictional Goethe's mind, and Koch represents his passion for Ulrike as the needed spur to do so. Goethe's Nobel address is entitled "The Perfect Moment"[11] in reference to the condition imposed by Faust on the agreement with Mephistopheles: that Mephistopheles must provide a moment that Faust would wish to last forever in order for Mephistopheles to win Faust's servitude in the afterlife (*F*, 1699–1711).[12] This condition is one of Goethe's important additions to the Faust tradition and a crucial element in the plot and the climactic conclusion of the drama. Koch thus astutely incorporates a highly significant and distinguishing feature of Goethe's *Faust* in his fictional primer on Goethe.

The most substantive references to *Faust* in the novel are an exposition of the fictional version of *Faust I* by the extradiegetic narrator, discussions of the meaning of the drama by Goethe and other characters, and a concluding fictional feuilleton essay on *Faust II* upon its publication after Goethe's death in 2002. By these means, Koch blends the exposition of the basic plot of both parts with modernizations such as having Faust discover DNA before Watson and Crick (but not publishing the result due in part to Mephistopheles' persuasion). In this way, all narrative levels seem designed to familiarize the North American readers of the novel with Goethe and *Faust* and to suggest their contemporary relevance. Koch even fantasizes about Goethe's popularity in Canada. A fellow Nobel laureate who is a Canadian invites Goethe to visit there: "It will be a major event, from coast to coast. I can see the headlines—'Goethe in Canada.' The schools will be closed. Kids will line the streets while you wave to them from behind a glass cage in the open stretch-limousine."[13] Once again, the didactic aspect of Koch's engagement with Goethe and *Faust* is foregrounded.

A very different form of interplay with the drama, in which didacticism is put in the service of and is subordinate to the search for individual and cultural identity, can be found in Robertson Davies' works. Davies held Goethe in great esteem. In 1970, the production of his Casanova play *General Confession* at the St. Lawrence Centre was postponed by director Leon Major in favor of the production of Fairley's *Faust* translation, upon which Davies commented: "If one has to be put to one side it is nice to have it done by Goethe, whom I worship."[14] Davies had a longstanding relationship to *Faust*: he read *Faust I* as a boy,[15] saw it performed in Edinburgh in 1949,[16] then both parts in Salzburg in 1965.[17] Somewhat surprisingly, however, the influence of Goethe's drama makes itself felt much more in Davies' narrative works rather than his plays.

Many important intertextual references to *Faust* can be found in Davies' novels. In a recent study, Richard Ilgner has explored the shared concerns with shamanism and the magus tradition in Goethe's drama and *The Rebel Angels* (1981), the first novel in Davies' Cornish Trilogy, which further includes *What's Bred in the Bone* (1985) and *The Lyre of Orpheus* (1988). Ilgner concludes that Davies "in his Faust novel *The Rebel Angels*, just like Goethe before him and the original shaman's story, is concerned with the recovery of the holistic, which entails first and foremost a recovery of nature and the feminine from their devalued status in patriarchal cultures."[18] In conjunction with this search for wholeness, a strong association between Goethe's drama, alchemy, and Jungian ideas pervades Davies' writings. He commented that seeing the Salzburg production put him "in the mood for some Jungian speculation" about the contribution that the artistic self's idiosyncratic search for its own path makes to humanity.[19] And thirty years later, in a 1994 letter written after having been shown alchemical manuscripts in the British Museum, Davies cites Jung's discussion of *Faust*:

> Goethe is really describing the experience of the alchemist who discovers that what he has projected into the retort is his own darkness, his unredeemed state, his passion, his struggles to reach the goal, i.e. to become what he really is, to fulfill the purpose for which his mother bore him and, after the peregrinations of a long life full of confusion and error, to become the *filius regius*, son of the supreme mother.[20]

Such associations between *Faust*, Jung, alchemy, and mother figures play an important role in *What's Bred in the Bone*. It has been argued that the three novels of the Cornish Trilogy "celebrated Canada's coming of age with stories that present Canadians as full participants in Western civilization."[21] One of these Canadians is Francis Cornish, whose quest for artistic inspiration and identity is at the heart of *What's Bred in the Bone*. His master and guide in this quest is the enigmatic expert restorer and forger of paintings

Tancred Saraceni. With regard to the art forgery scheme he and Saraceni are involved in at a castle in Nazi Germany, Francis has the following exchange with his lover Ruth Nibsmith about himself and Saraceni: "'I feel like Faust listening to Mephistopheles.' 'Lucky you. Would anybody ever have heard of Faust if it hadn't been for Mephistopheles?' 'All right. But he has in a high degree the trick of making the worse seem the better cause.'"[22] The setting of this scene might be intended as a reminder of the Nazi ideological appropriation of Goethe's *Faust* and the subsequent negative associations that were attached to the drama and the adjective "Faustian" ("*faustisch*"), particularly in immediate postwar Germany, a fact that Barker Fairley comments on in the introduction to his 1953 anthology of essays on the drama.[23] The exchange between Francis and Ruth, too, can be read as making reference to the Germans under Nazism listening to a Mephistophelean leader who could make the worse seem the better cause. The Faust reference here thus serves to explore ambivalences between fame ("Would anybody ever have heard of Faust . . . ?") and integrity and between good and evil.

Francis' explicit characterization of his relationship with Saraceni, however, is not the most significant reference to *Faust* in *What's Bred in the Bone*. The timeless Realm of the Mothers from *Faust II*, which Faust has to enter in order to bring back Helen of Troy as the quintessential image of human beauty, becomes one of the central metaphors in the novel. The Jungian ground for this is prepared in a discussion in which Saraceni proposes to Francis that modern painters cannot rely on mythology and religion anymore to find and express their inner vision: "So—the search for the inner vision must be direct. The artist solicits and implores something from the realm of what the psychoanalysts, who are the great magicians of our day, call the Unconscious, though it is actually the Most Conscious."[24] Having been issued the ultimate challenge by Saraceni to paint an original picture in the technique and spirit of the Old Masters and thus progress from disciple to companion of his mentor, Francis decides to "paint the myth of Francis Cornish. But how? . . . He could not descend, so far as his talent allowed, into the Realm of the Mothers and return with a picture" whose subject would be modern and whose style would be all his own.[25] Nonetheless, Saraceni calls the painting that results "something unquestionably from the Mothers. Reality of artistic creation, in fact. You have found a reality that is not part of the chronological present. Your here and now are not of our time."[26] Many years later, when Saraceni is called upon to explain the picture to a commission of experts, he describes it as an alchemical work and its supposedly anonymous creator as "The Alchemical Master."[27] In confidence he says to Francis, "You may not have a scholar's understanding of alchemy, but plainly you have lived alchemy; transformation of base elements and some sort of union of important elements has worked alchemically in your life."[28] At the close of the novel, in the moment of his death,

Francis slips into a different state of being: "Where was this? Unknown, yet familiar, more the true abode of his spirit than he had ever known before; a place never visited, but from which intimations had come that were the most precious gifts of his life. It must be—it was—the Realm of the Mothers. How lucky he was, at the last, to taste this transporting wine!"[29] In *What's Bred in the Bone,* Davies thus borrows from Goethe's *Faust* for a Jungian exploration of the unconscious elements of the human psyche that go into the alchemical process of forming both a self and a culture. The drama serves Davies as a key repository of cultural memory, unconscious but not forgotten in modernity, an "unknown, yet familiar" intimation of the search for wholeness.

VISUAL ART AND MUSIC

The fields of contemporary Canadian visual art and music have each brought forth at least one significant body of work relating to Goethe's *Faust,* with both oeuvres sharing the characteristic of representing artistic engagement over the course of a number of years. In 1996, Eva Brandl created a Faust installation entitled *La tentation du possible* (The temptation of the possible), first exhibited at the Christiane Chassay gallery, Montreal, where her *Faust, les sortilèges* had been exhibited in 1993. The reviewer for the *Montreal Gazette* wrote:

> Following the theme of Goethe's *Faust,* Eva Brandl's art explores the area between the possible and that which can only be dreamed. . . . The theme of Goethe's 18th-century update on the ancient myth, in which a man sells his soul to the devil, is humanity's struggle to situate itself in a world increasingly governed by physics and biology and seemingly stripped of anything sacred. Now, in our own time, even the certainties of science have begun to ring hollow, with people seeking solace in a myriad of therapies or in the kitsch remnants of religion. In such a perplexing period, Brandl's interest in Goethe's *Faust,* with its fluctuations between high hopes and bottomless despair, seems especially relevant.[30]

Whether or not one endorses the reviewer's characterization of the central theme of Goethe's *Faust,* which is certainly debatable, this passage makes clear that both Brandl's art and the reviewer's interpretation find relevance in the drama for questions and challenges confronting contemporary Western culture. For both, this relevance seems to reside particularly in the philosophical elements and qualities of the text.

In 1998, Brandl had an exhibition entitled *Faust: extraits et autres spéculations* (Faust: extracts and other speculations) at the Centre d'exposition, Saint-Hyacinthe, into which she incorporated elements of the earlier exhibit. Titles of the show's individual installations such as *Le drame du savant* (The drama of the sage), *Interlude d'Hélène* (Helen interlude), and *Blindman's Spell* strongly suggest echoes of *Faust I* and *II*, as do some of their central thematic concerns: the organization and "mutating quality"[31] of the material world, "the object's apparition and dissolution,"[32] the tension between ideals and the material world,[33] the tension between the belief in a purposeful (divine) design of the world and the idea of a creation without "inherent direction or purpose."[34] Eva Brandl's sustained engagement with Goethe's drama thus explores some of the fundamental constellations and philosophical questions of the text through the contemporary medium of installation art.[35] Here, it is precisely the rather distant and veiled memory echoes of Goethe's text that lend themselves to infusing the art with a polyvalent, somewhat mysterious aura.

In the field of Canadian music, the Faustian theme generally has been most prominent in opera. From the nineteenth century to the present, there have been scores of productions in Canada primarily of Charles Gounod's *Faust* (1859), but also of Hector Berlioz' *La damnation de Faust* (1846), and Arrigo Boito's *Mefistofele* (1868), in addition to concerts featuring a number of other operatic, vocal, and instrumental works around the Faust theme. In 1992, *Faust, an Alternative Opera,* composed by Jeff Corness, premiered in a production by Tamahnous Theatre and the Karen Jamieson Dance Company at the Vancouver East Cultural Centre.[36] The relationship of the opera to Goethe's text seems to be limited; in an article on his work, the composer discusses Goethe and Marlowe as precursors in general terms, but asserts that he is unable to identify any one particular influence.[37]

By contrast, the Canadian creators of another work of original music, albeit from a very different genre, make the influence of Goethe's *Faust* central and explicit. In 2003, Gilles Gobeil and René Lussier released their CD of electroacoustic music entitled *Le contrat* (The contract). This was the fruit of a project that the two Quebecois artists had collaborated on since 1996, and whose goal they define in the liner notes thus: "To compose a work inspired by Goethe's *Faust* and to build it according to the very architecture of the poem."[38] Over the course of the collaboration, whose long duration the two composers compare tongue-in-cheek with the "more than 30 years"[39] (*sic*) that it took Goethe to write *Faust,* three unfinished versions of the work-in-progress were presented at concerts in Montreal (1999), Paris (2000), and Victoriaville, Quebec (2000).

The CD contains seventeen tracks, bearing the following titles: 1. "Les remparts [The Ramparts]," 2. "La gageure [The Bet]," 3. "Le chapelet [The Rosary]," 4. "La nuit la plus longue [The Longest Night]," 5. "La forêt [The Forest]," 6. "Le cabinet d'étude [The Study]," 7. "Rats et contrat [Rats and Contract]," 8. "Le premier baiser; L'amour pointe [The First Kiss; Love Arises]," 9. "Le lavoir [The Wash House]," 10. "Le flagorneur"

[The Sycophant]," 11. "La chambre de Marguerite [Marguerite's Room]," 12. "Le duel [The Duel]," 13. "Les bijoux [The Jewels]," 14. "La caverne" [The Cavern]," 15. "Le jardin; Les chevaux noirs; L'entremetteuse [The Garden; The Black Horses; The Go-between]," 16. "La cathédrale [The Cathedral]," 17. "L'écolier [The Schoolboy]." Most of these track titles are evocative of scene titles or other aspects of Goethe's drama, especially once the project's avowed aim is taken into account. They also speak to the absence and changed sequence of scenes from the Goethe text, changes the composers acknowledge along with the influence of other sources.[40] The resulting compositions create soundscapes of various atmospheric valences (from silent, calm, or harmonious to loud, discordant, even aggressive) out of a dense texture of electronic and acoustic music, sound effects, recorded found sounds, spoken word, and intermittent silence. The abstract work does not provide clear narrative guidance, so the listener is dependent on the liner notes commentary and track titles in order to make the connection to Goethe's drama. As in Brandl's art, memory of the text and its connotations is evoked in subtle, abstract, almost dreamlike fashion.

DRAMA AND THEATER IN THE 1980s

The most obvious place to look for Canadian *Faust* reception is of course still the theater. The St. Lawrence Centre show in 1970 was followed by a 1977 production at the Glen Morris Studio, Toronto, directed by Allan F. Park, about which little is known. The next well-documented production of *Faust I* came in 1982, by Toronto's experimental theater Actor's Lab, adapted and directed by Richard Nieoczym. According to one reviewer, the production cast "Faust as a 60s hippie, unable to sustain the myths he believes in when he is confronted with contemporary reality."[41] The reviewer for the *Toronto Star* defined the subject matter of the drama as "alienation from society, the quest for the sublime, a look at life's rotten underbelly" and thought it suitable for the mix of experimental and traditional techniques presented by Actor's Lab.[42] In another review two weeks later, entitled "Freudians, Feminists and Faust," he expanded on the drama's relevance for a contemporary audience:

> There's a little bit of Faust in all of us. Deep down, there's a fearsome but hypnotic voice urging us to sell our souls to the devil—to give up the things we cherish most—for a fleeting chance at money or power or knowledge or some other elusive goal. Canadians have heard that voice. They're the ones who traded away control over their economic and cultural destinies for fatter wallets and fuller bellies, courtesy of the United States. The single trendies have heard that voice. They're the ones who gave up domestic security and lasting

romantic love for uncertain relationships and momentary sexual pleasures. The Fausts are everywhere we look.[43]

The reviewer criticizes "arbitrary changes unconnected with tradition" such as depicting God as a female trinity: "Feminism notwithstanding, the image is confusing and pointless."[44] Thus, the classical German drama provides the foil—both in its production and its reception—for meditations on a wide range of contemporary issues and developments in Canadian, North American, and global culture. These meditations blend what seem to be regarded as universal human traits and specific references to aspects of contemporary society. Of course, Goethe's drama is built from just such a blend (mixing, as it does, myths and archetypes with references to political, social, and artistic developments of the late eighteenth and early nineteenth centuries), making it suitable material for this form of interpretation and appropriation.

The 1980s saw few other notable theatrical *Faust* events. The first English-language production of *Faust I* in Vancouver in 1984 was plagued by technical problems and bad press.[45] In Toronto, Actor's Lab collaborated with Le Contre-Courante in 1988–1989 in a venture entitled *The Faust Quest/La quête de Faust*, produced by Richard Nieoczym. The program notes state that the "theatre experience for the audience and the actor is an immersion into the realm of the mythic," and the only indication in the notes that Goethe's version influenced this production is the fact that it features a character named "Goddess/Gretchen."[46]

DRAMA AND THEATER IN THE 1990s

As the discussion of two productions earlier in the chapter has already suggested, the 1990s turned out to be far more fertile theatrical ground, although some events contained only remote references to Goethe's version. In 1992, Sarah Harper created a carnivalesque street spectacle entitled *Méphistomania*, about which she commented on the occasion of its performance at the 2000 Shawinigan street theater festival: "What we do is more accessible than a *Faust* by Goethe performed in an indoor theatre."[47] Another popular spectacle containing plot elements reminiscent of Goethe's text was the puppet production *Faust: Pantin du diable* (Faust: Puppet of the devil) by the Quebec troupe Pupulus Mordicus, which employed larger-than-life-sized puppets in what a reviewer called "a joyously impertinent version of a secular myth touching on fundamental aspects of our human condition."[48] The show was created in 1995 and performed several times over the next years.

In the same year, the Milkman Theatre Group in Halifax produced *Faust: Philosopher, Demigod/Perpetual Motion Machine*. The group's director David

Kennedy, then a twenty-four-year-old Dalhousie University theatre graduate, saw the Faust myth as relevant to the spiritual crisis and uncertainties about the future he perceived in his generation. The group attempted to underline this relevance with a multimedia production that was placed ambivalently, in terms of the outcome for the protagonist, between the dramatic versions of the Faust myth by Christopher Marlowe and Goethe.[49] This shared influence of the two dramatic versions on the collective memory of the Faust theme is quite characteristic of the Anglophone world.

An original Canadian drama that also draws on Marlowe and Goethe, Andrew Kelm's *Faust* premiered in November 1993, produced by the Kensington Carnival Theatre Company at the Wellington Street Theatre Space under the direction of Ida Carnevali, and was published the same year. On the title page, Kelm calls it a "contemporary retelling of the Faust myth with particular acknowledgments to the work of Thomas [*sic*] Marlowe and Johann Wolfgang von Goethe."[50] The drama adapts elements of both parts of Goethe's drama and of Marlowe's version. It casts Faust as a bookish environmentalist and Mephistopheles as a foreigner and ends with Faust being born from a womb. The setting description of "Scene Two: The Famine," which introduces Mephistopheles, makes reference to events in Germany in the early 1990s:

> Hungry people break through a wall reminiscent of the Berlin Wall. They search for food, they fight. Right wing protectionist factions take on a Neo-Nazi character. A baby is killed. The man who will become MEPHISTOPHELES is beaten up and left lying in the street badly hurt.[51]

On the other hand, Mephistopheles' initial characterization of Faust puts him squarely into a North American context: "I know you. Your type . . . Dogooder, Liberal Christian, Politically correct! Environmentalist!"[52] "Scene Five: Magic," the equivalent of the "Witch's Kitchen" ("Hexenküche") scene in Goethe, is based on Native North American (Hopi) myths and rituals.[53] The drama is thus an eclectic cross-cultural negotiation of the Faust theme's mythical and historically specific interpretations.

A further original play with more far-reaching references to Goethe's *Faust* is Richard J. Léger's *Faust: Chroniques de la démesure* (Faust: Chronicles of immoderation), which premiered in November 1999 at the Ottawa theater La Nouvelle Scène in a production by the Théâtre La Catapulte under the direction of Joël Beddows. The play is based on the premise that a playwright tasked with adapting Goethe's drama for the stage has his wish to be guided by Goethe's (devilish) muse granted in order to achieve an original, modernized version of the Faust myth.[54] As the writing of this version gets under way, the playwright takes on the role of Faust, a brilliant biogeneticist with the ambition to clone human life in a more perfect form, while the muse, named Z, appears in the further Mephistophelean roles of psychiatrist Dr. Fuchsmann and Constance Phorkyadopoulos, chairwoman and president of a private biogenetics enterprise. Further characters include Wagner, professor of theology and chairman of the ethics committee at Faust's University of Toronto; a drug addict named Hélène, whom Faust grooms as surrogate mother for his experiments; and Marguerite Reinfach, an eminent biochemist, with whom Faust collaborates. Faust marries and impregnates Marguerite, but eventually betrays her, due to her refusal to aid him in his cloning plans. The complex plot is further complicated by Léger's textual technique of shifting between and blending the events around Faust with the plot level of the play being created and discussed by the playwright and Z, including exchanges with a lighting technician and two actresses taking on the roles of Hélène and Marguerite.

A multitude of intertextual references establish the relations of Léger's text to Goethe's. Like the source text, Léger's play contains a prologue in the theater, in which the playwright discusses the problems of adapting Goethe's *Faust* with the theater's artistic director and then summons Z by his wish to be inspired by Goethe's muse. A number of plot elements have equivalences in Goethe's text, in conjunction with articulating character names and traits evoking Goethe's Faust, Wagner, Margarete—whose last name Reinfach plays on German terms evoking Gretchen's characteristics of purity ("*rein*") and simplicity ("*einfach*")—Helen of Troy, and Mephistopheles' incarnation as the ugly Phorkyas, while Léger's Fuchsmann, to be played with a German accent, might be meant to evoke Mephistopheles' cunning by the inclusion of the German word for fox.

The structure of Léger's drama cannot be fully comprehended by reference to the play-within-the-play concept, but is rather linked to Goethe's drama through multiple intertextual layers in what David Blonde calls a "mise-en-abyme of the myth."[55] It thus creates a complex reflection on the philosophical and theatrical relevance of the Faustian bargain in contemporary Canada, and, as Blonde argues, for Franco-Ontarian theater and society in particular.[56]

In addition to such intertextual references (and reverences) to Goethe's version, the 1990s also saw a number of significant productions of his drama proper.[57] In February 1994, the German Theatre Group at Queen's University produced the only German-language staging of *Faust I* in Canada that I have been able to trace. Directed by Ruediger Mueller and Steven Kammerer, this production featured dance components (in an "Underworld" setting) and musical accompaniment by the band No Borders.[58]

In addition to Daniel Brooks' direction of *Faust I* discussed earlier in the chapter, the very rich year 1999, the 250th anniversary of Goethe's birth, saw another highly successful Canadian production, resulting in cross-cultural exchange between Canada and Germany. Théâtre UBU's *Urfaust, tragédie subjective* (Urfaust, subjective tragedy), an adaptation of Goethe's

Urfaust and Fernando Pessoa's *Faust* by director Denis Marleau, premièred in April 1999 in Montréal. It was performed by invitation in Weimar during the anniversary celebrations in June 1999 and toured Germany and France in the fall of that year. The production casts Faust as Ludwig Wittgenstein and Mephistopheles as Fernando Pessoa. It plays with doubles and doubling in a way that suggests that it is a *tragédie subjective* both in the sense of a subjective tragedy located in the human psyche and a tragedy of the subject. Many critics stressed the production's play with and reflections about the roles of doubling, mirroring, and illusion in questions of identity. These foci contributed much to the production's quality as a theatrical exploration of intercultural identity construction. Marleau himself is quoted in the newspaper *Tagesspiegel* as saying, "The proximity to the Anglo-Saxon world, the French enclave situation in North America and the phonetic dualism between the two languages, particularly in Montreal, have probably given us a particular affinity to the double, to the riddle of identity."[59] His *Urfaust, tragédie subjective* can thus be seen both as reflecting obliquely on this Canadian intercultural constellation and as opening a dialogue between French-Canadian and German culture. Once again, this adds a didactic dimension to Canadian interplay with *Faust*. The online newspaper of the German embassy in Canada called Théâtre UBU the "great explorer of German texts" and quotes its director of projects Hélène Dumas as saying that the German dramatic repertoire is underrepresented in Québec, and that Marleau wants to help the public discover lesser-known and atypical works.[60] In the Quebecois theater journal *Jeu*, Louise Vigeant writes that since she found Goethe's text difficult and convoluted, having read it in Gérard de Nerval's translation, she was apprehensive about the project, but she found that the dramaturgic work of Marleau and his use of the *Urfaust* have allowed Goethe's discourse to reach her.[61] A German critic wrote about the production: "That which is well-known and has not been questioned for a long time was alienated and became recognizable anew."[62] This enthusiastic reception in Goethe's homeland of the production, which was hailed as the best *Faust* of the season in the Weimar celebrations, attests to the fact that it brought home to the Germans new or forgotten aspects of *Faust*.

DRAMA AND THEATER 2000–2008

After repeat performances of Pupulus Mordicus' puppet show *Faust: Pantin du diable* and of Richard Léger's *Faust: Chroniques de la démesure* in 2001, Canadian theatrical Faust activity of the new millennium reached a first peak in 2003. In April of that year, the University of Calgary hosted a "Faustival," an international conference and festival examining the myriad manifestations of the Faust theme across eras, cultures, media, and disciplines. Aside from numerous scholarly examinations of Goethe's text, the Faustival featured two artistic contributions centrally concerned with his drama. Timothy Gosley and Petra Kixmöller from Quebec performed *Faust through the Shadows*, a production that brought shadow puppet techniques to Goethe's *Faust*. It blended human acting, shadow puppetry, video and sound projection, and contained references to the visual style of German Expressionist cinema (particularly F. W. Murnau's *Faust* and *Nosferatu*) and to contemporary popular culture (e.g., sound clips from William S. Burroughs, Tom Waits, and Frank Zappa's "Catholic Girls" to characterize Margarete). This irreverent postmodern parody emphasized the sexual and material underpinnings of the story, depicting Faust under the sway of his unfulfilled sexual desires and Margarete as a "material girl."

The centerpiece of the Faustival was the University of Calgary's Department of Drama production of *Faust I* and *Faust II* in British playwright Howard Brenton's English translation, under the direction of Barry Yzereef. This was the first Canadian production in which the drama had been shortened only in such a way and to such an extent that the structure and plot of both parts had been left intact. The production was limited to a $7,000 budget and had twenty-one student actors play 219 roles. Like Marleau's *tragédie subjective,* this production examined questions of identity: Mephistopheles was played by Jamie Konchak as an androgynous shape shifter, and according to the production's mask coach Brian Smith, one goal of the extensive use of masks was to address the question of the coherence and continuity of the ego. Marleau's and Davies' explorations of psychology and Jungian themes were echoed by the intentions of director Yzereef. He directed *Faust II* as a Jungian journey in Faust's mind, as part of his conviction that the drama as a whole "is nothing less than the story of mankind told through one man. 'He falls in love. The woman he falls in love with is eventually killed. He follows an individual (Mephistopheles) who is twisting and manipulating his life as he searches and strives for better things. He confronts aspects of himself, the world and his imagination.'"[63] This makes for the universal appeal of the drama for Yzereef: "Faust is us, with all our strengths, all our weaknesses. We all sell out at some point—we bend our principles and recognize ourselves doing it. I think that's why this story touches us."[64] Two of Yzereef's goals with this production were to overcome the prejudice that *Faust* is not suitable for the stage and to make the drama accessible to a North American audience. He notes that he had immediate success with the actors, who through their work discovered German theater and ideas.

Confirming the status of Alberta as the hub of Canadian Faust activity in 2003, in October the drama department of the University of Alberta produced an adaptation of both parts of Goethe's *Faust* by director Goesta Struve-Dencher.[65] Over the following years, this activity was dominated by further events blending academic with artistic explorations of the Faust theme: the international symposium and festival "Faust in the 21st Century" at the University of Toronto in September 2004, a FaustFest organized by Theatre Inconnu in Victoria in April–May 2005, and an international conference on the reception of Faust in non-Christian cultures at McGill University in Montreal in October 2006. In October 2008, Goethe's *Faust I* was produced collaboratively by the University of Waterloo and Wilfrid Laurier University in a performance blending human actors and shadow puppets. The production was initiated by Faust expert David G. John of the University of Waterloo and directed by Arlene Thomas, Mat Kelly, and Alexandra Zimmermann.[66] The performance was bilingual, being, in the words of one of the actors involved, "a German-English hybrid, where German is the language of raw emotion and love, and English is the intellectual language."[67] This reversal of the usual stereotypes about German in particular seems to suggest that the production was conceived as a deliberate, pedagogical act of intercultural mediation, an impression borne out by the production's origin in the two universities and its performance in schools and libraries of the region.[68] All these events underscore the close link between artistic, academic, and pedagogical interests in Canadian *Faust* reception. They, like most of the instances of reception discussed in this chapter, suggest that both re-activating collective memory of Goethe's drama and introducing it to new audiences can serve significant catalytic functions in Canadian culture.

CONCLUSION

The analysis of contemporary Canadian interplay with *Faust* presented in this chapter has shown that the drama has had a considerable impact on Canadian culture over the past four decades, sometimes subterraneously, sometimes directly. In this interplay, *Faust* has had a variety of functions: object of the didactic introduction of Canadians to a central piece of the German literary canon, source of metaphors for negotiations of Canadian identity, source of universal truths or psychological structures, source of artistic inspiration, or object of parody. As such, the drama has contributed to constructions and negotiations of a wide range of meanings in Canada and to some fertile exchanges between Canadian and German culture. Conversely, the artistic encounters with and appropriations of *Faust* under discussion here have been shown to elucidate key potential meanings and fruitful avenues of receptive interpretation of Goethe's text. Thus, while the wild popularity of Goethe in Canada imagined by Eric Koch will remain a fantasy, the reactivation of collective memory of his *Faust* as well as the artistic discovery of new aspects of the text account for surprisingly many and colorful tesserae in the Canadian cultural mosaic.

NOTES

1. For the earlier Canadian reception of the drama, see Jörg Esleben, "Goethe's *Faust* in Canada, 1834–1970," in *Refractions of Germany in Canadian Literature and Culture*, ed. Heinz Antor, Sylvia Brown, John Considine, and Klaus Stierstorfer (Berlin and New York: De Gruyter, 2003), 331–41. For commentary on some Canadian explorations of the Faust theme in the 1980s, see Richard Ilgner, "Faust and the Magus Tradition in Robertson Davies' *The Rebel Angels*," in *International Faust Studies: Adaptation, Reception, Translation*, ed. Lorna Fitzsimmons (London and New York: Continuum, 2008), 205–15.

2. Esleben, "Goethe's *Faust* in Canada, 1834–1970," 338–41.

3. Barker Fairley, "On Translating *Faust*," in *Barker Fairley: Selected Essays on German Literature*, ed. Rodney Symington (New York: Lang, 1984), 144.

4. Kate Taylor, "Faust's Fall Rather Flat," *Globe and Mail*, December 2, 1995, C4; Vit Wagner, "Faust Artful But Lacks Soul," *Toronto Star*, December 3, 1995, F4.

5. Wagner, "Faust Artful But Lacks Soul," F4.

6. Vit Wagner, "Faust Ignites the Stage," *Toronto Star*, November 13, 1999, n.p.

7. Robert Cushman, "The Devil Sure Is a Smooth One," *National Post*, Toronto Edition, November 12, 1999, B6.

8. Mira Friedlander, "The Devil and Mr. Brooks: Faust: Director Well Aware of Goethe Script's Challenges," *National Post*, November 6, 1999, E10.

9. Eric Koch, *Icon in Love: A Novel about Goethe* (Oakville, Ontario: Mosaic, 1998).

10. Koch, *Icon in Love*, 11.

11. Koch, *Icon in Love*, 65.

12. The English translation of *Faust* (*F*) consulted for this chapter is Johann Wolfgang von Goethe, *Faust: A Tragedy*, trans. Walter Arndt (New York: Norton, 1976).

13. Koch, *Icon in Love*, 180.

14. Davies, *Discoveries: Early Letters 1938–1975*, ed. Judith S. Grant (Toronto: McClelland and Stewart, 2002), 231.

15. Judith S. Grant, *Robertson Davies: Man of Myth* (Toronto: Viking, 1994), 73.

16. Davies, *Discoveries*, 130.

17. Grant, *Robertson Davies*, 479.

18. Ilgner, "Faust and the Magus Tradition," 213.

19. Cited in Grant, *Robertson Davies*, 479.

20. Jung cited in Robertson Davies, *For Your Eye Alone: Letters 1976–1995*, ed. Judith S. Grant (Toronto: McClelland and Stewart, 1999), 298–99.

21. Judith S. Grant, "Davies, Robertson," in *Oxford Companion to Canadian Literature*, 2d ed., ed. Eugene Benson and William Toye (Toronto: Oxford University Press, 1997), 279.

22. Robertson Davies, *What's Bred in the Bone* (London: Penguin, 1987), 338–39.

23. Barker Fairley, *Goethe's Faust: Six Essays* (Oxford: Clarendon, 1953), v.

24. Davies, *What's Bred in the Bone*, 333.
25. Davies, *What's Bred in the Bone*, 359.
26. Davies, *What's Bred in the Bone*, 361.
27. Davies, *What's Bred in the Bone*, 395–97.
28. Davies, *What's Bred in the Bone*, 398.
29. Davies, *What's Bred in the Bone*, 434.
30. Henry Lehmann, "A Faust for the Eyes: Eva Brandl Installation Recalls Goethe's Classic," *Montreal Gazette*, September 21, 1996, 16.
31. Lehmann, "A Faust for the Eyes," 16.
32. Yvonne Lammerich, "Eva Brandl: Expression, Centre d'exposition de Saint-Hyacinthe, November 15 – December 21," *Parachute* 95 (1999): 43.
33. See Sylvie Parent, Exhibition notes for *Faust: Extraits et autres spéculations* (Saint-Hyacinthe, Quebec: Expression Centre d'exposition, 1999).
34. Lammerich, "Eva Brandl," 43.
35. See Centre for Contemporary Canadian Art, "Eva Brandl," artist file in the Canadian Database, http://www.ccca.ca/artists, for photographs of Brandl's installation and a brief biography on the artist (accessed March 10, 2009).
36. Gordon Armstrong, Review of *Faust, an Alternative Opera*, *Theatrum* 28 (April/May 1992): 32.
37. Jeff Corness, "*Faust*: A Theatre That Feels Like Music," *Canadian Theatre Review*, 72 (1992): 16.
38. Gilles Gobeil and René Lussier, *Le contrat*, Audio CD and liner notes (Montreal: Empreintes DIGITALes, 2003). See also http://www.electrocd.com/en/cat/imed_0372/pistes/ (accessed March 2, 2009).
39. Gobeil and Lussier, *Le contrat*.
40. Gobeil and Lussier, *Le contrat*.
41. Jon Kaplan, "Actor's Lab Theatre Endures as Thriving Ensemble," *Now*, March 3, 1982, 14.
42. Henry Mietkiewicz, "Actor's Lab Is Blunted by a Conventional Faust," *Toronto Star*, February 28, 1982, C2.
43. Henry Mietkiewicz, "Freudians, Feminists and Faust," *Toronto Star*, March 14, 1982, 69.
44. Mietkiewicz, "Freudians, Feminists and Faust," 69.
45. Lloyd Dykk, "Truly the Very Devil of a Time," *The Vancouver Sun*, October 27, 1984, E4.
46. *The Faust Quest/La quête de Faust*, program notes, Actor's Lab and Le Contre-Courant, Toronto, 1988–1989.
47. "Faust et le bateau des Aquarves en visite à Shawinigan," *tempo*, July 26, 2000, http://www.canoe.qc.ca/TempoSceneArchives/juil26_rue.html (accessed July 18, 2002). All translations are mine unless noted otherwise.
48. Marie Laliberté, "Pupulus Mordicus: *Faust, pantin du diable*," *Voir Québec*, February 1, 2001, http://www.pupulusmordicus.qc.ca/voir.html (accessed March 7, 2009).
49. Andy Pedersen, "Resurrecting Faust: Halifax's Milkman Theatre Group Adapts a Classic for the Late 20th Century," *Halifax Daily News*, November 30, 1995, 43.
50. Andrew Kelm, *Faust* (Toronto: Playwrights Union of Canada, 1993).
51. Kelm, *Faust*, 2.

52. Kelm, *Faust*, 4.

53. Kelm, *Faust*, 18–21.

54. Richard J. Léger, *Faust: Chroniques de la démesure* (Ottawa: Le Nordir, 2001).

55. David Blonde, "Pactiser avec le mythe. Stratégies théâtrales de la modernisation du mythe de Faust dans *Faust, chroniques de la démesure* de Richard J. Léger," in *Écritures hors-foyer. Actes du Ve Colloque des jeunes chercheurs en sociocritique et en analyse du discours et du colloque 'Écritures hors-foyer: Comment penser la littérature actuelle?' 25 et 26 octobre 2001, Université de Montréal*, ed. Pascal Brissette et al. *Discours social / Social Discourse* 7 (2002): 36.

56. Blonde, "Pactiser avec le mythe," 41–44.

57. In 1993, Sylvie Chaloux directed *Faust* (*La danse de Faust et Mephisto* [The dance of Faust and Mephisto]) at the Université de Québec à Montréal, starring Jean Turcotte in the role of Mephistopheles. I have been unable to find further information on this production and the nature of its relationship to Goethe's text.

58. Program notes.

59. Jean-Claude Desfons, "Ich ist immer ein Anderer: Der frankokanadische Regisseur Denis Marleau verzaubert mit seiner Urfaust-Montage die Theaterwelt," *Tagesspiegel*, September 10, 1999, http://www2.tagesspiegel.de/archiv/1999/09/09/ak-ku-bu-12376.html (accessed March 25, 2003).

60. Patrice Bergeron, "L'Urfaust d'Ubu à Weimar et Berlin," *Embassy Newspaper Online* 6, no. 1 (1998–1989), http://www.germanembassyottawa.org/news/Perspectives/winter99/urfaust.html (accessed March 25, 2003).

61. Michel Vaïs et al., "Urfaust, papiers collés," *Jeu* 91 (1999): 98.

62. Claus-Henning Bachmann, "Tagebuch," *Neue Musikzeitung* 49 (December/January 1999–2000): 6.

63. Bob Clark, Preview of University of Calgary Production of Goethe's *Faust I* and *Faust II*, *Calgary Herald*, March 22, 2003, ES12.

64. Martin Morrow, "A Mephistopheles of a Production: U of C Tackles the Monstrous, Complex and Dramatic World of Goethe's *Faust*," *Fast Forward*, March 27–April 2, 2003, 43.

65. Goesta Struve-Dencher, http://goestas.com/Faust/Faust_index.html (accessed March 7, 2009).

66. Anna Gerber, "'Zwei Seelen wohnen, ach! in meiner Brust' – Goethes *Faust* Part 1 ein Theater- und Schattenspiel," *Waterloo Centre for German Studies Newsletter* 9 (December 2008), 3.

67. Gerber, "'Zwei Seelen wohnen, ach! in meiner Brust,'" 3.

68. Gerber, "'Zwei Seelen wohnen, ach! in meiner Brust,'" 3.

BIBLIOGRAPHY

Armstrong, Gordon. Review of *Faust, an Alternative Opera*. *Theatrum* 28 (April/May 1992): 32.

Bachmann, Claus-Henning. "Tagebuch." *Neue Musikzeitung* 49 (December/January 1999–2000): 6.

Bergeron, Patrice. "L'Urfaust d'Ubu à Weimar et Berlin." *Embassy Newspaper Online* 6, no.1 (1998–1999). http://www.germanembassyottawa.org/news/Perspectives/winter99/urfaust.html (accessed March 25, 2003).

Blonde, David. "Pactiser avec le mythe. Stratégies théâtrales de la modernisation du mythe de Faust dans *Faust, chroniques de la démesure* de Richard J. Léger." In *Écritures hors-foyer. Actes du Ve Colloque des jeunes chercheurs en sociocritique et en analyse du discours et du colloque 'Écritures hors-foyer: Comment penser la littérature actuelle?' 25 et 26 octobre 2001, Université de Montréal,* edited by Pascal Brissette et al. *Discours social / Social Discourse* 7 (2002): 35–44.

Centre for Contemporary Canadian Art. "Eva Brandl." Artist file in the Canadian Art Database. http://www.ccca.ca/artists (accessed March 10, 2009).

Clark, Bob. Preview of University of Calgary Production of Goethe's *Faust I* and *Faust II*. *Calgary Herald,* March 22, 2003, ES12.

Corness, Jeff. "*Faust*: A Theatre That Feels Like Music." *Canadian Theatre Review* 72 (1992): 16–20.

Cushman, Robert. "The Devil Sure Is a Smooth One." *National Post* Toronto Edition, November 12, 1999, B6.

Davies, Robertson. *Discoveries: Early Letters 1938–1975*. Edited by Judith S. Grant. Toronto: McClelland and Stewart, 2002.

———. *For Your Eye Alone: Letters 1976–1995*. Edited by Judith S. Grant. Toronto: McClelland and Stewart, 1999.

———. *What's Bred in the Bone*. 1985. London: Penguin, 1987.

Desfons, Jean-Claude. "Ich ist immer ein Anderer: Der frankokanadische Regisseur Denis Marleau verzaubert mit seiner Urfaust-Montage die Theaterwelt." *Tagesspiegel,* September 10, 1999. http://www2.tagesspiegel.de/archiv/1999/09/09/ak-ku-bu-12376.html (accessed March 25, 2003).

Dykk, Lloyd. "Truly the Very Devil of a Time." *Vancouver Sun,* October 27, 1984, E4.

Esleben, Jörg. "Goethe's *Faust* in Canada, 1834–1970." In *Refractions of Germany in Canadian Literature and Culture,* edited by Heinz Antor, Sylvia Brown, John Considine, and Klaus Stierstorfer, 331–41. Berlin and New York: De Gruyter, 2003.

"Faust et le bateau des Aquarves en visite à Shawinigan." *Tempo,* July 26, 2000. http://www.canoe.qc.ca/TempoSceneArchives/juil26_rue.html (accessed July 18, 2002).

The Faust Quest/La quête de Faust. Program. Actor's Lab and Le Contre-Courant. Toronto, 1988–1989.

Fairley, Barker, trans. *Goethe's Faust*. Illustrations by Randy Jones. Toronto: University of Toronto Press, 1970.

———. *Goethe's Faust: Six Essays*. Oxford: Clarendon, 1953.

———. "On Translating Faust." 1969. Reprinted in *Barker Fairley: Selected Essays on German Literature,* edited by Rodney Symington, 143–54. New York: Lang, 1984.

Friedlander, Mira. "The Devil and Mr. Brooks. *Faust*: Director Well Aware of Goethe Script's Challenges." *National Post,* November 6, 1999, E10.

Gerber, Anna. "'Zwei Seelen wohnen, ach! in meiner Brust' – Goethes Faust Part 1 ein Theater- und Schattenspiel." *Waterloo Centre for German Studies Newsletter* 9 (December 2008): 3.

Gobeil, Gilles, and René Lussier. *Le contrat*. Audio CD and liner notes. Montreal: Empreintes DIGITALes, 2003.

———. "*Le contrat*: Track Detail." http://www.electrocd.com/en/cat/imed_0372/pistes/ (accessed March 2, 2009).

Goethe, Johann Wolfgang von. *Faust: A Tragedy*. Translated by Walter Arndt. New York: Norton, 1976.

Grant, Judith S. "Davies, Robertson." In *Oxford Companion to Canadian Literature*. 2d ed. Edited by Eugene Benson and William Toye, 277–80. Toronto: Oxford University Press, 1997.

———. *Robertson Davies: Man of Myth*. Toronto: Viking, 1994.

Ilgner, Richard. "Faust and the Magus Tradition in Robertson Davies' *The Rebel Angels*." In *International Faust Studies: Adaptation, Reception, Translation*, edited by Lorna Fitzsimmons, 205–15. London and New York: Continuum, 2008.

Kaplan, Jon. "Actor's Lab Theatre Endures as Thriving Ensemble." *Now*, March 3, 1982, 14.

Kelm, Andrew. *Faust*. Toronto: Playwrights Union of Canada, 1993.

Koch, Eric. *Icon in Love: A Novel about Goethe*. Oakville, Ontario: Mosaic Press, 1998.

Lafon, Dominique. "Le diabolique et le théâtral, ou comment la démesure s'empara du dramaturge." In *Faust: Chroniques de la démesure*, by Richard J. Léger, 7–10. Ottawa: Le Nordir, 2001.

Laliberté, Marie. "Pupulus Mordicus: *Faust, pantin du diable*." *Voir Québec*, February 1, 2001. http://www.pupulusmordicus.qc.ca/voir.html (accessed March 7, 2009).

Lammerich, Yvonne. "Eva Brandl: Expression, Centre d'exposition de Saint-Hyacinthe, November 15 - December 21." *Parachute* 95 (1999): 43–44.

Léger, Richard J. *Faust: Chroniques de la démesure*. Ottawa: Le Nordir, 2001.

Lehmann, Henry. "A Faust for the Eyes: Eva Brandl Installation Recalls Goethe's Classic." *Montreal Gazette*, September 21, 1996, I6.

Mietkiewicz, Henry. "Actor's Lab Is Blunted by a Conventional Faust." *Toronto Star*, February 28, 1982, C2.

———. "Freudians, Feminists and Faust." *Toronto Star*, March 14, 1982, 69.

Morrow, Martin. "A Mephistopheles of a Production: U of C Tackles the Monstrous, Complex and Dramatic World of Goethe's *Faust*." *Fast Forward*, March 27–April 2, 2003, 43.

Parent, Sylvie. Exhibition Notes for *Faust: Extraits et autres spéculations*. Saint-Hyacinthe, Quebec: Expression Centre d'exposition, 1999.

Pedersen, Andy. "Resurrecting Faust: Halifax's Milkman Theatre Group Adapts a Classic for the Late 20th Century." *Halifax Daily News*, November 30, 1995, 43.

Pupulus Mordicus. http://www.pupulusmordicus.qc.ca/faust.html (accessed February 19, 2009).

Struve-Dencher, Goesta. http://goestas.com/Faust/Faust_index.html (accessed March 7, 2009).

Taylor, Kate. "Faust's Fall Rather Flat." *Globe and Mail*, December 2, 1995, C4.

Theatre Inconnu. http://www.theatreinconnu.com/faustfest.html (accessed May 21, 2006).

Vaïs, Michel, et al. "Urfaust, papiers collés." *Jeu* 91 (1999): 97–101.

Wagner, Vit. "Faust Artful but Lacks Soul." *Toronto Star*, December 3, 1995, F4.

———. "Faust Ignites the Stage." *Toronto Star*, November 13, 1999, n.p.

8

Goethe's *Faust* in Werner Fritsch's "Theater of the Now"

Susanne Ledanff

Contemporary German writer and multimedia artist Werner Fritsch's "Theater of the Now" is deeply imbricated with the conception of the moment in Goethe's *Faust*. Fritsch is a passionate collector of momentary visions from world cultural history, and he positions his writing under the poetics of the magical and consciousness-altering moment. The "Theater of the Now," as he envisages it, is not to be confused with the contemporary theater and its ephemeral prevailing themes. His theater has been deemed "an anti-space and a place of epiphany."[1] Fritsch explains,

> No further opinions should be acted out in the Theater of the Now. Rather, a space should be created in which an aura materializes and the spectator himself forges ahead into finer regions of perception, as long as there is still any hope at all. The decisive factor is not that which is shown, but rather that which can materialize in the spectator beyond the shown.[2]

Fritsch's poetic language is often characterized by a cryptic and metaphorical density, and dreamlike, visionary intensity. The poetic cues that he provides in interviews, project sketches, and, not last, his *Die Alchemie der Utopie: Frankfurter Poetikvorlesungen 2009* (The alchemy of utopia: Frankfurt poetics lectures 2009) suggest Fritsch's sense of the significance of the "Now," the experience which transcends the present, for the spectator. Fritsch wants to tap into the meanderings of the spectator's brain, activating the process by which the poetic word is "projected onto the internal screen."[3] In the "Theater of the Now" there is an attempt to stimulate the spectator's own regions of memory and emotion.[4] The author wants to create words and images that lead the spectator beyond the media terror of the present.

In this context of Fritsch's avant-gardism, his "translation" of Goethe's *Faust* "into the Now"[5] is an unusual project which reflects his sustained interest in the Faust theme and his poetic utopianism.[6] I speak of Fritsch's multimedia project *Faust Sonnengesang* (Faust song of the sun), which includes the theatrical work *Faust. Im Anfang ist das Wort. Ein Stück aus Augenblicken und Träumen* (Faust: In the beginning is the word. A play of moments and dreams) (2009), and the film *Faust Sonnengesang* (Faust song of the sun). Fritsch's project sketch "*Faust Sonnengesang*—The Multimedia Installation" from 2009 is a useful introduction to the goals of this comprehensive project.[7] He explains,

> It seemed important to me to transform this material, which is ultimately an archive into which Goethe poured the essence of thousands of books, into our Now. By this I mean that transforming the material into the Now does not mean transforming historical facts philologically, but poetically—into our present age. This means reformulating it anew with one's own language, and fermenting it by means of one's own experience.[8]

In his reinterpretation of the Faust myth, which originates from his criticism of the dissipation of "cultural memory," the author explains further,

> *Faust Sonnengesang* seeks to raise the Faust myth to a new level. Our age is threatened not least by the loss of our cultural memory; in addition, our perception is becoming increasingly splintered. For this reason *Faust Sonnengesang* aims to approach people today in different ways (various media)—specifically in the form of this multimedia installation.[9]

The point of departure for Frisch's writing is, then, the present cultural situation and the threats to "cultural memory." Interestingly, this concept links him to contemporary research on cultural memory, such as that of Jan and Aleida Assmann, as I will discuss.[10]

There is another cue which Fritsch articulates in his project sketches and poetology for his *Faust Sonnengesang*, namely, Goethe's "fulfilled" or "eternal" moment, which is indeed central to Fritsch's bold multimedial theatrical and filmic production. The author aims to create a "Now" to which one says "linger a while, you are so beautiful."[11] The "translation" of Goethe's *Faust* "into the Now" emanates from the central motif of the wager in which Faust's soul falls to the devil should he wish the climactic moment to remain. It will be necessary to come back to the fact that Fritsch is fully cognizant of making fundamental departures from the plot of Goethe's *Faust*. He reinterprets Goethe's ambiguous concept of the possible fulfillment of happiness and draws from it an aesthetic and a dramaturgy through which today's spectator can experience a "vision of the Golden Age, myths of paradise, notions of the afterworld, and teachings of wisdom from foreign cultures" brought together "with images of individual happiness."[12] The distance from the Goethean model could not be more clear, for, as Fritsch explains, "*Faust Sonnengesang* picks up where Goethe's *Faust* leaves off."[13]

Yet there is also an earlier work by this author that confirms his preoccupation with *Faust* as an undertaking subject to transformations and illustrates a different approach to the Faustian sources: *Chroma. Farbenlehre für Chamäleons* (Chroma. Color theory for chameleons), first staged at the Expo in Hanover on September 2, 2000, as part of the theatrical program on the theme of Goethe's *Faust*, which included Peter Stein's *Faust* production.[14] Fritsch's preoccupation with the Faust myth as it is predominantly represented in Goethe's *Faust* represents a dynamic and increasingly intercultural phase in the evolution of the myth, which Peter Werres encapsulates as "one of the archetypal manifestations" of "Western hubris."[15]

In a way, *Chroma* is more traditional than the aesthetically free and subjective treatment of the Faust material in *Faust Sonnengesang*. *Chroma* allows the allusion to the plot of the devil's pact to be unambiguously recognizable. The work places the Gustaf Gründgens figure, the cult star behind the Mephisto actor of the Third Reich, at the "intersection of the threads of German history"[16]—at the high point of German culture in Goethe's work and its abyss in the Nazi era.

The purpose of this chapter is to explore Fritsch's use of the Goethean Faust myth in his Faust works, with an emphasis on the *Faust Sonnengesang* project. The author has occupied himself with the Faust material since 1995. One can add to *Chroma* the preform *Gründgens. Libretto*, a choreographical production at the Deutsches Schauspielhaus in Hamburg in 1995 written for Austrian director Johann Kresnik.[17] Thus Fritsch's *Faust* adaptations alternate between the German national myth and political themes in *Chroma* and the universal archive in *Faust Sonnengesang*. They enable comprehension of a metamorphosis of the tragic into the hymnlike. Fritsch himself admits that the national-historical perspective in *Chroma* could no longer satisfy him.[18] Indeed, it is in *Faust Sonnengesang* that the liberation from the "tragic" material comes to light, evincing unusual visionary and critical positions.

To begin, I shall overview the emergence of Fritsch's aesthetic and indicate his role for a new postdramatic theater in Germany. After that, I will explore his political transposition of the Goethean *Faust* in *Chroma*. This will be followed by an analysis of the most recent "utopian" turn in Fritsch's *Faust* reception in the *Sonnengesang* project. As I will show, the development of the author's *Faust* "translation" leads to an incorporation of concepts of intercultural memory in his latest artistic productions, which can be conceived of as avant-garde and multimedia.

THE EMERGENCE OF FRITSCH'S AESTHETIC

Werner Fritsch was born in 1960 in Waldsassen, Upper Palatinate, and grew up on an isolated farm. The landscape of Upper Palatinate brought forth worlds of images and spaces of memory, a "topography" and "linguistic-visual cosmos,"[19] and this landscape is indeed the point of departure for Fritsch's writing since the novel *Cherubim* (1987; theatrical production of the *Cherubim Monolog*, 1988, 1998, 2003; film: *Das sind die Gewitter in der Natur*, 1988). The novel was awarded the Robert Walser Prize—the first of a number of prizes Fritsch has received. Not less important for Fritsch's literary career was his contact, at age fifteen, with Bavarian author and filmmaker Herbert Achternbusch, who recognized the beginnings of *Cherubim* as worthy of publication by Suhrkamp[20] and later ushered Fritsch into the art of filmmaking.

The conception of Fritsch as the "outsider" in German contemporary literature is not easy to brush aside. Wolfgang Höbel perceives the production of *Chroma* in 2001 at the Berliner Theatertreffen as the turning point at which Fritsch's image moved beyond that of a regional writer.[21] *Chroma* was followed by *Nico. Sphinx aus Eis* (Nico. Sphinx of ice) (2001), which depicts a New York heroin addict whose traumatic monologue is positioned between the rock scene and the shadows of a Nazi childhood. Stefan Pokroppa observes a "poetics of distance" in Fritsch's focus on historical figures such as Gründgens and Nico, whereby the place of *Heimat* loses cohesive strength.[22] Instead, Fritsch's expressions of postmodern *Zeitkritik* have become more pronounced.

I do not want to recapitulate Fritsch's collective works, but rather to discuss these themes for his project *Faust Sonnengesang*. When we think of the author's youthful point of departure, the visionary narrations of the farm hand, then there are further religious texts worthy of mention: the visions of Anna Katharina Emmerick in the tradition of Mechthild von Magdeburg.[23] It is not surprising that Fritsch's ambitious hunger for education, which had not been "destroyed" by study of *Germanistik* and philosophy,[24] allows "literary house gods" to come to the surface: Kafka, Weiss, Beckett, Joyce, Faulkner, Céline, Burroughs, Huchel.[25] Yet it goes against the impression of a solely modernist influence to note that Fritsch strives against abstract "modernist dogma"[26] and, indeed, his work has postmodernist affinities in its use of collage, quoted voices, historical documents (as in *Chroma* and *Nico*), and the theme of the divided self. There is certainly a strong element of surrealistic writing in his work. Antonin Artaud is especially influential, but also the Polish author Tadeusz Kantor with his "Theater of the Dead" and the elements of dreamlike dialogue.[27]

Also of interest is the critical reception of Fritsch's aesthetic utopias in the spectrum of similar contemporary theatrical art. Anna Opel situates

Fritsch's work in the context of a "theater art focused on linguistic bodies," like the work of Rainald Goetz and Sarah Kane, in which "[l]anguage supplants the theatrical figure as a continuity of language and body, becoming a linguistic body in itself."[28] "A wild, palpable, but certainly no longer an intellectually graspable attitude towards life is what constitutes . . . Fritsch's cosmos," Pokroppa contends.[29] This is certainly an indication of Fritsch's avoidance of traditional psychological dramaturgy in his "postdramatic" theater.[30]

CHROMA AND GOETHE'S *FAUST*

The play *Chroma* clearly demonstrates Fritsch's self-conscious grappling with the Goethean Faust myth.[31] Among his more or less veiled references to the Goethean model, Fritsch mainly draws from *Faust I*, including the rejuvenation ("*Verjüngung*") in "Witch's Kitchen" ("Hexenküche"), yet there are also references to *Faust II*, such as Wagner's Homunculus creation in "Laboratory" ("Laboratorium"). *Chroma* depicts a "HOMUNCULUS FAUST," under the alias of Gründgens, who receives medical treatment to purge his homosexuality. Maria Morphium/Mephisto appears here as a concentration camp physician.[32] Such significant departures from the Goethean model intensify the effects of recognizing echoes from it. But the echoes are used rather sparingly in individual scenes of the script, such as in the Faust/Gretchen dialogue.[33] What makes these quotes possible, and constitutes the most important structural element of the play, is that these are the biographical stations in the life of actor and director Gustaf Gründgens—and his "Faust pact" with the Nazis. There is a nod here toward the historical *Faust* productions in the Nazi era, even an episode from Gründgens' beginnings as an actor in a *Faust* production in the Fronttheater of World War I, in a scene in which the humanistic cultural heritage of *Faust* is confronted with the brutality of war. In the Darmstadt production, loudspeakers emit the sound of canon fire, but even linguistically the text tips into the apocalyptic. The scenes might seem to be ambiguously real or dreamed in the nightmarish retrospective of Gründgens' life. A further highly symbolic scene is a shocking torture fantasy: the monologue of the Gretchen figure, which is carried out on stage with Gretchen "head down and disgraced" ("kopfunter und geschändet").[34] The scene is a disturbing high point of the reinterpretation of the Faust material in Fritsch's selected political context: the torture methods of the Gestapo under National Socialism. The dramaturgy is still dominated by the appearance of friends and colleagues from Gründgens' circle: Erika and Klaus Mann, Hermann (Göring), Emmy (Göring—the actress who played Gretchen in the Nazi era), Flicki (Elisabeth Flickenschildt)—and not least Hitler himself as patron of the Gründgens era. Mephisto appears as an SA/SS man, as a concentration camp physician, and finally as a boy in a coral red dress, embodying the dying Gründgens' lust. This is an allusion to the fact that Fritsch's Mephisto only functions as a projection surface for Gründgens' imagination. On the one hand, then, we see the transposition of Goethe's *Faust* within a clearly political framework. On the other hand, and I would like to come here to the poetological premises of Fritsch's "Theater of the Now," *Chroma* is already a drama of consciousness that contains the thought of the "last film" of one's own life story at the moment of death, a motif which Fritsch will also use in *Faust Sonnengesang.*

The work begins with the death scene of morphine-addicted Gründgens in Manila in 1963. From the abyss of this "Place of the Underworld" and its drug scene, Gründgens calls upon Mephisto, the boy in the coral red dress, a projection of his own ego. The introduction to Gründgens' retrospective of his life happens with Mephisto's words:

> Then you will be forgotten forever!
> Give up, Gustaf, submit,
> Right in this hour you will obtain
> More for your senses than you gain
> In a whole year's monotony
> What tender spirits now will sing
> The lovely pictures that they bring
> Are not mere magic for the eye.
>
> (Bist du vergessen—
> für immer!
> Gib auf, Gustaf! Gib dich hin;
> Du wirst, mein Freund, für deine Sinnen
> In diesen Stunden mehr gewinnen
> Als in des Lebens Einerlei
> Was dir die zarten Geister singen,
> Die schönen Bilder, die sie bringen
> Sind nicht ein leeres Zauberspiel.)[35]

Mephisto points out that all that follows is the "final film" of Gründgens, an overview of his life at the moment of death. Cynically, he plays here with the idea that a harmonizing view can be drawn from the "lovely pictures" of a life's synopsis, which are presented in the style of Goethe's verses. With that, Goethe's idea of "[w]isdom's last verdict" ("der Weisheit letzter Schluss") (*F*, 11574) is thwarted.[36] The famous passage from Goethe's play is pertinent, as the concept of the "fulfilled" moment is of particular relevance also for *Faust Sonnengesang*:

> I might entreat the fleeting minute:
> Oh tarry yet, thou art so fair!

> My path on earth, the trace I leave within it
> Eons untold cannot impair.
> Foretasting such high happiness to come,
> I savor now my striving's crown and sum.
>
> (Zum Augenblicke dürft' ich sagen:
> Verweile doch, Du bist so schön!
> Es kann die Spur von meinen Erdetagen
> Nicht in Äonen untergehn. –
> Im Vorgefühl von solchem hohen Glück
> Genieß ich jetzt den höchsten Augenblick) (*F*, 11581–86)

Let us maintain that it is the parameters of the "last film" with which the *Chroma* work is held together, but there is clearly a political meta-level of reflection on the Faust material. On Fritsch's reinterpretation of the Faust/Mephisto binary, Pokroppa contends that the "transcendent symbols of God and the devil can no longer be maintained as in Goethe's day. God becomes relativized."[37] Mephisto triumphs when he declares the manifold contaminated Gretchen figure (Gretchen, Emmy, Hermann) to be "rescued."[38] The contaminated era of art and acting from the Nazi period is also "rescued" in the transfiguration of "timeless art" in the postwar period.

In looking back at Fritsch's work on *Chroma*, principlal considerations of the adaptation of *Faust* for the present can certainly be found.

> How does one quote, how does one quote tokenistically, how does one quote so that the transitional quote—one's own contrivance—can no longer be felt? Where does Goethe stop—and where does Fritsch begin? . . . In *Chroma* there comes a shred of Goethe and then some extemporaneous Goethean meter, and then the conversation between the dying man and his soul in the figure of Mephisto, soon accompanied by the choirs of war dead, and soon some whore joke on the soundtrack. And don't forget—Fritsch is coming, too.[39]

What makes these heterogeneous allusions plausible is Faust's (Gründgens') journey through consciousness, which takes place through a process of recapitulation and assembly. Fritsch's politically accented adaptation of *Faust* is in no way new. *Chroma* is clearly related to the antagonistic interpretations with which the processing of the Faust material reacted to the social, political, ideological, and philosophical themes and discourses of the twentieth century. Here, the themes of National Socialism and science protrude.[40] The Gründgens material had already been staged in Ariane Mnouchkine's *Mephisto* (1979), with her Théâtre du Soleil, using the novel by Klaus Mann, which is a point of contention due to the biographically motivated accusations of Gründgens within its transposition of Goethe's *Faust*. Fritsch's interpretation of the Faustian Gründgens is certainly much more aesthetically diverse, which can be attributed to the surreal spaces of consciousness of the leading figure and the painstakingly researched voice material of Gründgens' friends Hermann and Emmy Göring.[41] The piece also includes an expression of the competition between Gründgens and Klaus Mann: "You, hero in a novel, which creates for you more memory than a treacherous rat would deserve" ("Du, Held eines Romans, der dir mehr Gedächtnis verschafft, als eine verräterische Ratte wie du es verdient").[42]

Of the instances of innovation which Fritsch creates through the use of his own video clips on stage, the aesthetic function of the film *Chroma Faust Passion*, shot in the Philippines on Good Friday 2000, is intriguing. This film depicts a crucifixion in which young men flagellate themselves bloody and are crucified—in reality, not as in a passion play or Hollywood films, as the author notes.[43] Fritsch explains his intention in blending this film into *Chroma* as follows: "These images of real pain are the counterpoint to the actor who portrays pain and death."[44] The question remains as to what extent Fritsch's theater, imbued with audiovisual effects, is capable of drawing contemporary audiences out of their media-laden consumerist behaviors. Phrases like "real pain" may evoke skepticism in light of both the dulling effects of "authentic" death and violence on reality TV and the nerve-tingling of contemporary theater. However, the crucifixion scene in the *Chroma Faust Passion* film deals with one of the most important ritualized forms of cultural memory.[45] Locating an "authentic" violence scene in a crucifixion ritual, which serves to thwart and elucidate a "Faustian" biography such as that of Gründgens, demonstrates a high level of reflection on the mise-en-scène of cultural icons—which may, to some, appear quite different from the effect-grabbing of the contemporary theater. One should be reminded that Fritsch's collected work aims toward his "utopia" of a "polymedial narration" freed from discrete genres.[46] But will this contemporary, avant-gardist aesthetic distinguish itself from the tradition of theatricalized Faust themes?

Goethe himself broke new ground in the use of new media in the theater. For the appearance of the Earth Spirit ("Geist"), he approached the painter Wilhelm Zahn about the use of the Laterna Magica in the course of preparing for the Weimar production in 1828.[47] In the scene "Hall of Chivalry" ("Kaiserliche Pfalz – Rittersaal") there was to be a slightly concealed Laterna Magica for the phantasmagorical appearance of Paris and Helena.[48] In the twentieth century, numerous avant-gardist *Faust* performances have been staged with the aid of modern technologies: from Max Reinhardt's productions using the revolving stage in Berlin in 1909 and 1911, to the challenging installation of a sound stage for Peter Stein's production in 2000.[49] Bold theatricalizations of the Faust theme can serve as a vehicle for postmodern criticism. In the case of the theatrical and filmic work *Faust Sonnengesang*, Fritsch's argumentation is vehemently critical of civilization, and the utopianism of the enterprise is contingent upon the multimedia performance.

THE MULTIMEDIA *FAUST SONNENGESANG* PROJECT

Let us explore now the aesthetic forms through which Fritsch seeks to express his ideas of a spiritual experience of the "Theater of the Now" and subsequently his spiritual re-interpretation of the motif of the moment in Goethe's *Faust*. The theatrical piece *Faust Sonnengesang* is a multimedia project in several respects.[50] The stage text of the theatrical work *Faust. Im Anfang ist das Wort* is referred to in various scenes in the screenplay of the film *Faust Sonnengesang*, as discussed below.[51] But already by looking at the stage text and the stage directions of *Faust. Im Anfang ist das Wort*, it becomes clear why *Faust Sonnengesang* must be constructed with multiple media—especially in light of the aesthetic of the "picture cave" ("*Bilderhöhle*") in which human dreams of happiness should also be present.[52] Fritsch's spatial composition is dominated by the Tryptichon figure. On both sides of the stage there is a screen, with the left illustrating "the river Eunoe, rising up from the moment of happiness." On the right side we see the river Lethe, "in which everything drives away that which is terrible and unchangeable."[53] The Tryptichon figure is now also mirrored at the level of the protagonists. At stage center are Faust and the figures whom he encounters during his journey from remembrance to the "Golden Age." Here we also see the division of Mephisto/Mephista, working from the sideline, being ascribed to the symbolic opposition of the rivers Eunoe and Lethe. Mephisto is connected to the river Lethe, which allows the apocalyptic underground noise of the present to be driven away. At Mephisto's signal, we hear "a tornado of sound from all radio and television channels currently running at this moment."[54] Mephista is ascribed to the river Eunoe, which calls forth quietude, reflection, and rapture, regaining silence through pantomime by placing a finger on her mouth, thus allowing Faust to speak. The stage direction that Mephisto "again and again allows the deluge of meaning to break in over the heads of the audience," his domain being that of "distraction"—the "domain of the demons"—is relativized, with the apocalyptic experience of "distraction" intermittent. The "tornado of sound" opens each scene, but is quickly silenced by Mephista. This silence creates the prerequisite for the intensity of the creations of Fritsch's *Faust*, a "paradisical" anti-world in the past and present. With that, Fritsch's adaptation certainly presents a reinterpretation of prior Mephistopheles figures. In its duplicity, this figure transcends the artistic concept of a Mephisto portrayed by a female actor (which Thomas Krupa already used in his production of *Chroma*). In *Faust. Im Anfang ist das Wort*, though, Fritsch's interpretation of the projective character of Mephisto in *Chroma* is transgressed. One cannot even say that the male Mephisto, who operates the board for the inferno of sound, is the vestige of the "demonic" Mephisto. Nor can one say that Fritsch's Mephista embodies the "good" side of the soul in the metaphysical traditions of the Faust theme, ultimately responsible for inner transformations toward absolution and contemplation. More radically than in *Chroma*, Fritsch points toward the surreal character of the Mephisto figure. "Mephisto—or Mephista—is not genuinely evil but is as Faust imagines him or her to be."[55]

At present, we see that the *Faust* film is at the fore of Fritsch's *Faust Sonnengesang* project. Fritsch's various film, drama, and sound installations are now more closely connected than ever in his work, especially considering that the project has taken several years. Fritsch began work on his *Faust* film in 1998 while traveling to many areas, including Madagascar, Venezuela, Mexico, Ecuador, India, Tibet, China, Japan, the Czech Republic, Italy, Greece, Norway, and New Zealand. It evolved into the film-poem *Faust Sonnengesang*, with promotional funding from the Media Board Berlin-Brandenburg and Bayerischer Rundfunk, and, in 2008–2009, an Arno Schmidt grant.[56] Broadcast by the Bayerischer Rundfunk-alpha TV channel on January 6, 2011, featuring the voices of well-known German actors such as Corinna Harfouch, Angela Winkler, and Ulrich Matthes, the three-hour film received enthusiastic reviews.[57]

In his attempt to create a utopian alternative to contemporary media distractions, Fritsch has adapted the Goethean *Faust* into a richly intercultural work in which concentrated natural-lyrical and cosmological imagery suggests the "immortality" of the poetic magician's creative spirit. Fritsch's most recent work starting from the stage version of *Faust. Im Anfang ist das Wort. Ein Stück aus Augenblicken und Träumen* is exemplified by a number of lyrical passages which suggest feelings of intoxication in their symphonies of color and their synesthesia. Also, the hermetic imagery of the text points not only to the Christian-inspired spirituality of the author, but also to religious traditions of Asia, of which the author has intimate knowledge. Furthermore, while in *Faust. Im Anfang ist das Wort* Fritsch goes beyond the cryptically written passages of earlier works, which permitted a recognition of certain contemporary or historical references through montage and the blending of fragments of reality, in the new work this is barely possible, as the current work is indeed a treatment of a spiritual experience. Faust is seen again and again as a "divinely" inspired writer.

Faust is accompanied by mythological figures on his journey through his own unconscious and the dreams of humanity. In this way, a rudimentary form of the plot emerges: the central motifs are Faust's catharsis. He sees "the earthly paradise" (in the sense of Dante's *Paradiso*) at the peak of "Mount Purgatorio," where the rivers Lethe and Eunoe flow.[58] Faust's decision while at the crossroads is to create a "divine comedy" ("*göttliche Komödie*") instead of a "diabolical tragedy" ("*teuflische Tragödie*").[59] His writing is dedicated to the muse Mnemosyne:

> I want to create a work
> Not only from the maelstrom of my day
> For day dispersed at night anew
> Ark for dream-rubble
> They tarry on the river
> from the flowing light of divinity
> Ark for spirits
> Memory theater
> Mnemosyne mother of the muses
>
> (Ich aber will ein Werk schaffen
> Nicht allein aus dem Mahlstrom meiner ichs Tag
> Für Tag neu Nacht zerstreut
> Arche für Traumtrümmer
> Die treiben auf dem Fluß
> aus dem fließenden Licht der Gottheit
> Arche für Geister
> Gedächtnis Theater
> Mnemosyne Mutter der Musen)[60]

Figure 2. Still from the film *Faust Sonnengesang* (November 12, 2009). By permission of Werner Fritsch Filmproduktion.[61]

Some mythological figures are inspired by the muse Mnemosyne, such as King Midas in the scene "Dream of the Golden Age" ("Traum vom goldenen Zeitalter"). The scene "Dream of the Mothers' Realm" ("Traum vom Reich der Mütter") is also a reinterpretation of the myth of Persephone/Demeter, based on the legend that Demeter was permitted to fetch her daughter up from Hades each year. The text not only plays with Greek mythology, but also emphasizes the traditions of feminine strength and wisdom. The mothers—obviously a play on Goethe's *Faust II*—are an archetype that we have known since Bachofen's research on the chthonic abysses from Greek mythology. Symbols such as the snake goddess Persephone/Medusa used in the play represent the rising up from deformations and eviscerations and promise magical transformations.

The play does not lack a certain dramatic tension in the representation of the dichotomy of the soul. Visions of salvation and the abyss are dependent upon each other. In no way is there a dominating hymnlike language in Faust's poetic monologues. We hear in the incantation of the "great challenge of FAUST SONG OF THE SUN" ("das große Wagnis FAUST SONNENGESANG")[62] the experience of the abysmal and the threatening, of death and suffering. This is most apparent in the use of the fire imagery in the scene "Dream of the Theater. Under This Skullcap: Moment" ("Traum vom Theater. Unter dieser Schädeldecke: Augenblick") in which both Mephistos bombard Faust with images of the "burning book of the Now" ("brennendes Buch des Jetzt"),[63] a central metaphor in the *Faust Sonnengesang* project. In the mystical tradition, fire imagery refers to the powers of purification and healing. Faust sees "metamorphosis in the fire" ("Im Feuer seh ich die Metamorphose")[64] and makes peace with his dead (Fritsch is alluding here to the personal experience of his sister's death in 2004). It is not difficult to see that Fritsch is drawing from the poetic tradition of the "ecstasies of time" ("*Ekstasen der Zeit*"),[65] the mystical suddenness of recognition, which stands in contrast to Goethe's "fulfilled" or "eternal" moment and might be illustrated by Meister Eckhardt's showing of God through the tiny glimmer of the soul in the "Nû," or even Jakob Böhme's mystical recognition of God, and the idea of the return of the Golden Age.

The variations of the incantation of the images of paradise are linguistically diverse. Sometimes they appear in iambic meter, drawing on antiquity, and sometimes in a childlike language which paints a picture of how paradise could look. Sometimes they appear in an idyllic family scene, and sometimes, such as at the end of the play, in scenes which bring about the memory of the archetypal image of the *locus amoenus,* once in the images of the Egyptian eon and then in the lyrical depiction of the New Zealand landscape (pronounced by a Nefertiti/Persephone figure and a voice called the "light of New Zealand/young woman" ["Das Licht Neuseelands/Junge Frau"]). One asks, though, how the audience could be able to absorb such a complex variety of voices, and how they could possibly be swept along on this mystical journey to the myths of human paradise. Within its extreme execution of the poetics of the "linguistic body," in Opel's terms, on stage, the play does engage in self-reflection upon its reception. This happens at many points, in the form which Fritsch has already described in his *Faust Sonnengesang* sketches in his *Die Alchemie der Utopie*.

> MEPHISTA. In the Theater of the Now
> It is enough if you come to
> It is enough if a spectator
> Comes to
> If a spectator takes along
> A moment, a dream
> Into his life
>
> (MEPHISTA. Im Theater des Jetzt
> Genügt es wenn Sie zu sich kommen
> Es genügt wenn ein Zuschauer
> Zu sich kommt
> Wenn ein Zuschauer einen Gedanken
> Einen Augenblick einen Traum
> Mit in sein Leben nimmt)[66]

Within the experience of such moments, recognition of the Faustian theme is no doubt important, yet the play's relation to the Faustian plot is ambivalent, as when Mephista says, "A Faust play not a Faust play" ("Ein Faust-Stück kein Faust-Stück").[67] On the one hand, the "Faust play" stems from an echoing of the Goethean figures and motifs. On the other hand, Fritsch is well aware that the eschatological message, which he delivers through the momentary visions of his Faustian poet figure, constitutes a fundamental departure from the historical model.

For example, what comprises the decisive reinterpretation of the Faust material, be it that of the chapbook or Goethe's *Faust*, is readily apparent:

> In contrast to the Johann Faust of the chapbook
> And Goethe's Heinrich Faust, the Faust
> Of this play
> Works with white magic
>
> (Im Gegensatz zum Johann Faust des Volksbuchs
> Und Goethes Heinrich Faust wirkt der Faust
> Dieses Stücks
> Mit weißer Magie)[68]

It is without a doubt that Fritsch wants to introduce a cultural-historical caesura in imagining the Faust myth. The "translation of *Faust* into the

Now" is ambiguous, as we can see. It speaks not only to symptoms of crisis in the present, but also to the ecstatic-eschatological moments of *Faust Sonnengesang*—Faust's "white magic." In the Goethean Faust's resignation to "magic's art" ("Drum hab' ich mich der Magie ergeben") (*F*, 377), both "black," demonic, magic and "white" magic come into play.[69] The spiritual and religious traditions in Fritsch's "white magic" are intended in a more radical way. Indeed, this is the actual occasion for his "*Faust* translation," *Faust Sonnengesang*. It gives rise to an about-face in the metaphysical traditions of Faust and his "alienation of the soul," and the changing references since the sixteenth century to "the performative sign [which] has been defined as a magical, and thus satanic, phenomenon."[70] As we have just seen, Fritsch is not only true to the symbol of the one who seeks meaning in questions of human existence in Faust writing. He accords to Goethe's *Faust* a special reverence in that the dream potential of the Goethean symbol of the moment becomes the center of attraction for Fritsch's *Faust Sonnengesang*.

How does Fritsch's archival maintenance of the images of happiness from literary, religious, and spiritual traditions in *Faust Sonnengesang* relate to the conception of the moment in Goethe's *Faust*? The Faustian inner conflict we see with Goethe locates the experience of the moment in a fundamentally different way. It arises from restless striving, not only after deep recognition, but from the widening of boundaries through an active and relishing experience of the world and for this reason renders the Faust bet superfluous at the end of the piece. Therefore the "climactic moment" refers back to the "restless striving" of human nature, even in the moment of death. It is precisely this which makes Faust worthy of redemption, making it justifiable that the "linger a while" phrase is only spoken in the subjunctive, "I might entreat the fleeting minute: Oh tarry yet, thou art so fair!" ("Zum Augenblicke dürft' ich sagen: / Verweile doch, Du bist so schön!") (*F*, 11581–82).[71] Goethe's profound skepticism in his *Faust* of the ability to fulfill the climactic moment of happiness is fundamentally different from Fritsch's message that it is time to offer alternatives to the apocalyptic conditions of the present—through the collection of "happy moments" in a work of art.

However, Fritsch rightly perceives the importance of the "happy moment" in the Goethean version of the myth. It is the concept of the moment which largely determines Goethe's *Faust*, distinguishing it from other traditions of Faust writing. The concept establishes the horizon for Faustian restlessness. Without the singular meaning which Goethe ascribes to the "fulfilled" moment, the Faustian search for the soul would not have been possible. It is well known that the "fulfilled," the "eternal," the "concise" moment is a central image for Goethe, in that the ephemerality of the present moment is overcome and transcended by qualitative super-elevation—a meaningful, fulfilling point in time which elevates itself above the flow of time. The writings of Goethe in which this "concise" moment has "duration" need not be explored here.[72] In *Faust*, Goethe comes closest to representing the happiness of the moment in the Helena/Faust encounter. It is an Arcadian image in which the fantastic-dreamlike action of the Helena act seems hypothetical.[73] The earthly Arcadia, already depicted in Faust's recuperation scene at the beginning of Part II, is also a climax of a dream, "where Faust awakens from his recuperative sleep to the music of the Elves' chorus accompanied by Aeolian harps."[74]

Fritsch is particularly interested in such ideas within the complex system of the Goethean *Faust*. The author certainly does not treat the text model philologically. His central metaphors must now be clarified, and it must be pointed out how different *Faust Sonnengesang* is from the failing retrospective on life in the "last film" in *Chroma*, with its cynical reference to the Goethean "eternal" moment. Fritsch's titular concept of the "Song of the Sun" can be related to two scenes of Goethe's *Faust*. In the "Prologue in Heaven" ("Prolog im Himmel"), "The sun contends in age-old fashion / With brother spheres in hymnic sound" ("Die Sonne tönt nach alter Weise / In Brudersphären Wettgesang") (*F*, 243–44). In "Charming Landscape" ("Anmutige Gegend"), the Horae, the guardians of Heaven, drive Phoebus' sun chariot through the celestial gates: "What great din the dawning brings!" ("Welch Getöse bringt das Licht!") (*F*, 4671). At both points there appears the symbol of "celestial music," which alludes to Dante's *Divine Comedy* and the Pythagorean teaching on spherical harmony.[75]

The Egyptian images of the hereafter are perhaps more central. Fritsch's Faust has come to know "white" magic in Egypt. His journey can also be seen as the journey of the sun god, Ra, on the solar barque, which rises again each morning from night into day.[76] Knowledge of the Egyptian sun myth is, as Fritsch says, an "overriding image for FAUST SONG OF THE SUN. Similarly, FAUST SONG OF THE SUN casts light on the life-giving knowledge of the past."[77] The Egyptian *Book of the Dead*, with its sayings to accompany the dead into the hereafter, is an important document of the psychological-religious treatment of the sun symbol. The belief in the possibility of renewal is expressed, for example, in the couplet found in dictum 115: "He who looks to the sun is embraced by the essence of darkness."[78]

INTERCULTURAL MEMORY AND GOETHE'S "WORLD THEATER" IN *FAUST SONNENGESANG*

The allusiveness of Fritsch's work is related to the importance of the concept of cultural memory in his aesthetics. In the *Faust Sonnengesang* project, one comes across multiple references to Goethe, the Egyptian *Book of the Dead*, and Dante's *Divine Comedy*. The manner in which Fritsch evokes the past is poetically suggestive of the concept of cultural memory introduced by German Egyptologists Jan and Aleida Assmann. Crucial in understanding cultural memory as a phenomenon is the distinction between memory and history. The latter concerns an historian's objectivity and the factual reconstruction of the past. Memory aims for collective knowledge from one generation to the next, rendering it possible for later generations to reconstruct their cultural identity.[79] Fritsch's poetic concepts can be connected with the Assmanns' concern with "structural anamnesis" or "culture as a space of reflection."[80] These concepts were already established in the ancient Greek images of the muses. The Assmanns write, "Culture owes to memory the ability to construct a world with meaning, which is accessible to the individual and society through consciousness. [Memory acts] through the capability of remembrance of the meaningful, and forgetting of the contingencies of day-to-day life."[81] To be sure, Fritsch also finds importance in the written traditions of culture in texts and images (as in the esteem afforded Egyptian hieroglyphs), yet it is the intuitive, oral tradition of memory practices which motivates his concept of the moment and his understanding of the epiphanies of memory. In looking at Fritsch, we see examples of the topoi of the Assmanns' "imagery of memory," the temporal metaphors, such as awakening and waking, and especially the fire, light, and lightning imagery of "suddenly accessible recognition."[82] Fritsch's project aims to collect selectively the moments of happiness of human knowledge and experience. At the same time his poetic project echoes cultural studies related to what Aleida Assmann considers the "crisis of cultural memory," even though in the end she does not believe that "electronic media and their potential of distraction" can completely drive out the human capacity for "deliberateness" ("*Besonnenheit*").[83] It is precisely this hope that Fritsch wants to bring to life in his utopian *Faust Sonnengesang* project.

The concepts of "world theater" or "world poetry," redolent of Goethe's *Faust,* are also pertinent to Fritsch's project. The concept of the world poem is present in Fritsch's project outline for his *Faust* film: "In a time-dissolving span of three hours, an attempt will be made—ideally on three separate picture-levels— to create a kind of world poem."[84] The Goethean "world theater" is characterized as a "[c]osmos of the theater, of theatrical forms, of theatrical genres, and also of theatrical transformation."[85] It could be that Fritsch's *Faust Sonnengesang* aims to be included in the idea of Goethe's "world poem," which is introduced in the "Prelude in the Theater" ("Vorspiel auf dem Theater"): "So in this narrow house of boarded space / Creation fullest circle go to pace" ("So schreitet in dem engen Bretterhaus / Den ganzen Kreis der Schöpfung aus") (*F*, 239–40).[86]

Interpretations of Goethe's *Faust* as a "world poem" of the same rank as the *Divine Comedy* span from the work of Romanist Karl Vossler all the way to Ulrich Gaier's *Faust* commentary.[87] It is noteworthy that the earlier interpretations emphasize the "intertextually constructed topography" of Goethe's *Faust*, based on the Dantean model.[88] It is precisely this merging of the two works that we also find in Fritsch's *Faust Sonnengesang*, inspired by his concept of an arklike archive of thoughts and dreams.

THE *FAUST SONNENGESANG* FILM

The *Faust Sonnengesang* film is a fusion of the stage project and the vast material from Fritsch's filming of *Sonnengesang* over the last ten years.[89] Similarly to the theatrical text and the stage directions of the play, the images from Fritsch's "film poem" serve to round out the theatrical "picture cave" aesthetics. In the film, the "global archive" of scenes from Faust's itinerary through a number of countries on all five continents now becomes more universal. Intercultural encounters on a mythological-cultural level include—besides the reminiscences of Greek mythology and the Egyptian cultural symbols already discussed in the play—the Norse myth of the world tree Yggdrasil, the nature myths of South Pacific cultures, a Mexican All Saints procession, and a multitude of references to Asian (Buddhist, Taoist) spirituality, just to name a few. In one sequence, there is an encounter of the Polynesian goddess Marama and the Egyptian god Ra. The film is a road movie with almost psychedelic qualities created by alienating images which are hallucinatory in nature (the aesthetic is achieved by Fritsch's preference for the gently cracked image and its light effects). It is obvious that the experimental film allows Fritsch to oscillate between places of his travels, mythologies, religions, and documents of a broad literary-cultural heritage. In one sequence, Kuan Yin, Buddhist bodhisattva of mercy, addresses Faust with the following lines, which emphasize Fritsch's belief in the interrelatedness of Eastern and Western spirituality:

> Know that East
> And West are interchangeable
>
> (Wissen daß Osten
> Und Westen vertauschbar sind)[90]

Originally Fritsch had planned the figure of the tryptichon for the film just as in the theatrical script. The idea was that on the right side of the screen the oldest images of humanity could be seen, while on the left we are presented with contemporary scenes from the various continents. This concept has been changed in most parts of the film because of technological considerations (it has been maintained in eight minutes of the Walpurgis Night scene toward the end of the film). Instead, Fritsch suggests leaps in time through the overlapping of his film material and voices from off. An example of this is the Shanghai sequence showing the modern metropolis, which is highlighted in the film by Chinese song.[91] Fritsch finds the ambiguity of mythological and deliberately chosen contemporary figures to be important. For example, Kuan Yin appears in the beginning as an old woman in the Himalayas, then as another old woman at the prayer wheel, and she finally metamorphoses into the Asian muse.

In any case, it is the filmic medium which serves the sensory complexity of Fritsch's "dream labyrinth" of magical moments.[92] At one point Faust delivers the poetics of Fritsch's film project when he remarks,

> In this dream
> The sun turns to a hieroglyph
> The light to script
> I wield the camera
> Like a Faust-wedge
> Which connects the oldest symbols
> To those of the present
>
> (In diesem Traum
> Wird die Sonne zur Hieroglyphe
> Das Licht zur Schrift
> Ich handhabe die Kamera
> Wie einen Faust-Keil
> Der die ältesten Zeichen
> Mit denen der Gegenwart verbindet)[93]

The film is based not only on visual effects, though. It also assimilates readings of historical texts from Taoist philosophy to one of the two oldest documents of Old High German epic poetry, the *Muspilli* text, which Fritsch, in turn, also "translates into the Now," imbuing it with his own lyricism. In the film, this is borne by the unmistakable voice of the actor Ulrich Matthes. Other voices in the highly lyrical screenplay belong to Corinna Harfouch and Angela Winkler. It should be mentioned briefly that the "actors" in the film are mainly Fritsch himself (as Faust), and, furthermore, his friends and his daughters.

Critics have qualified Fritsch's film as a synthesis of theater, radio play, film, and poetry. Together with the musical accompaniment one can speak of the highly dense *Gesamtkunstwerk* which the film envisages.[94] Similarly, Wolfgang Höbel praises the return of the auteurist avant-garde film and the "motley, dazzling, many-voiced chorus of images."[95]

A more detailed analysis of this most recent, and I would venture, most radical "translation" of Goethe's *Faust* into the Now cannot be given here. My last observations deal, however, with the question of the transparency of the Goethean subtext in the film. Similar to the theater script, the allusions to the Goethean "fulfilled moment" are numerous and certainly recognizable for the educated audience of the educational Bayerischer Rundfunk-alpha channel. Some words of Faust in the film are literally the same as in the play, as, for example, in the solitary meditation of "Faust perched on a rock" (this is, of course, a reference to Walther von der Vogelweide's poem "Sitting on a Stone"). This scene and many others hint at Faust's introspection, which is in Fritsch's "translation" a utopia of magical moments and spiritual regeneration. There is also a further development of the role of Mephisto in the film as compared to the play. Mephisto (who appears in the costume of the Gründgens production in a series of momentary glimpses) has a powerful performance in a sequence entitled "Everything Burns" which alludes to fire metaphors and the "burning" of traumatic memories of mankind. After that he disappears and is replaced by the female Mephista figures (taken from various mythological and religious traditions) who guide Faust on his spiritual journey—emphasizing the Goethean idea of the Eternal-Feminine ("das Ewig-Weibliche").

Perhaps the monumental three-hour spiritual journey in the film is the most Faustian element of Fritsch's enterprise after all. The film concludes with a reference to the idea of the "last film"—a retrospective of fulfilled moments in the moment of death:

> In the darkroom of the perfect
> This film of this life is
> Cut from death
> Mature ecstasies of the Now
> Projected in the cinema
> Beneath my cranium
> Echoes from the Garden of Eden
> Rain on the soundtrack
>
> (In der Dunkelkammer des Perfekts
> Wird der Film dieses Lebens
> Geschnitten vom Tod
> Entwickelte Ekstasen des Jetzt
> Projiziert im Kino
> Unter meiner Schädeldecke
> Echos aus dem Garten Eden
> Auf der Tonspur Regen)[96]

OPENING THE FIST: A "TRANSLATION" OF GOETHE'S *FAUST* THROUGH AVANT-GARDE CONCEPTS OF INTERCULTURAL MEMORY

To conclude, I would like to return to Fritsch's comprehensive project of the "Theater of the Now" and his *Faust* "translation" into the Now. In *Die Alchemie der Utopie*, which outlines the poetics of his entire Faust project, Fritsch

Figure 3. Still from the film *Faust Sonnengesang* (November 12, 2009). By permission of Werner Fritsch Filmproduktion.

speaks of a Faust figure who is able to establish "an empathic counterforce" that "affects the world from Germany," even causing a "compensation" for the catastrophes of the Hitler era.[97] He speaks further of a "globally empathic communication of thoughts" which he hopes to gain from the *Faust Sonnengesang* project.[98] Fritsch uses the beautiful metaphor of the "Faust" opening up, where "Faust" is the German for "fist": "From a visual as well as a literal perspective: Faust, the German myth itself, means a clenched fist. FAUST SONG OF THE SUN is an attempt to open this hand and, starting with our German culture, to make contact with all five continents, without denying its roots."[99]A connection can be drawn between Fritsch's utopian "Theater of the Now," which is a collection of world knowledge, and Goethe's hope that "general humanness is being advanced [in the writings of] writers of all nations."[100] Fritsch's *Faust* "translation" *Faust Sonnengesang* thus participates in the tendency to interpret *Faust*, according to Goethe's concept of "world literature," as less a "German" than a "world" text.

Fritsch's new work does not come without this intellectual pathos. The culturally critical goals and avant-gardist poetic concepts of the author are aimed at the creation of the most unusual "translation" of the Faust theme in contemporary literature, and this according to an international benchmark. The *Faust Sonnengesang* project contains a radical vision of a "cosmopolitan" Faustian explorer of the dreams of humanity, but eventually, as can be seen from some of the statements of the author, it is still closely connected to the historical consciousness of a German writer.

In a way, Fritsch varies the Faust theme with an approach following and transcending Goethe. He replaces the Goethean vocabulary of the "Deed"—"In the beginning was the Deed" ("im Anfang war die Tat") (*F*, 1237)—with the "Word," pointing here most seriously to the power of poetic enunciation, which authenticates an opening up of the meaning of human existence in the present and past. On the other hand, as I have shown in this chapter, Fritsch's "translation" of *Faust* also opens up levels of meaning of the Goethean *Faust* unlike that attempted by any other author. I am speaking of his interest in the motif of the moment in Goethe's *Faust* and his inspiration by the form of the "world poem."

I find it to be an especially noteworthy result of Fritsch's bold interpretation of *Faust* that multiple media are the means of realizing a poetics of "cultural memory," or more specifically "culture as a space of reflection." The utopian dream of *Faust Sonnengesang* is the requirement for this kind of multimedia performance, something which also includes the three-hour film and its multilayered audiovisual effects. Remarkably, this new reflection on Goethe's *Faust* in light of intercultural memory arises from the midst of contemporary German culture and its multiple interfaces. Goethe's *Faust* is very much alive in its homeland.

NOTES

1. Wolfgang Höbel, "Vorletztes Gericht in Manila," in Werner Fritsch, *Chroma. Eulen: Spiegel - Farbenlehre für Chamäleons. Deutsche Geschichte* (Frankfurt: Suhrkamp, 2002), 173.
2. Werner Fritsch, *Die Alchemie der Utopie: Frankfurter Poetikvorlesungen 2009* (Frankfurt: Suhrkamp, 2009), 113.
3. Werner Fritsch in Stephanie Junge, "Der letzte Film. Werner Fritsch im Gespräch mit Stephanie Junge," in *Chroma. Eulen: Spiegel - Farbenlehre für Chamäleons*, 180.
4. Fritsch, *Die Alchemie der Utopie*, 114.
5. Fritsch, *Die Alchemie der Utopie*, 169.
6. The term "poetic utopianism" as it is used with regard to Fritsch's writing, particularly his *Faust Sonnengesang* project, does not imply a theoretical framework of utopian discourse, such as Marxism. Rather, Fritsch's utopian counter-vision stems from purely aesthetic concepts. Fritsch's emphasis on the momentary visions of the "divinely" inspired poet and his belief in the quasi-religious mind-changing power of the poetic word can be related to a number of literary traditions—from mystical revelations such as those of Jacob Böhme (which were influential for the early German Romantics) to modernist and surrealistic writing.
7. I have known Werner Fritsch since February 2007 when he visited New Zealand. Fritsch was very helpful in supplying me with unpublished texts such as the script for the planned performance of the play *Faust. Im Anfang ist das Wort*, which is part of the *Sonnengesang* project. He also provided some project sketches in English

translation, and we had longer discussions of his project during my stay in Berlin from September to December 2009. The English project sketch "Faust Song of the Sun - A Multi Media Installation" contains translations from the chapter "Faust Sonnengesang" in *Die Alchemie der Utopie*, 169–90. Almost all texts from Fritsch's plays, as well as this entire chapter, have been translated from the German by Timothy Dail, Ph.D. student in the German Program at the University of Canterbury.

8. Fritsch, *Die Alchemie der Utopie*, 169.

9. Fritsch, *Die Alchemie der Utopie*, 175.

10. I refer mainly to Aleida Assmann and Dietrich Harth, eds., *Mnemosyne: Formen und Funktionen der kulturellen Erinnerung* (Frankfurt: Fischer, 1991); Aleida Assmann, *Erinnerungsräume. Formen und Wandlungen des kulturellen Gedächtnisses* (Munich: Beck, 2006); Aleida and Jan Assmann and Christof Hardmeier, eds., *Schrift und Gedächtnis. Beiträge zur Archäologie der literarischen Kommunikation* (Munich: Wilhelm Fink, 1983).

11. Fritsch, *Die Alchemie der Utopie*, 174.

12. Fritsch, *Die Alchemie der Utopie*, 173.

13. Fritsch, *Die Alchemie der Utopie*, 177.

14. See Stefan Pokroppa, *Sprache jenseits von Sprache. Textanalysen zu Werner Fritschs Steinbruch, Fleischwolf, Cherubim und Chroma* (Bielefeld: Aisthesis, 2003), 83.

15. Peter Werres, "The Changing Faces of Dr. Faustus," in *Lives of Faust: The Faust Theme in Literature and Music. A Reader*, ed. Lorna Fitzsimmons (Berlin and New York: Walter de Gruyter, 2008), 2.

16. Fritsch, "Das Mephisto-Jahrhundert," in *Chroma. Eulen: Spiegel - Farbenlehre für Chamäleons*, 163.

17. Although Höbel ("Vorletztes Gericht in Manila," 174) claims that the libretto has little in common with *Chroma* other than the main character, one can date Fritsch's earliest preoccupations with the "Gründgens-Faust" material to 1995. See Fritsch, *Die Alchemie der Utopie*, 169.

18. Fritsch, *Die Alchemie der Utopie*, 169.

19. Lisa Marie Küssner, *Sprach-Bilder versus Theater-Bilder. Möglichkeiten eines szenischen Umgangs mit den 'Bilderwelten' von Werner Fritsch* (Marburg: Tectum, 2006), 7.

20. Fritsch, *Die Alchemie der Utopie*, 42.

21. Höbel, "Vorletztes Gericht in Manila," 175.

22. Pokroppa, *Sprache jenseits von Sprache*, 116; Höbel, "Vorletztes Gericht in Manila," 175.

23. Fritsch, *Die Alchemie der Utopie*, 15.

24. Fritsch, *Die Alchemie der Utopie*, 54.

25. Fritsch, *Die Alchemie der Utopie*, 41.

26. Fritsch, *Die Alchemie der Utopie*, 153.

27. See Klaus Dermutz, "Umschmelzungen gesprengter Fragmente – Zu einigen Motiven im Werk von Werner Fritsch," in Werner Fritsch, *Hieroglyphen des Jetzt. Materialien und Werkstattberichte*, ed. Hans-Jürgen Drescher and Bert Scharpenberg (Frankfurt: Suhrkamp, 2002), 45.

28. Anna Opel, *Sprachkörper. Zur Relation von Sprache und Körper in der zeitgenössischen Dramatik – Werner Fritsch, Rainald Goetz, Sarah Kane* (Bielefeld: Aisthesis, 2002), 9.

29. Pokroppa, *Sprache jenseits von Sprache*, 7.

30. See Opel, *Sprachkörper*, 33.

31. In order to comprehend *Chroma* in detail one must consider the production by the Darmstädter Staatstheater with the congenial director Krupa. See Pokroppa's discussion of this rather true-to-work production in *Sprache jenseits von Sprache*, 93. I have seen a performance in New Zealand in February 2007, directed by Peter Falkenberg and performed by the actors of the University of Canterbury's Free Theatre, with the author present. Falkenberg's translations of parts of the *Chroma* script into English are used for this chapter.

32. Fritsch, *Chroma*, in *Chroma. Eulen: Spiegel - Farbenlehre für Chamäleons*, 45.

33. Fritsch, *Chroma*, in *Chroma*, 32.

34. Fritsch, *Chroma*, in *Chroma*, 59.

35. Fritsch, *Chroma*, in *Chroma*, 17.

36. Johann Wolfgang von Goethe, *Faust: Texte*, vol. 7, pt. 1, *Sämtliche Werke. Briefe, Tagebücher und Gespräche*, ed. Albrecht Schöne (Frankfurt: Deutscher Klassiker Verlag, 1994). Quotations from this edition appear in the text abbreviated as *F*. The English translation used is *Faust. A Tragedy*, trans. Walter Arndt, ed. Cyrus Hamlin (New York: W. W. Norton, 1976).

37. Pokroppa, *Sprache jenseits von Sprache*, 111.

38. Pokroppa, *Sprache jenseits von Sprache*, 111.

39. Fritsch in Markus Mayer, "Sense & Sound. Werner Fritsch im Gespräch mit Markus Mayer," in *Chroma. Eulen: Spiegel - Farbenlehre für Chamäleons*, 186.

40. See Horst Hartmann, *Faustgestalt. Faustsage. Faustdichtung* (Aachen: Shaker, 1998), 110.

41. See Pokroppa, *Sprache jenseits von Sprache*, 105.

42. Fritsch, *Chroma*, in *Chroma*, 67.

43. Fritsch in Junge, "Der letzte Film," 180.

44. Fritsch in Junge, "Der letzte Film," 180.

45. The distinction between the "written," "ritualized" forms of rendering memory ("*Schrift*") and "oral" forms of memory practices ("*Gedächtnis*") is at the center of the research of Alcida and Jan Assmann. See later in this chapter references to Aleida and Jan Assmann, "Schrift und Gedächtnis," in *Schrift und Gedächtnis*, 265–84.

46. Fritsch, *Die Alchemie der Utopie*, 65.

47. See Albrecht Schöne, ed., *Faust: Kommentare*, vol. 7, pt. 2, Johann Wolfgang von Goethe, *Sämtliche Werke. Briefe, Tagebücher und Gespräche* (Frankfurt: Deutscher Klassiker Verlag, 1999), 479.

48. Schöne, *Faust: Kommentare*, 478.

49. Alan Corkhill, "'Why all this noise?': Reading Sound in Goethe's *Faust I* and *II*," in *International Faust Studies: Adaptation, Reception, Translation*, ed. Lorna Fitzsimmons (London and New York: Continuum, 2008), 66; Bree Hadley, "Reality Just Arrived—Mark Ravenhill's *Faust Is Dead*," in *International Faust Studies*, 267–68.

50. For the following discussion of the multimedia performance of the *Faust Sonnengesang* project, I have focused on the material from the script, the stage directions, and the project sketches that have been provided to me, as well as information on the film project.

51. The *Im Anfang ist das Wort* play was performed as a scenic reading at the Theatre Gütersloh on the occasion of the festival *Wege durch das Land* on May 29, 2010.

52. Fritsch, *Die Alchemie der Utopie*, 178. For the concept of "human dreams of happiness," see note 12.

53. Werner Fritsch, "Faust. Im Anfang ist das Wort," 1.

54. Fritsch, "Faust. Im Anfang ist das Wort," 2.

55. Fritsch, *Die Alchemie der Utopie*, 177.

56. See interview with Wolfgang Habermeyer, "Werner Fritsch, Autor und Regisseur, im Gespräch mit Dr. Wolfgang Habermeyer," July 28, 2008, http://www.br-online.de/content/cms/Universalseite/2008/06/10/cumulus/BR-online-Publikation--141943-20080610131234.pdf (accessed June 12, 2010). Further information was provided by Werner Fritsch in March 2010.

57. After the broadcast on Bayerischer Rundfunk on January 6, 2011, reviews included Thomas Irmer, "Ein Mutakt des Fernsehens. Das Filmgedicht *Faust Sonnengesang* von Werner Fritsch bei BR-alpha," January 21, 2011, http://funkkorrespondenz.kim-info.de/print.php?kat=ARTIKEL&nr=8426 (accessed May 20, 2011); Wolfgang Höbel, "Furioses Fernsehexperiment: Faust hebt ab," January 14, 2011, http://www.spiegel.de/kultur/tv/0,1518,druck-738062,00.html (accessed September 22, 2011).

58. Fritsch, "Faust. Im Anfang ist das Wort," 33.

59. Fritsch, "Faust. Im Anfang ist das Wort," 8.

60. Fritsch, "Faust. Im Anfang ist das Wort," 36.

61. See also "Werner Fritsch: 'Sonnentanz' (2009)," http://www.youtube.com/watch?v=PmzZRBnSy9s (accessed October 4, 2011).

62. "Faust. Im Anfang ist das Wort," 21.

63. "Faust. Im Anfang ist das Wort," 41.

64. "Faust. Im Anfang ist das Wort," 37.

65. Karl Heinz Bohrer investigates this concept mainly with regard to twentieth-century world literature in *Ekstasen der Zeit. Augenblick, Gegenwart, Erinnerung* (Munich: Hanser, 2008). The term is also used by Fritsch, *Die Alchemie der Utopie*, 172.

66. Fritsch, "Faust. Im Anfang ist das Wort," 5.

67. Fritsch, "Faust. Im Anfang ist das Wort," 5.

68. Fritsch, "Faust. Im Anfang ist das Wort," 6.

69. Schöne, *Faust: Kommentare*, 212.

70. David Hawkes, *The Faust Myth: Religion and the Rise of Representation* (New York: Palgrave Macmillan, 2007), 7.

71. For this interpretation of Faust's final words, see also Schöne, *Faust: Kommentare*, 752.

72. I touch upon Goethe's symbolism of the moment in my *Die Augenblicksmetapher. Über Bildlichkeit und Spontaneität in der Lyrik* (Munich: Hanser, 1981), 57–77, and "Augenblick" and "Stunde" in *Metzler Lexikon literarischer Symbole*, ed. Günter Butzer and Joachim Jacob (Stuttgart: Metzler, 2008), 30–31, 373–75. In his comprehensive study of the concept of the moment in Goethe's complete works, Andreas Anglet investigates in detail the motifs of the "eternal" moment in *Faust I and II* and comes to the conclusion, "Faust's partial search for redemption is determined by the concept of the 'eternal' moment," *Der 'ewige' Augenblick: Studien zur Struktur und Funktion eines Denkbilds bei Goethe* (Cologne: Böhlau, 1991), 192.

73. See Schöne, *Faust: Kommentare*, 612.

74. Corkhill, "'Why all this noise?'" 57.

75. Corkhill, "'Why all this noise?'" 56.

76. Fritsch, *Die Alchemie der Utopie*, 176.

77. Fritsch, "Faust Song of the Sun: The Film" (Project Outline, 2009).

78. *Das Totenbuch der Ägypter*, trans. and ed. Erik Hornung (Zurich and Munich: Artemis, 1979), 26.

79. See Jan Assmann, *Das kulturelle Gedächtnis. Schrift, Erinnerung und politische Identität in frühen Hochkulturen* (Munich: Beck, 1992).

80. Assmanns, "Schrift und Gedächtnis," 266.

81. Assmanns, "Schrift und Gedächtnis," 267.

82. Aleida Assmann, "Zur Metaphorik der Erinnerung," in *Mnemosyne*, 22.

83. Aleida Assmann, *Erinnerungsräume*, 412–13.

84. Fritsch, "Faust Song of the Sun: The Film."

85. Klaus Manger, "Goethes Welttheater," in *Goethe und die Weltkultur*, ed. Klaus Manger (Heidelberg: Winter, 2003), 365.

86. See Manger, "Goethes Welttheater," 379.

87. See Stefan Matuschek, "Weltgedicht und Weltliteratur," in *Goethe und die Weltkultur*, 391–402.

88. Matuschek, "Weltgedicht und Weltliteratur," 394.

89. In addition to the broadcast on Bayerischer Rundfunk on January 6, 1011, the film was shown at the ARD Hörspieltage in the ZKM [Zentrum für Kunst und Medientechnologie] Media Theater on November 11, 2011.

90. Werner Fritsch, "Faust Sonnengesang. Ein Filmgedicht" (Faust song of the sun. A filmic poem) (Screenplay, 2010), 24.

91. A segment of this sequence under the title "Werner Fritsch: '*Shanghai: All Gates open* [*sic*], June 11, 2010'" is available online, http://www.youtube.com/watch?v=x7xTMIx3jAg (accessed September 28, 2011).

92. One can get an idea of the avant-gardist film techniques of the author by looking at the older "dream film" *Labyrinth*, which contains scenes of everyday life and images of nature, as well as archetypal symbolism.

93. Fitsch, "Faust Sonnengesang. Ein Filmgedicht," 18.

94. Irmer, "Ein Mutakt des Fernsehens."

95. Höbel, "Furioses Fernsehexperiment."

96. Fritsch, "Faust Sonnengesang. Ein Filmgedicht," 34.

97. Fritsch, *Die Alchemie der Utopie*, 185.

98. Fritsch, *Die Alchemie der Utopie*, 186.

99. Fritsch, *Die Alchemie der Utopie*, 173. With his "hand" metaphor, Fritsch comes close to an East Asian interpretation of the Faust tradition by Adrian Hsia. Hsia suggests that, according to Taoist or Confucianist principles and their beliefs in the cycles of nature, "Faust" should be renamed "Hand": "This East Asian Faust or rather, 'Hand,' would absolutely be a contemporary, universal figure of the post-Faustian world." Adrian Hsia, "Einführung oder Konstruktion einer 'anderen' Faust-Gestalt," in *Zur Rezeption von Goethes "Faust" in Ostasian*, ed. Adrian Hsia (Bern: Peter Lang, 1993), 20.

100. Thesis at the meeting of scientists in Berlin 1828, Schöne, *Faust: Kommentare*, 35.

BIBLIOGRAPHY

Anglet, Andreas. *Der 'ewige' Augenblick: Studien zur Struktur und Funktion eines Denkbilds bei Goethe*. Cologne: Böhlau, 1991.

Assmann, Aleida. *Erinnerungsräume. Formen und Wandlungen des kulturellen Gedächtnisses*. Munich: Beck, 2006.

——. "Zur Metaphorik der Erinnerung." In *Mnemosyne: Formen und Funktionen der kulturellen Erinnerung*, edited by Aleida Assmann and Dietrich Harth, 13–35. Frankfurt: Fischer, 1991.

Assmann, Aleida, and Jan Assmann. "Schrift und Gedächtnis." In *Schrift und Gedächtnis. Beiträge zur Archäologie der literarischen Kommunikation*, edited by Aleida Assmann, Jan Assmann, and Christof Hardmeier, 265–84. Munich: Wilhelm Fink, 1983.

Assmann, Jan. *Das kulturelle Gedächtnis. Schrift, Erinnerung und politische Identität in frühen Hochkulturen*. Munich: Beck, 1992.

Bohrer, Karl Heinz. *Ekstasen der Zeit. Augenblick, Gegenwart, Erinnerung*. Munich: Hanser, 2008.

Corkhill, Alan. "'Why all this noise?': Reading Sound in Goethe's *Faust I* and *II*." In Fitzsimmons, *International Faust Studies*, 55–69.

Dermutz, Klaus. "Umschmelzungen gesprengter Fragmente – Zu einigen Motiven im Werk von Werner Fritsch." In Fritsch, *Hieroglyphen des Jetzt. Materialien und Werkstattberichte*, 40–51.

Fitzsimmons, Lorna, ed. *International Faust Studies: Adaptation, Reception, Translation*. London and New York: Continuum, 2008.

Fritsch, Werner. *Die Alchemie der Utopie: Frankfurter Poetikvorlesungen 2009*. Frankfurt: Suhrkamp, 2009.

——. *Chroma. Eulen: Spiegel - Farbenlehre für Chamäleons. Deutsche Geschichte*. Frankfurt: Suhrkamp, 2002.

——. Faust. Im Anfang ist das Wort. Ein Stück aus Augenblicken und Träumen (Stage Text, 2009).

——. Faust Song of the Sun - A Multimedia Installation (Project Outline, 2009).

——. Faust Song of the Sun: The Film (Project Outline, 2009).

——. Faust Sonnengesang. Ein Filmgedicht (Screenplay, 2010).

——, dir. *Faust Sonnengesang. Filmgedicht von Werner Fritsch* (DVD). Werner Fritsch Filmproduktion, 2010.

——. *Hieroglyphen des Jetzt. Materialien und Werkstattberichte*. Edited by Hans-Jürgen Drescher and Bert Scharpenberg. Frankfurt: Suhrkamp, 2002.

——. "Werner Fritsch: '*Shanghai: All Gates open* [*sic*], June 11, 2010.'" http://www.youtube.com/watch?v=x7xTMIx3jAg (accessed September 28, 2011).

——. "Werner Fritsch: 'Sonnentanz' (2009)." http://www.youtube.com/watch?v=PmzZRBnSy9s (accessed October 4, 2011).

Goethe, Johann Wolfgang von. *Faust. A Tragedy*. Translated by Walter Arndt. Edited by Cyrus Hamlin. New York: W. W. Norton, 1976.

——. *Faust: Texte*. Vol. 7, pt. 1, *Sämtliche Werke. Briefe, Tagebücher und Gespräche*, edited by Albrecht Schöne. Frankfurt: Deutscher Klassiker Verlag, 1994.

Habermeyer, Wolfgang. "Werner Fritsch, Autor und Regisseur, im Gespräch mit Dr. Wolfgang Habermeyer." July 28, 2008. http://www.br-online.de/

content/cms/Universalseite/2008/06/10/cumulus/BR-online-Publikation--141943 -20080610131234.pdf (accessed June 12, 2010).

Hadley, Bree. "Reality Just Arrived—Mark Ravenhill's *Faust Is Dead*." In Fitzsimmons, *International Faust Studies*, 259–75.

Hartmann, Horst. *Faustgestalt. Faustsage. Faustdichtung*. Aachen: Shaker, 1998.

Hawkes, David. *The Faust Myth: Religion and the Rise of Representation*. New York: Palgrave Macmillan, 2007.

Höbel, Wolfgang. "Furioses Fernsehexperiment: Faust hebt ab." January 14, 2011. http://www.spiegel.de/kultur/tv/0,1518,druck-738062,00.html (accessed September 22, 2011).

———. "Vorletztes Gericht in Manila." In Fritsch, *Chroma. Eulen: Spiegel - Farbenlehre für Chamäleons*, 171–78.

Hornung, Erik, trans. and ed. *Das Totenbuch der Ägypter*. Zurich and Munich: Artemis, 1979.

Hsia, Adrian. "Einführung oder Konstruktion einer 'anderen' Faust-Gestalt." In *Zur Rezeption von Goethes "Faust" in Ostasian*, edited by Adrian Hsia, 15–20. Bern: Peter Lang, 1993.

Irmer, Thomas. "Ein Mutakt des Fernsehens. Das Filmgedicht *Faust Sonnengesang* von Werner Fritsch bei BR-alpha." January 21, 2011. http://funkkorrespondenz .kim-info.de/print.php?kat=ARTIKEL&nr=8426 (accessed May 20, 2011).

Junge, Stephanie. "Der letzte Film. Werner Fritsch im Gespräch mit Stephanie Junge." In Fritsch, *Chroma. Eulen: Spiegel - Farbenlehre für Chamäleons*, 179–80.

Küssner, Lisa Marie. *Sprach-Bilder versus Theater-Bilder. Möglichkeiten eines szenischen Umgangs mit den 'Bilderwelten' von Werner Fritsch*. Marburg: Tectum, 2006.

Ledanff, Susanne. "Augenblick" and "Stunde." In *Metzler Lexikon literarische Symbole*, edited by Günter Butzer and Joachim Jacob, 30–31, 373–75. Stuttgart: Metzler, 2008.

———. *Die Augenblicksmetapher. Über Bildlichkeit und Spontaneität in der Lyrik*. Munich: Hanser, 1981.

Manger, Klaus. "Goethes Welttheater." In *Goethe und die Weltkultur*, edited by Klaus Manger, 365–90. Heidelberg: Winter, 2003.

Matuschek, Stefan. "Weltgedicht und Weltliteratur." In Manger, *Goethe und die Weltkultur*, 391–402.

Mayer, Markus. "Sense & Sound. Werner Fritsch im Gespräch mit Markus Mayer." In Fritsch, *Chroma. Eulen: Spiegel - Farbenlehre für Chamäleons*, 184–95.

Opel, Anna. *Sprachkörper. Zur Relation von Sprache und Körper in der zeitgenössischen Dramatik – Werner Fritsch, Rainald Goetz, Sarah Kane*. Bielefeld: Aisthesis, 2002.

Pokroppa, Stefan. *Sprache jenseits von Sprache. Textanalysen zu Werner Fritschs Steinbruch, Fleischwolf, Cherubim und Chroma*. Bielefeld: Aisthesis, 2003.

Schöne, Albrecht, ed. *Kommentare: Faust*. Vol. 7, pt. 2, Johann Wolfgang von Goethe, *Sämtliche Werke. Briefe, Tagebücher und Gespräche*. Frankfurt: Deutscher Klassiker Verlag, 1999.

Werres, Peter. "The Changing Faces of Dr. Faustus." In *Lives of Faust. The Faust Theme in Literature and Music. A Reader*, edited by Lorna Fitzsimmons, 1–18. Berlin and New York: Walter de Gruyter, 2008.

9

Homunculus' Quest for a Body

Bruce J. MacLennan

Goethe's *Faust* strikes resonant chords in any thoughtful modern person, but for those of us employed in Faustian endeavors, it is difficult not to take the drama personally. Therefore, at the risk of adding to the numerous subjective interpretations of *Faust*, in this chapter I will explore some of its intimations and implications for several Faustian technologies with which I am involved: artificial intelligence, autonomous robotics, artificial life, and artificial morphogenesis. *Faust* has relevance to science and technology beyond these specific disciplines, of course, but they are beyond the scope of this chapter. First, however, it is necessary to define these technological pursuits and their goals.

Artificial intelligence (*AI*) is perhaps best known; it seeks to design artificial systems that have a behavior that would be called intelligent if exhibited by humans.[1] Much current research is devoted to relatively specific behaviors, such as recognizing faces, controlling vehicles, and scanning images or text for patterns of interest. This is largely an engineering activity, and greater insight into natural (human and animal) intelligence is neither an explicit goal nor an inevitable result. Nevertheless, research continues in *artificial general intelligence* (*AGI*), which refers to the creation of an artificial intelligence comparable to human intelligence in scope, flexibility, and generality.[2] Although we are still many years from developing an AGI, even the possibility raises questions in the philosophy of mind, such as whether such an artificial intelligence could or would exhibit consciousness or free will. Our inability to give clear, defensible answers to such questions reveals gaps and aporia in contemporary philosophy and psychology.[3]

Autonomous robotics is an active research area. Literally, an autonomous robot would be self-governing (*autos* + *nomos*), a law unto itself,[4] but in common usage the autonomy of a robot may be limited to its ability to operate without direct human control. In this context, "Autonomy refers to systems capable of operating in the real-world environment without any form of external control for extended periods of time."[5] The longer-range goal is to develop robots that are truly autonomous, able to take care of themselves, to pursue their own goals, and, to this end, to be able to co-operate with each other or with humans and other animals. Successfully implementing truly autonomous robots would help us to understand our own autonomy.

The discipline of *artificial life* (*alife*) seeks to create "sufficiently life-like" artificial systems out of non-biological materials. In this it may be contrasted with *synthetic biology*, which seeks to re-engineer living matter for technological purposes. Some alife organisms are implemented with robotic technology, but many live in virtual environments that exist in a computer's memory (computer viruses and worms are simple, but all too familiar, examples). Current alife systems are not literally alive, but they display many lifelike attributes, such as reproduction, heritable traits, sensorimotor coordination, decision-making, competition, and cooperation. These lifelike systems allow us to explore the characteristics and boundary conditions of life. Nevertheless, most alife researchers expect that, in the long run, true artificial life will be developed and that this accomplishment will help us to understand the necessary and sufficient conditions of life.

Artificial morphogenesis is a promising approach to nanotechnology.[6] Current nanotechnology focuses on the development of new, nanostructured materials, which, for the most part, are assembled into macroscopic products by conventional manufacturing techniques. Unfortunately, this approach is limited in its ability to assemble complex hierarchical systems with significant structure from the nanoscale up to the macroscale. Organisms display this hierarchical structure, with complex structures at every length scale, and we can anticipate that future autonomous robots and alife systems will have to be similarly structured (see below). Fortunately, nature shows an alternative assembly process in embryological morphogenesis, by which cells proliferate, differentiate, and coordinate their activity to create complex three-dimensional forms. Thus we expect future nanostructured systems to assemble themselves by processes of growth, differentiation, and self-organized motion.[7]

These disciplines—artificial intelligence, autonomous robotics, artificial life, and artificial morphogenesis—merge in the project of developing truly autonomous, intelligent robots able to behave independently and competently in the real world. Our current understanding of intelligence is that it depends on dense, intricately connected neural networks, which cannot be efficiently implemented on conventional digital computers. Conventional manufacturing techniques are unlikely to be able to assemble sufficiently intricate artificial neural networks, and therefore artificial morphogenesis will be required to "grow" (self-assemble) them. Furthermore, the creation of complex sense organs and effectors (such as artificial muscles) will require artificial morphogenesis. Research in autonomous robotics and artificial life will show us how to make these robots cooperate with each other and with us.[8]

Since these technologies promise many benefits, we might go groping blindly forward, like Faust, "foretasting such high happiness to come" ("Im Vorgefühl von solchem hohen Glück") (*F*, 11585), and exclaim, "Abide, you are so fair" ("Verweile doch! du bist so schön!") (*F*, 1700),[9] sealing our fate. The Faustian character of these technologies is apparent; what might we have to bargain away to obtain them? What might machines with more than human intelligence mean for the future of humankind? What are the ethical implications of using autonomous robots in warfare?[10] What are the environmental implications of artificial organisms, which might be microscopic in size? And so on. Aside from their obviously Faustian character, these technological and social issues might seem remote from Goethe's drama, but his deep insights into nature and human nature allowed him to anticipate many of the problems and sometimes their solutions. In particular, Homunculus' quest for a body symbolically prefigures the history of AI in the twentieth century, including the emergence of theories of embodied and situated intelligence, and offers new insights into the relation of mind and matter. Therefore, in this chapter I will limit myself to this issue and leave *Faust*'s broader implications to a book in preparation.

WORDS AND DEEDS

Symbolic AI

The discipline of artificial intelligence arose in the late 1950s, although it has much deeper roots, stretching back through Aristotelian logic into Pythagorean numerology.[11] Its history may be divided into two overlapping phases, *symbolic AI* (also known as *traditional AI* or *GOFAI*, "good old-fashioned AI") and, since the mid-1980s, *connectionist AI*. The latter takes seriously the embodiment of natural intelligence, both in the brain and, as more recently recognized, in a body situated in its physical environment. These developments were impeded by background assumptions about the nature of intelligence that were grounded in European traditions such as rationalism, idealism, Cartesian dualism, and the mechanical philosophy. As a consequence researchers focused on human intelligence (supposedly the only intelligence truly worthy of study) and in particular on the faculties considered most characteristic of human intelligence: language and abstract reason. Symbolic AI gets its name from its focus on "symbols," in this context: words, concepts, and abstract categories.

Symbolic AI is a direct outgrowth of developments in symbolic logic and formalist mathematics in the late nineteenth and early twentieth centuries. For example, in his *Investigation of the Laws of Thought* (1854) George Boole expressed logic in a formal algebraic notation, which is the ancestor of modern symbolic logic as developed by Bertrand Russell, Alfred North Whitehead, and others. Further, in the years leading up to 1900 mathematicians were successful in reducing much of mathematics to a system of axioms from which, in principle, all the truths of mathematics could be deduced by formal inference expressible in symbolic logic. David Hilbert is well known for advocating a *formalist* philosophy of mathematics, in which the truths of mathematics consist entirely in the formal relations among contentless symbolic structures (words, sentences, formulas, etc.). Thus Ludwig Wittgenstein famously remarked, "all propositions of logic say the same thing, to wit nothing" ("Alle Sätze der Logik sagen aber dasselbe. Nämlich nichts"); he called them senseless ("*Sinnlos*"), but not nonsense ("*Unsinn*").[12]

In the early twentieth century philosophers of science, especially those of the Vienna Circle, such as Rudolph Carnap, began to apply symbolic logic to scientific knowledge, thus laying the foundations of *logical positivism* and *logical empiricism*, which dominated the philosophy of science in the first half of the century. In this approach, the structure of knowledge is formal and logical, but the empirical content resides in primitive terms and properties defined in terms of physical measurement. Anything that could not be expressed in these logical-empirical terms was taken to be meaningless or at least nonscientific.

Logical empiricism provided what seemed to be an ideal foundation for artificial intelligence, since it was supposed that any "genuine knowledge" could be expressed in these symbolic structures and that cognition was essentially reasoning, which could be reduced to the mechanical manipulation of formal symbols.[13]

Formal logic and formalist mathematics do not depend on empirical data; they are *purely* formal. Thus, as Wittgenstein observed, the knowledge structures in a purely symbolic AI system are apparently not *about* anything. Stevan Harnad has called this the *symbol grounding problem*: how do the symbols in an AI system—or in our minds, if we suppose they are like a symbolic AI system—get their meanings? One answer is that there is no primary content, and the only meaning resides in the formal (contentless) relationships among "ungrounded" symbols. In the words of the "formalists' motto," widely accepted in AI, "If you take care of the syntax, the semantics will take care of itself."[14] Or as Mephistopheles observes, "Men usually believe, if only there be words, / That there must also be some sort of meaning" ("Gewöhnlich glaubt der Mensch, wenn er nur Worte hört, / Es müsse sich dabei doch auch was denken lassen") (*F*, 2565–66).[15] However, when applied to human cognition this is an unsatisfactory resolution, and Harnad and others have argued that symbols are grounded ultimately in sensory perception. Goethe, too, observed, "How difficult it is . . . to refrain from replacing the thing with its sign, to keep the object alive before us instead of killing it with the word" ("Jedoch wie schwer ist es, das Zeichen nicht an die Stelle der Sache zu setzen, das Wesen immer lebendig vor sich zu haben und es nicht durch das Wort zu töten").[16] This issue brings us back to *Faust.*

Word and Sense

The drama regularly reminds us of the power and limitations of *senseless* discourse. Examples include the familiar parodies of the Schoolmen's logic-chopping and the Humanists' empty rhetoric and pedantic antiquarianism;[17] both are examples where form dominates content. In contrast, Faust understands that meaningful language, significant speech, is grounded in one's inmost understanding.[18] Sometimes the substitution of form for meaning is successful, at least for a time, as in Mephistopheles' institution of fiat money to cure the Emperor's economic woes and his use of illusion to rout the rival emperor.[19] In both cases we have only the appearance of something real, but the appearance is sufficient to the purpose.

Not limited to senseless knowledge structures, however, the problems in symbolic AI also stemmed from formal logical deduction as a model of cognition. Mephistopheles accurately describes the limitations of sequential formal reasoning in his colloquy with the Student in Part I, "Study" ("Studierzimmer II"):

> My friend, I shall be pedagogic,
> And say you ought to start with Logic.
> For thus your mind is trained and braced,
> In Spanish boots it will be laced,
> That on the road of thought maybe
> It henceforth creep more thoughtfully,
> And does not crisscross here and there,
> Will-o'-the-wisping through the air.
>
> (Mein teurer Freund, ich rat' euch drum
> Zuerst Collegium Logicum.
> Da wird der Geist euch wohl dressiert,
> In spanische Stiefeln eingeschnürt,
> Daß er bedächtiger so fort an
> Hinschleiche die Gedankenbahn,

Und nicht etwa, die Kreuz' und Quer,
Irrlichteliere hin und her.) (*F*, 1910–17)[20]

Creeping along the "*Gedankenbahn*" ("road of thought") has proven to be the Achilles' heel of many symbolic AI systems, for the more knowledge in the system, the more the combinations of formulae the reasoning engine must sequentially evaluate. This is called the problem of *combinatorial explosion*, and it defeats even the fastest computers. Early robots were extremely slow, sometimes taking an hour to make a movement, because they used sequential, discursive logic, analysis, and planning to coordinate their behavior, but animals and insects with very simple brains behave competently and quickly in the world. As Mephistopheles recognizes, sometimes we must resort to such tortured methodical and analytical reasoning, but it is inefficient, and in most cases we are better served by holistic embodied behavior:

They teach you for a year or so
That what you did all at one go,
Like eating and drinking, fancy-free,
Needs stages one, and two, and three.

(Dann lehret man euch manchen Tag,
Daß, was ihr sonst auf einen Schlag
Getrieben, wie Essen und Trinken frei,
Eins! Zwei! Drei! dazu nötig sei.) (*F*, 1918–21)[21]

Mephistopheles next uses the metaphor of weaving for thinking, which reminds computer scientists of the Jacquard loom (dating from 1801), which used punched cards to control an automatic weaving machine. Charles Babbage intended to use this technology to control his "analytical engine," perhaps the first automatic computer (under development from 1837 to 1871), and punched card technology continued to dominate automatic data processing through much of the twentieth century. But this is what Mephistopheles says:

Yet the web of thought has no such creases
And is more like a weaver's masterpieces:
One step, a thousand threads arise,
Hither and thither shoots each shuttle,
The threads flow on, unseen and subtle,
Each blow effects a thousand ties.

(Zwar ist's mit der Gedanken-Fabrik
Wie mit einem Weber-Meisterstück,
Wo Ein Tritt tausend Fäden regt,

Die Schifflein herüber hinüber schießen,
Die Fäden ungesehen fließen,
Ein Schlag tausend Verbindungen schlägt.) (*F*, 1922–27)[22]

This does not describe the slow sequential mechanism of a symbolic AI system, but rather the spreading activity in a connectionist neural network (a web of thought), in which thousands of nerve fibers converge on each neuron, which then influences thousands of others, to create a continuous field of activity in the cortical "*Gedanken-Fabrik*" ("thought factory").[23] Thus in his 1937–1938 Gifford Lectures on Natural Religion the pioneer neurophysiologist Sir Charles Sherrington, whose own poetry was inspired by Goethe's, described the brain as "an enchanted loom where millions of flashing shuttles weave a dissolving pattern, always a meaningful pattern though never an abiding one; a shifting harmony of subpatterns."[24]

Logos—Idea—Dynamis—Energeia

Faust's efforts (*F*, 1224–37) at translating logos in the first verse of the Gospel of John are not unprecedented; as Jantz observes, "he was being an excellent classical philologist, solidly traditional and thoroughly grounded in the history of the concept from Heraclitus to St. John."[25] His attempts reflect, according to Jantz, a progressively deeper penetration into the phenomenology of the symbol ("*Wort*"), the comprehension ("*Sinn*") of which gives the Renaissance mage power ("*Kraft*") over nature, which is actualized ("*Tat*") in the magical operation.[26] Faust's successive translations also anticipate the use of computational models in AI and cognitive science, for computing submits a formal symbolic structure (the program) to a mechanical interpreter (the computer) so that, *ex opere operata*, the potential computation is actualized in specific behavior to achieve some end: word, interpretation, power, action.

The semiotician and logical empiricist Charles Morris divided semiotics into *syntax*, *semantics*, and *pragmatics*; the first studies the structure of linguistic forms independently of their meanings, the second studies their relationships to their meanings, and the third addresses the effects of linguistic expressions on interpreters in the context of communicative situations. Formal syntax and semantics have been studied extensively by logicians and, when semantics is grounded in measurement, syntax and semantics correspond to the "logical" and "empirical" parts of logical empiricism. Pragmatics, due to its resistance to mathematical analysis, has been the neglected stepchild.[27]

Following in this tradition, symbolic AI at first adopted the formalists' motto; that is, if the semantic relations are completely encoded by the syntax (formal relations), then, from a formalist perspective, there is no further need to consider semantics. This is ideal from the perspective of symbolic AI, since computers are purely syntactic: the symbols in the computer are meaningless (to the computer); they lack *original intentionality*.[28] Likewise, the computer's "thinking" is purely formal, like formal logic, and depends only on the formal structure of knowledge representations (their syntax), not on their meanings. Similarly, early attempts at machine translation focused on syntax to the exclusion of semantics.

In brief, it was eventually discovered that syntax was insufficient on its own, and that machine translation and other AI applications had to take meaning into account. As Faust recognized, "Wort" ("word," Gk. *logos*) was overvalued until the importance of "Sinn" ("sense," "meaning," Gk. *idea*) was recognized. However, while syntax and semantics may be adequate for disembodied cogitation (itself a debatable supposition),[29] they are pragmatically impotent. Thus Faust anticipates recent work in AI, cognitive science, and philosophy showing that true intelligence is *embodied* and *situated* in a pragmatic background of concerns, purposes, needs, and so on.[30] This corresponds to the last two refinements in Faust's translation: "Kraft" ("force," "power"), which expresses the power of logos as potentiality (Lat. *potentia*, Gk. *dynamis*), and then "Tat" ("deed," "act"), which expresses it as purposeful activity or effect (Lat. *actio*, Gk. *energeia*). AI and cognitive science are following a similar path, from the superficiality of syntax, through disembodied semantics, to pragmatic, goal-directed action in the world: "striving" ("*Streben*"). As for Faust and Mephistopheles, so for AI, Homunculus lights the way toward embodiment (*F*, 6987).

THE LITTLE MAN WITHIN

The Modern Quest for the Homunculus

The economist Hans Christoph Binswanger, with explicit reference to *Faust*, has described the modern economy as "a continuation of alchemy by other means."[31] The same description applies to AI and alife, for they effectively seek to create a homunculus, an artificial mind or person. More generally the goal of alchemy may be described as *the materialization of spirit and the spiritualization of matter*.[32] That is, spirit is to be drawn down into matter at the same time as matter is spiritually elevated. Thus base *prima materia* (symbolized by lead) is purified, ennobled, made incorruptible (symbolized by gold).

In AI the goal is to arrange material processes (e.g., by programming a computer) so that they exhibit genuine intelligence. According to the criteria of *strong AI* (reflected in the well-known Turing Test and ultimately rooted in logical empiricism), if an AI system is behaviorally indistinguishable from a human, then we are scientifically obliged to consider it genuinely intelligent and literally to have a mind.[33] From this perspective, the goal of AGI is to "spiritualize" matter, in the sense of imparting a mind to otherwise mindless matter. Conversely, such an artificial intelligence would accomplish the materialization of spirit by producing mind through material processes.

The goals of artificial life are similar: the animation of matter and the materialization of life. In one sense this has been accomplished already, for the techniques of synthetic biology have been used to assemble two viruses according to their genetic codes.[34] This in vitro creation of life is only a beginning, however, since viruses occupy a gray area between living and nonliving and because organic materials were used as a basis. More generally alife is directed toward the creation of definitely living artifacts from non-biological materials, perhaps within a computer.

Nowadays we commonly distinguish in vivo ("in life") and in vitro ("in glass") experiments, but many scientists now describe three sorts of experiments: in vivo, in vitro, and *in silico* ("in silicon"). The latter refers to *computational science*: the simulation of actual or hypothetical physical systems in a computer. This method has become the indispensable third branch of twenty-first-century science, complementing theory and experiment (whether in vivo or in vitro).

Traditionally alchemy has sought to create the homunculus in a hermetically sealed alchemical vessel (symbolically spherical—a microcosm—or egg-shaped), such as we find Wagner using in the Laboratory of Act II.[35] Synthetic biology still seeks in vitro creation of life, but AI and alife make greater use of in silico methods. In some cases these are mere simulations of intelligence or life, but the more ambitious goal is to make the real thing. However, the fact that a process takes place in silico does not imply that it is a simulation and thus unreal. It's important to keep in mind that computers are physical devices and that computations are physical processes. If a computer (or robot) exhibits genuine intelligence or life, then it is *physically real* intelligence or life.

Some thirty-five years ago I was given a tour of Intel's fabrication facilities. At one place my guide introduced me to a highly skilled technician who was rinsing the silicon wafers in a solution. "She is watching," I was told, "for a sign that not everyone can see, a certain iridescent sheen, which tells her the process is done." "The peacock's tail!" I thought, but didn't say.[36] It is also interesting that the raw material of most semiconductor devices is silica (silicon dioxide, quartz), that is, *sand*, one of the commonest substances on earth; as the alchemists note, "The prima materia has the quality of ubiquity: it can be found always and everywhere."[37] It "is found everywhere, being a stone, and also not a stone; common and precious; hidden and concealed, yet known by everyone."[38]

Of course, semiconductor manufacturing has other, less romantic similarities to alchemical practice, including the use of noxious, toxic, and corrosive chemicals, to which workers are exposed and which contaminate the environment. Both activities involve high temperatures, molten metals, poisonous gases, and toxic wastes.

Masculine Creation

It is significant that Wagner's accomplishment was a purely masculine affair, as was much of "good old-fashioned AI," in fact as well as spirit. Normally the alchemical *Magnum Opus* requires cooperation between the alchemist and his *Soror Mystica,* a woman who provides the required sexual polarity and gender balance, which symbolizes on the level of the operators the necessary *coniunctio oppositorum* necessary on the level of the operation.[39] Perhaps this is why Wagner has been hitherto unsuccessful in this operation, for I expect he is celibate in mind as well as body.[40] The necessity of synthesizing the masculine and feminine perspectives is an important psychological insight, not confined to alchemy.[41] Alice Raphael explains:

> According to legend, Pythagoras received the greater part of his ethical knowledge from a Delphic priestess. Historically, the relationships of Plutarch to Klea and of Socrates to Diotima illustrate that a serious exchange of thought and feeling existed between men and women of superior philosophic interests in antiquity. The Soror Mystica was manifest also in the alchemical tradition, for many an alchemist had as disciple either his wife or a Mystical Sister, who assisted him in his laboratory and represented the all-important feminine principle in the production of the philosophers' stone.[42]

More directly relevant to *Faust,* we may add the example of Simon Magus and *his* Helena, with all its "tantric" implications, for she was simultaneously courtesan, muse, and embodied divine Wisdom. Thus the Gnostic mage was known as Faustus (Lat. "fortunate"), and Helena incarnated divine Thought or Sophia, the fallen World-Soul, whose ascent to the Godhead would redeem the world.[43] Simon also claimed to have created a homunculus nobler than God's creation, with a purer soul than ordinary people, because conjured from subtle air rather than molded from earth.[44] *Faust*'s Homunculus, like traditional AI systems, is similarly subtle and ungrounded.

When Mephistopheles drops in on Wagner's alchemical laboratory and inquires what he is up to, Wagner announces that a man is being made. The devil playfully asks, "And what loving pair / Have you got hidden in the smoke-hole there?" ("Und welch verliebtes Paar / Habt ihr in's Rauchloch eingeschlossen?") (*F,* 6836–37),[45] but there is neither love nor sexual union in Wagner's machinations, who disdains such irrational messiness:

No God forbid! That old style we declare
A poor begetting in a foolish fashion.
The tender core from which life used to surge,
The gracious force that came from inward urge,
Which took and gave, for self-delineation,
Blending near traits with far in new mutation,
To this we now deny its lordly height;
What if beasts still find it their delight,
In future man, as fits his lofty mind,
Must have a source more noble and refined.

(Behüte Gott! wie sonst das Zeugen Mode war
Erklären wir für eitel Possen.
Der zarte Punkt aus dem das Leben sprang,
Die holde Kraft die aus dem Innern drang
Und nahm und gab, bestimmt sich selbst zu zeichnen,
Erst Nächstes, dann sich Fremdes anzueignen,
Die ist von ihrer Würde nun entsetzt;
Wenn sich das Tier noch weiter dran ergötzt,
So muß der Mensch mit seinen großen Gaben
Doch künftig höhern, höhern Ursprung haben.) (*F*, 6838–47)[46]

Wagner ridicules the delicate process, of which Goethe was so aware, of organic growth and development, by which the organism defines itself out of its own inner necessity, a self-organizing process that, as we now know, has evolved by random mutation and recombination of traits.[47] Similarly, in the past we tried to engineer AI and robotic systems, rather than to grow them, but despite Wagner's optimism (or arrogance), we often reach the limits of our ability to design complex systems and must resort to various forms of *evolutionary computation*, which use selective retention in combination with random mutation and recombination, aping biology to achieve what rational design cannot. Nevertheless, Wagner predicts,

What men as Nature's mysteries would hold,
All that to test by reason we make bold
And what she once was wont to organize,
That we bid now to crystallize.

(Was man an der Natur geheimnisvolles pries,
Das wagen wir verständig zu probieren,
Und was sie sonst organisieren ließ,
Das lassen wir kristallisieren.) (*F*, 6857–60)[48]

Crystals are closely connected to computing. Of course semiconductor devices are made from silicon crystals, but crystals are also a good metaphor for computers and computation, for, like crystals, computers are highly organized and regular in structure, and programs and data structures have the austere beauty of crystals.[49] We also find crystal-like structures in living nature, but as implied in the title of Donna Haraway's history of embryology, *Crystals, Fabrics, and Fields*,[50] other metaphors also apply, and self-organizing organic material, especially during embryological development, is better characterized as *soft matter* (or *viscoelastic material*).[51] Roughly, these are materials that stretch elastically when you pull on them weakly, but deform and flow when you pull on them strongly enough. These are the characteristics of most living tissues, and they are likely to be the characteristics of robots grown by artificial morphogenesis. (So far, however, the crystal metaphor has dominated research on self-reconfigurable robotics and programmable matter, which often is based on fixed "lattice architectures.") We will look further at the flexibility of living matter below.

The distinction between rigid crystals and soft matter also applies at a more metaphorical level, for symbolic AI viewed knowledge as rigid, formula-like structures constructed from atomic wordlike units, that is, as formal, logical, abstract objects. Their inflexibility led to "brittle" behavior; minor exceptions or unexpected circumstances could break the systems (cause them to behave unintelligently). Furthermore, the rigidity of these structures complicated learning and adaptation, since these processes could not be gradual. Dissatisfied with brittle, inflexible behavior, AI researchers have returned to organic intelligence and the brain (sometimes called "wetware" to distinguish it from hardware and software), and developed new *connectionist* techniques, which permit flexible, adaptable, deformable, and fluid ways of representing knowledge and cognition. Metaphorically, organic knowledge is soft.[52]

Moreover this organic knowledge is grounded in an organic body, and recent work in AI and cognitive science has shown the importance of the physical body and its physical environment in structuring and molding these knowledge structures.[53] It has become apparent that intelligence is as inseparable from its physical embodiment as the hole is from the doughnut.

But Wagner, the pedantic academic, has not learned this lesson, for he has created an artificial, idealized version of himself: an intellect without a body, a talking head. Homunculus is not so much a "little man" as a little brain in a vat. As Charles Passage states, "he is without substance, the mere 'idea' of a man, though the chemicals in the retort have apparently assumed the crinkled half-a-walnut-meat appearance of an extracted brain."[54] This chemical brain comes stocked with universal knowledge, according to Goethe in his second Helena sketch,[55] nor does Homunculus have to learn language, for it is also preloaded in his artificial brain.[56] As will be discussed in more detail below, much AI research has been directed to the production of disembodied (or minimally embodied) "brains in vats," which, it was hoped, would be intellectually developed from the moment of their creation and could be preloaded with knowledge by their creators. (The Cyc project, which is attempting to encode all of common sense into a comprehensive AI knowledge-base, is an excellent example.)[57] Behind these projects is the widespread Western intellectualist assumption that the mind comprises facts and inferential processes and that the body is an unfortunate impediment to our swift soaring rational intellects.[58]

Is intellect all there is to being human? Some futurists interested in AGI talk of an eventual *technological singularity*, when artificial intelligence surpasses human intelligence.[59] The idea is that this achievement would mark "the end of the human era," since such an artificial intelligence would be better able to design AI systems than we are, and therefore a self-reinforcing acceleration of AI technology would leave us behind.[60] While some, such as Bill McKibben and Bill Joy, have seen the singularity as catastrophic for humankind, others, such as AI researchers Ray Kurzweil and Hans Moravec, have hailed it as humanity's destined self-transcendence.[61] They argue that we should not feel sad if humans are superseded, for by designing our successors we are fulfilling our role in the evolution of intelligent life on earth. Moravec writes,

> At the same time, by performing better and cheaper, the robots will displace humans from essential roles. If their capacities come to include self-replication (and why not?), they may displace us altogether. . . . Personally, I am not alarmed at this; these future machines will be our progeny, our mind children, built in our image and likeness, ourselves less flawed, more potent.[62]

Homunculus is nothing if not a "mind child."

Wagner, the intellectualist technologist hiding in his laboratory, is of course in agreement. He sees the random processes of evolution being bettered by scientific technology:

> Insane, at first, appears a great intent;
> We yet shall laugh at chance in generation;
> A brain like this, for genuine thinking meant,
> Will henceforth be a thinker's sure creation.
>
> (Ein großer Vorsatz scheint im Anfang toll,
> Doch wollen wir des Zufalls künftig lachen,
> Und so ein Hirn, das trefflich denken soll,
> Wird künftig auch ein Denker machen.) (*F*, 6867–70)[63]

Likewise, "good old-fashioned AI" attempted the rational design of intelligent systems, whereas now we depend more on biologically inspired self-organization, which can result in systems that are effective but may not be intellectually comprehensible.

Moravec advises that for our mind children, as for our biological children, "It behooves us to give them every advantage and, when we have passed evolution's torch, bow out."[64] With foresight, our twilight need not be unpleasant; he contends,

> As with biological children . . . we probably can bargain for some consideration in our retirement. Good children like to see their parents comfortable in their later years. "Tame" super intelligences could be created and induced to protect and support us, at least for awhile. The relationship, however, requires advance planning and diligent maintenance. It is not too early to start paying attention.[65]

As superintelligent Homunculus abandons his creator, leaving him to dot his "i"s, Mephistopheles reminds us, "Upon the creatures we have made / We are, ourselves, at last, dependent" ("Am Ende hängen wir doch ab / Von Kreaturen die wir machten") (*F*, 7003–4).[66]

Since Mephistopheles has just acknowledged his dependence on Homunculus in their immanent journey to the classical world (*F*, 7001–2), these lines hint that he has had a hand in Homunculus' creation, which Goethe acknowledged in his December 16, 1829, conversation with Eckermann.[67] Wagner's learned experimentation had been impotent until the devil's well-timed arrival, as Homunculus recognized (*F*, 6885–88). Mephistopheles brought the needed shadow element, an urge to embodiment and physical activity, to Wagner's intellectual but inanimate creation, and at exactly the right psychological moment (the *kairos* or *occasio*). As Edward Edinger explains, "Psychologically, the homunculus signifies the birth of the conscious realization of the autonomous psyche."[68] That is, a new psychic center has been constellated that is independent from the conscious ego, represented by Faust. It represents "the ego's dawning awareness of the existence of a second psychic center, the [unconscious] Self."[69] Homunculus is enlightened consciousness, which has the wisdom to seek union in the depths of the unconscious. Thus his illumination leads Faust/Ego and Mephistopheles/Shadow into the archetypal world of the Aegean Festival, where the beauty at the heart of nature will revive Faust.

Mephistopheles and Homunculus are akin; they are both *daemones* (*Dämonen*), as Goethe told Eckermann.[70] In psychological terms, a daemon (Gk. *daimôn*) is a subconscious complex, which can behave as an autonomous personality.[71] The two share "clearness of intellect" ("*geistiger Klarheit*"), as Goethe said,[72] and a disposition to act. They are also akin in that, as Denton Snider observes,[73] Mephistopheles is "the spirit of negation" ("der Geist der stets verneint") (*F*, 1338) and Homunculus is defined by limitation, for he is confined to his little flask, at least until his final immolation. "Thus Homunculus is related to Mephisto by his limit."[74] Homunculus' strict determination is nothing other than Mephistopheles' negation, according to the Spinozan principle, "omnis determinatio est negatio" ("all determination is negation").[75]

Indeed, as Snider also points out, all three personalities present at Homunculus' genesis contribute to his character.[76] We may call them Man, Devil, and Professor (or Scientist or Engineer). Professor Wagner contributes theory, technical skill, and raw materials, as well as the little man's intellectual endowments, the light that will guide the others, but also his tendency to trust authority over personal experience.[77] This benefactor is left behind, for Homunculus is also motivated by Mephistopheles' contribution of "negation, activity, and life," and by his own Faustian aspiration to transcend limitation and seek beauty and embodiment.[78] For Faust, though hailing from the Professor's environment, has escaped the academic cloister and contributes "aspiration [and] freedom from the narrow world of Wagner."[79] Nevertheless, Faust the Man, as conscious ego, remains unconscious while these archetypal forces mobilize.

These psychological considerations may seem far removed from AI, but they suggest the neglect of embodiment and the unconscious mind that characterized AI, cognitive science, and philosophy throughout so much of their history. They are relevant also to our disembodied, intellectualist relation with nature and to how we understand it. Homunculus' quest for a body is also ours.

Fiery Spirit

It is worthwhile to dwell a little more on the nature of Homunculus and what it suggests about a disembodied artificial intelligence, for he is consistently described as a flame, fiery, brilliant, flashing, shining, and so on.[80] This is certainly appropriate to his nature, for both fire and light are subtle and immaterial, and in alchemy fire is the element of transformation.[81] Thus we can get additional insight into Homunculus' nature by recalling that traditionally fire is characterized by two *qualities* or *powers* (Lat. *potentiae*, Gk. *dynameis*): it is hot and dry.[82] Heat is the power that decomposes mixtures into their constituents, for it causes unalike to separate and like to cling to like—think of distillation.[83] Thus heat is the power of discrimination; it makes distinctions and thus symbolizes analysis. Therefore heat and light are appropriate to Homunculus as an active intellectual spirit. The traditionally masculine warm elements (fire and air) always strive upward, whereas the traditionally feminine cool elements (water and earth) sink into the depths.[84]

The other quality of fire is dryness, which, as Aristotle explains, gives form to things, and is opposed to the formlessness of fluids.[85] Thus dryness represents determination, but it is the fixed determination of a static form, as opposed to the active discrimination of heat. Thus the combined qualities of fire suggest active analysis leading to rigid systemization (as might be expected of Wagner's creation).

Symbolic AI systems are similarly fiery, acting through the fundamental discrimination of 1 and 0 (true and false) to operate on rigid symbolic structures, often representing logical propositions of one sort or another. Even machine learning systems, if they are symbolic (based on fixed, wordlike symbols), are ultimately inflexible and brittle, for they can only rearrange the fixed parts of these knowledge structures. Therefore it is symbolically consistent that Homunculus' body is a rigid crystalline vessel, which confines and delimits him. Likewise, the electrical currents in our computers (which suggest fire and are physically akin to light) are confined within their silicon crystals.

Living things, in contrast, are characterized by moistness, which is the opposite quality to dryness. Dry things are rigid, moist things are supple, and life requires such flexibility. Most organisms are either soft on the outside or soft on the inside (or both), and the physics of soft matter is especially appropriate to living things.[86] Likewise water is expansive, but conforms to its surroundings, adapting to its environment.[87] Therefore, it is appropriate that Homunculus' quest for an organic body ends in the Aegean Sea. This suggests that AI's quest for embodiment will end likewise in structures that are soft, both literally and figuratively.[88]

Minimal Embodiment

Of course AI systems are not literally disembodied—existing only in a mental realm—for computers are physical objects, but they are *minimally embodied*; they have trivial bodies capable of only impoverished interaction with their environments, like brains in vats. In this they are very like Homunculus.

For example, Thales notices an embarrassing aspect of Homunculus' inadequate embodiment:

> Another aspect would seem critical —
> He is, I think, hermaphroditical.
>
> (Auch scheint es mir von andrer Seite kritisch,
> Er ist, mich dünkt, hermaphroditisch.) (*F*, 8255–56)[89]

This is to be expected from alchemical tradition, for the homunculus is a *rebis* ("two-thing") resulting from a coniunctio oppositorum, especially of male and female.[90] More to the point, Homunculus is a thinking machine. The rational mind is traditionally sexless, and while the issue is not closed, contemporary research supports the fact that there are no sex-linked differences in adult cognition.[91] Be that as it may, sexual dimorphism is more significant in the body and "lower" psychological faculties, including the nonrational and unconscious minds, where the drives reside, than it is in the idealized intellect represented by Homunculus.

Second, although Homunculus can apparently perceive his environment, we cannot conclude that he must have sense organs, for he may be clairvoyant, as mentioned in some alchemical sources.[92] Even if he does have sense organs, he does not have limbs with which he can interact with his environment. Limbs are important not only for locomotion and manipulating physical objects, but also as a prerequisite to active perception, which, in contrast to passive observation, is essential to embodied intelligence in humans and other animals. Physical interaction with the environment structures the information in our brains and creates knowledge. As Bergson said, "Intellectuality and materiality have been constituted, in detail, by reciprocal adaptation."[93]

Finally, Homunculus' means of locomotion is to float in the air in his crystalline vehicle; he is literally *ungrounded*, minimally connected with the physical world. Similarly, most AI systems have resided in immobile computers. Even most robots, at least until very recently, have been very limited in their ability to interact with their environment. Typically they roll around on wheels and have simple grippers for manipulating objects.

Thus Homunculus has much in common with traditional disembodied AI systems, which are like brains in vats in that they have little or no significant interaction with their environments. For example, since much AI research has focused on higher cognitive capacities, such as language understanding, abstract reasoning, playing board games, and so on, the input-output medium was often textual, some formal artificial language, or formal approximation to a natural language. Even systems that did process sensory information, such as computer vision systems, did so in a remarkably passive and disembodied way. For example, such a system might take a digitized photographic image and attempt to segment the scene into discrete objects and to identify these objects (i.e., to attach words to them). In contrast, natural perception is usually a more active process in which perceptual structures are revealed by the organism's purposeful motion in and interaction with its environment.[94]

In part, this AI research strategy was a manifestation of an intellectualist bias in Western psychology, but it was also a consequence of incorrect assumptions about the relative difficulty of "pure thought" and interaction with the physical world. For example, it was supposed that it would be easier to understand typed text than situated spoken language, and that parsing a static scene would be easier than a situated agent's extraction of relevant information from an environment with which it was purposefully interacting. In fact the opposite is the case, and it is often easier for a situated embodied agent to behave competently in its environment than for a disinterested observer to make sense of it. For example, an embodied agent does not need a complete mental model or description of its environment; it is sufficient to be able to identify *affordances* (perceivable potential actions) that enable its intended behavior. (Thus insects and other simple organisms behave very effectively, in spite of their tiny brains.) As the phenomenologist philosopher Hubert Dreyfus observed long ago, there are many things that we "know" simply by virtue of having a body, and therefore an embodied intelligence does not have to explicitly represent or process this "knowledge."[95]

Fortunately there has been a sea change in AI research, and a growing number of theoreticians and experimenters understand the importance of embodiment as a foundation for intelligence.[96] In particular, we now understand that genuine information is not simply a given (datum), but that it is created by agents' embodied purposeful interaction with an environment in which they are situated.[97]

Embodiment is becoming an important and indeed transformative concept in contemporary philosophy, psychology, cognitive science, and linguistics, as well as in AI. Although the significance of embodiment has roots in Kant, and more recently in the pragmatism of Dewey and James, and in phenomenology and existentialism (e.g., Merleau-Ponty, Heidegger, and Dreyfus), it has been increasing in importance since about 1990.[98]Among the recent contributors are Terry Winograd and Fernando Flores in AI, Rodney Brooks, Hans Morovec, and Rolf Pfeifer in robotics, and George Lakoff, Mark Johnson, and Raphael Núñez in cognitive science.

Fluid Morphogenesis

Homunculus' apotheosis is achieved in the Aegean Festival, the climax of Part II, Act II, a "mythical festival of life and love, procreation and organic evolution."[99] Here Galatea appears as a goddess of nature, but also as a surrogate for sea-born Aphrodite.[100] Thus, she is surrounded by Erotes in Raphael's *Triumph of Galatea*, which Goethe knew. As a goddess of both nature and beauty, she is the goal of the striving of Homunculus, who is possessed by Eros; the two are *desire* and *the object of desire*. But why does Homunculus seek his consummation in the sea?

Water is a common symbol of matter, the flux of material existence, and the realm of Becoming.[101] For example, in Porphyry's commentary *On the Cave of the Nymphs*, which allegorizes Odysseus' wanderings over the sea as the soul's sojourn in matter,[102] we read, "Again, according to Plato, the deep, the sea, and a tempest are images of material reality. And on this account, I think, the poet called the port by the name of Phorcys. For he says, 'It is the port of the ancient marine Phorcys.'"[103] Of Phorcys, to whom Plato attributes generation, Proclus remarks, "as the Jupiter in this ennead causes the unapparent divisions and separation of forms made by Saturn to become apparent, and as Rhea calls them forth into motion and generation, so Phorcys inserts them into matter, produces sensible natures and adorns the visible essence."[104] The daughters of Phorcys are the Phocyads, "sprung forth from Night" ("In Nacht geboren"), who "stem from Chaos by undoubted right" ("Des Chaos Töchter sind wir unbestritten") (*F*, 8010, 8028), whom Mephistopheles met on the Upper Peneios, and of whom he became an honorary member as Phorcyas (*F*, 8012–33). Rhea, the Great Mother, was connected with *rheô* ("to flow") and its derivatives, *rhoê* ("flux"), and *rhythmos* ("measured motion," "order"), and thus with the cycles and processes of nature.[105]

Porphyry also describes the descent of souls into fluid material reality, which is Homunculus' goal as well:

> Since, however, [matter] is continually flowing, and is of itself destitute of the supervening investments of form, through which it participates of *morphe*, and becomes visible, the flowing waters, darkness, or, as the poet says, obscurity of the cavern, were considered by the ancients as apt symbols of what the world contains, on account of the matter with which it is connected.[106]

He further observes that this is the cave of not just any Nymphs, but those whom Homer calls Naiads,[107] whose name comes from the verb *naô* ("to flow").[108] Porphyry continues,

> For we peculiarly call them Naiades, and the powers that preside over waters, Nymphs; and this term, also, is commonly applied to all souls descending into generation. For the ancients thought that these souls are incumbent on water which is inspired by divinity.[109]

Likewise, Homunculus descends into generation, an artificial being eager to be reborn through organic evolution and development.[110] Here, the bountiful sea is a symbol of fruitful matter, as Thales' paean (*F*, 8433–43) reminds us: "From the water has sprung all life! / All is sustained by its endeavor!" ("Alles ist aus dem Wasser entsprungen!! / Alles wird durch was Wasser erhalten!") (*F*, 8435–36).[111] Everyone sings, "Of life's renewal you are the fount" ("Du bists dem das frischeste Leben entquellt") (*F*, 8444).[112] Homunculus immerses his fiery spirit into Galatea's fluid depths, but the opposites do not cancel, for fire and water have been intensified in the persons of Eros and Galatea, and thus their union creates a new synthesis. As Goethe explains,

> Whatever appears in the world must divide if it is to appear at all. What has been divided seeks itself again, can return to itself and reunite. This happens in a lower sense when it merely intermingles with its opposite, combines with it; here the phenomenon is nullified or at least neutralized. However, the union

may occur in a higher sense if what has been divided is first intensified; then in the union of the intensified halves it will produce a third thing, something new, higher, unexpected.

(Was in die Erscheinung tritt, muß sich trennen, um nur zu erscheinen. Das Getrennte sucht sich wieder und es kann sich wieder finden und vereinigen; im niedern Sinne, indem es sich nur mit seinem Entgegengestellten vermischt, mit demselben zusammentritt, wobei die Erscheinung Null oder wenigstens gleichgültig wird. Die Vereinigung kann aber auch im höhern Sinne geschehen, indem das Getrennte sich zuerst steigert und durch die Verbindung der gesteigerten Seiten ein Drittes, Neues, Höheres, Unerwartetes hervorbringt.)[113]

Further, in their debate about the relative merits of fire and water as creative forces, Anaxagoras praises the rapidity with which fire can cause change, but Thales answers that the sea creates forms gently:

Never was Nature and her fluid power
Indentured yet to day and night and hour.
She shapes each form to her controlling course
And be the scale immense, eschews all force.

(Nie war Natur und ihr lebendiges Fließen
Auf Tag und Nacht und Stunden angewiesen;
Sie bildet regelnd jegliche Gestalt,
Und selbst im Großen ist es nicht Gewalt.) (*F*, 7861–64)[114]

Fire is an active agent of change and discrimination, and so it leads to sudden transformation and phase changes, as when water boils or ice melts; it is ultimately violent, as we witness on the Upper Peneios, which recalls the hellish technology (*"Flämmchen"* [*F*, 11125]; *"Feuergluten"* [*F*, 11129]) of Faust's project to drive the ocean from his land.[115] Water, in contrast, is a more passive catalyst of union, mixture, and adaptation. Thales says that, while fire can create inanimate objects, life came to be through moisture (*F*, 7856), which Homunculus realizes is precisely his objective (*F*, 7858). In practice, both fiery and watery processes are required for the self-organization of complex, organic forms, an insight we can apply in AI, alife, and artificial morphogenesis.

Before his *hieros gamos*, Homunculus' embodiment had been minimal (just enough to contain his form); it was transparent, thin, and fragile (easily broken by contact with matter)—rather like a sperm, which must break itself on the egg in the womb; only the nucleic acid, encoding the genotype, penetrates through the egg's membrane. The fusion of the information-bearing sperm with the egg, which provides substance as well as information, triggers the developmental process (*Bildung*) by which cells divide, proliferate, and rearrange flexibly and fluidly to create the embodied organism. Morphogenesis is watery, because water is synthetic, cooperative, and coordinating, as opposed to fire, which is analytic, competitive, and isolating.

The zygote (fertilized egg) polarizes, into animal and vegetable poles (above and below), which then interpenetrate, leading to successive stages of polarization and spiraling differentiation governed by mutually interacting cooperation and competition.[116] The process is characterized by *circular causation*, a fundamental law of self-organization by which local interactions among the cells create global patterns and fields, which in turn govern the behavior of the cells.[117] We find analogous processes in Goethe's theory of morphology and in his alchemical inspirations, which are, however, outside the scope of this chapter. We are applying these insights in artificial self-organizing systems.

Embryological morphogenesis, and many other natural processes of formation, transformation, and re-creation,[118] are fundamentally fluidic.[119] Cells proliferate and move according to the laws of viscous fluids; they coordinate their activity and create physical form by processes such as chemical reactions, growth, diffusion, and chemotaxis (following differences in chemical concentration). Embryology is best understood in terms of soft matter,[120] and this understanding can be applied to artificial morphogenesis.[121]

Homunculus' self-immolation unites his fiery spirit with Galatea's watery nature. In addition to tempering his discriminative heat with integrative coolness, it allows him to dissolve his crystalline limitations and boundaries because formless moisture opposes rigid dryness. Conversely, Homunculus is the agent of transformation:

> this is Eros, Love, the first of the Gods, according to Plato (Symposium 178, 6), who came out of Chaos, hence the primitive form and maker of forms. Love is, then, really the ultimate shape, the little demiurge at work in Nature and in Man, transforming them both, breaking the hard limits of all that is fixed and throwing them into his flame for a new creation.[122]

This process is an alchemical "blending and fusion of opposites—of fire and water, of spirit and substance, of the masculine and the feminine—through which life is created in the sea."[123] An alchemical text in which Goethe "found particular pleasure,"[124] the *Aurea Catena Homeri* (*Golden Chain of Homer*), states:

> God has ordained it so that the Universal spirit by means of Humidity should work all things, because Humidity mixes easily with everything, by means of which the spirit can soften, penetrate, generate, destroy and regenerate all things. Thus Humidity or water is the Body, the Vehicle and Tool, but the spirit or fire is the Operator, the Universal Agent and fabricator of all Natural Things.[125]

> Whosoever wishes to arrive at the Fountain of Secret Wisdom, let him mind this well; and let him go with this Central Point of Truth to the circumference, and forever imprint in his memory: that from fire and water, or spirit enclosed in Humidity all things in the World are generated, preserved, destroyed and regenerated.[126]

In summary, fire is hot and dry, but water is cool and moist. Coolness reflects a lack of discrimination (hot), and so a mixture of diverse qualities, integration, blending, even chaos.[127] Moistness reflects a lack of rigidity or fixed form (dryness), and so conformability and adaptability to surroundings.[128] Organisms are characterized by integration, coordination, cooperation, and adaptability; thus the qualities of water are especially characteristic of life, and should be a basis for alife as well, but fire cannot be omitted. For Homunculus and Galatea effect a coniunctio oppositorum, an alchemical union of all the opposites (fire+water = hot+dry + cold+moist), which provides the foundation of life: activity (hot = discrimination) + structure (dry = rigidity) + integration (cold) + adaptability (moist). In this way the quintessence is created from the union of all four elements (fire, water, air, earth), which the Sirens and then the chorus hymn:

> Let Eros who wrought it be honored and crowned!
> Hail to the Ocean! Hail the wave,
> The flood with holy fire to lave!
> Waters hail! All hail the fire!
> The strange event hail we in choir!
>
> ALL VOICES IN CONCERT:
> Hail light airs now floating free!
> Hail earth's caves of mystery!
> Held in honor evermore
> Be the elemental four!
>
> (So herrsche denn Eros, der alles begonnen!
> Heil dem Meere! Heil den Wogen!
> Von dem heilgen Feuer umzogen;
> Heil dem Wasser! Heil dem Feuer!
> Heil dem seltnen Abenteuer!
>
> ALL-ALLE!
> Heil den mildgewogenen Lüften!
> Heil geheimnisreichen Grüften!
> Hochgefeiert seid allhier
> Element' ihr alle vier!) (*F*, 8479–87)[129]

New approaches to computing, called *natural computation*, are more suggestive of organic fluidity and embodied action than of fiery words and pure spirit. These include new forms of analog computing (which admits a continuum between 0 and 1), soft computing, DNA and molecular computing and self-assembly (which actually take place in solutions), swarm intelligence, fluid computation, field computation, evolutionary computing, and artificial morphogenesis, as well as algorithms such as simulated annealing and particle swarm optimization, which is inspired by the fluid motions of flocks of birds and schools of fish.[130] Polarity and intensification play an important role in these self-organizing and form-creating systems. Like Homunculus, AI and computing have taken the plunge.

Eros and the Orphic Egg

Deeper insights into the "spiritualization of matter and the materialization of spirit" and the basis for a true artificial mind come from further penetration into the symbolism of the sea. Goethe commented that he had special sympathy for Hesiod, the Orphic poems, and Stoic philosophy.[131] Therefore, unlike the Herald, we are not surprised when the Orphic Egg makes an unscheduled appearance in the masque for the Emperor ("Spacious Hall" ["Weitläufiger Saal"]).

Although the Orphic poems differ among themselves, in most Orphic cosmologies either Night or Water (but sometimes Matter, Gk. *hulê*) is the ultimate origin.[132] From this first principle an Egg is produced, often by means of Aithêr or Chaos as an intermediary. The Egg splits, its halves becoming Heaven and Earth, and from it emerges an incorporeal (Gk. *asômatos*) god described as "winged, bisexual and self-fertilizing, bright and aitherial."[133] He is most often called Phanês ("the one who appears") and Eros, but also Protogonos ("first-born"), and Mêtis ("practical wisdom").[134]

In the Emperor's masque there was a premature, aborted, or false birth from the cosmic egg, perhaps because it was a diabolical affair engineered by Mephistopheles, who, with a stroke from the Herald's wand, transforms himself into dark and chaotic prima materia. The Herald describes the events:

> Lo, how this double-dwarf, this ape,
> Curls in a ball, a loathsome shape!
> The shape turns egg-like! Wondrous view!
> Puffs itself out, and breaks in two!
> And strange twin-progeny appear;
> A bat, an adder have we here:
> The one in dust-tracks slides and curls,
> The dark thing round the ceiling whirls,
> Now out to join her mate she's whirred,
> I would not care to make a third.
>
> (Wie sich die Doppelzwerggestalt
> So schnell zum eklen Klumpen ballt!—
> —Doch Wunder!—Klumpen wird zum Ei,

> Das bläht sich auf und platzt entzwei.
> Nun fällt ein Zwillingspaar heraus,
> Die Otter und die Fledermaus.
> Die eine fort im Staube kriecht,
> Die andre schwarz zur Decke fliegt.
> Sie eilen draußen zum Verein,
> Da möcht' ich nicht der Dritte sein.) (*F*, 5474–83)[135]

The Herald, sensing the shadiness of the operation, does not want to be the Third to effect reunification of this polarity, opposed creatures of earth and air. As Raphael says on this passage, "Goethe has inducted us gently into Orphic theology."[136]

Perhaps the Boy Charioteer, who unexpectedly appears at this point, was born like Phanes from the egg. His character suggests the alchemical quintessence, since he is driving a levitating chariot pulled by four dragons, which could correspond to the elements, which he has mastered. The Herald thinks he looks effeminate (*F*, 5548–51), and symbolically he is hermaphroditical, an alchemical rebis uniting the opposites, as do Homunculus and Euphorion, who are his later manifestations; the three are spirits of inspiration.[137] Faust calls him "spirit of my spirit" ("Geist von meinem Geiste") (*F*, 5623), suggesting the highest essence of the mind. Raphael explains that this "soul-daemon came as a stranger-guest from the distant land of the gods, entering into man in order to give him a soul"; it is "active in the higher mode of knowledge, in ecstatic inspiration."[138] In Jung's terms, he is the unconscious self, the innermost archetypal core, unification with which is the goal of the lifelong process that he called "individuation" ("becoming undivided," Lat. *individuus*). But apropos artificial minds, Jung stresses that "our consciousness does not create itself—it wells up from the unknown depths . . . out of the primordial womb of the unconscious."[139] Is this possible in an artificial intelligence?

The Depths of the Embodied Mind

Artificial intelligence, like cognitive science, has focused primarily on the conscious mind, but it is discovering the mind's necessary material embodiment. Even here, however, it has focused on the *faculties* of the conscious mind, such as discursive reason, rather than on conscious experience itself. Fortunately, after a long period of neglect, neuroscience and allied disciplines are taking consciousness seriously, but a coherent theory of the relation between conscious experience and physical processes, which Chalmers calls the *Hard Problem*,[140] eludes us. The issue is salient in AI, and the problem of artificial consciousness provides a useful test case for natural consciousness.[141] The problem is not restricted to rational cognition, and the importance of emotions in autonomous robotics has been recognized,[142] but whether it is possible for robots to *feel* their emotions, and under what conditions they might do so, is an open question.[143]

What can we learn from Homunculus' quest? The sea is a traditional symbol of material existence, but it is also a potent symbol of the unconscious mind. Anthony Stevens, a Jungian analyst, writes, "As the source of life, the sea is equated with the mother and the unconscious psyche. . . . This association stresses the life-generating potential of the unconscious."[144] The unconscious mind (both personal and collective) is the Third between the polarities of the conscious mind and materiality, for as Jung says,

> The deeper "layers" of the psyche lose their individual uniqueness as they retreat further and further into darkness. "Lower down," that is to say as they approach the autonomous functional systems, they become increasingly collective until they are universalized and extinguished in the body's materiality, i.e., in chemical substances. The body's carbon is simply carbon. Hence "at bottom" the psyche is simply "world."[145]

Thus Homunculus' immersion of his brilliant light into dark watery depths is also a reunification of the conscious and unconscious minds, which is essential to individuation.[146] Therefore Mephistopheles is correct when he explains that he (as Shadow, part of the unconscious mind, grounded in matter) is prior to the light of consciousness, which thus depends on matter:

> I am a part of the part that once was everything,
> Part of the darkness which gave birth to light,
> That haughty light which envies mother night
> Her ancient rank and place and would be king—
> Yet it does not succeed: however it contend,
> It sticks to bodies in the end.
> It streams from bodies, it lends bodies beauty,
> A body won't let it progress;
> So it will not take long, I guess,
> And with the bodies it will perish, too.
>
> (Ich bin ein Teil des Teils, der Anfangs alles war,
> Ein Teil der Finsternis, die sich das Licht gebar,
> Das stolze Licht, das nun der Mutter Nacht
> Den alten Rang, den Raum ihr streitig macht,
> Und doch gelingt's ihm nicht, da es, so viel es strebt,
> Verhaftet an den Körpern klebt.
> Von Körpern strömt's, die Körper macht es schön,
> Ein Körper hemmt's auf seinem Gange,
> So, hoff' ich, dauert es nicht lange
> Und mit den Körpern wird's zu Grunde gehn.) (*F*, 1349–58)[147]

Spirit and matter are a polarity (included in Goethe's list in "Polarity"),[148] and their higher reunion requires a Third, with a necessary connection to each of the poles. This Third is the unconscious mind. On the one hand, it is psychical, like consciousness. On the other, like material reality, it is never completely illuminated by consciousness; it is the inner darkness corresponding to the outer darkness of the unperceived physical world.[149] Although the Herald declined to be the Third in Mephistopheles' attempted coniunctio oppositorum, he is perhaps the alchemist who can do the job. As master of ceremonies of the masque, a phantasmagoria of often archetypal figures, he stands in for Goethe,[150] but we cannot fail to see him also as Hermes, herald of the gods and interpreter (*hermêneus*) of their signs, the psychopomp who with his sleep-inducing wand leads souls into the archetypal realms.

CONCLUSIONS

The challenge of modern embodied philosophy, theory of the mind, and artificial intelligence is to understand the necessary interrelation of mind and matter (a polarity, connected by the unconscious as a Third), without a simplistic reduction of one to the other. For this, traditional science, which looks outward, must be supplemented with phenomenology, which looks inward. But phenomenology can look only as deeply as the light of consciousness can penetrate; it too must be supplemented, by depth psychology. By thus filling in the gap between conscious mind and unconscious matter we will see better how to create an artificial mind.

Traditional symbolic AI was akin to Wagner's scholasticism and to Homunculus' inadequate embodiment. The focus was on words devoid of content and on intellect divorced from action. Contemporary developments of embodied AI and cognitive science have shadowed Faust's progression from dry intellectualism to embodied striving, and Homunculus' union of his subtle thought with the oceanic depths of the unconscious mind and the material body. In both cases the agent of change was Mephistopheles, the archetypal Shadow and Spirit of Negation, creating an antithesis to the word and catalyzing the synthesis.

Because of his deep insights into nature, the mind, and biological form and development, Goethe was able to see beyond some of the problems that AI and alife would encounter and to anticipate solutions that we are still learning to apply. These insights informed *Faust*, his life's work, his alchemical magnum opus, which explores our relations with nature, both seen and unseen, and the conscious ego's relation with the unconscious self, which is continuous with nature. Therefore it continues to be a fount of inspiration for those of us frequenting the shoreline where mind meets matter.

NOTES

1. Marvin Minsky, ed., *Semantic Information Processing* (Cambridge: MIT Press, 1968), v.

2. See, for example, Ben Goertzel and Cassio Pennachin, eds., *Artificial General Intelligence* (Berlin: Springer, 2007).

3. See, for example, Bruce J. MacLennan, "Consciousness: Natural and Artificial," *Synthesis Philosophica* 22, no. 2 (2008): 401; Bruce J. MacLennan, "Robots React But Can They Feel? A Protophenomenological Analysis," in *Handbook of Research on Synthetic Emotions and Sociable Robotics: New Applications in Affective Computing and Artificial Intelligence*, ed. Jordi Vallverdú and David Casacuberta (Hershey: IGI Global, 2009), 133.

4. See, for example, the *Oxford English Dictionary*.

5. George A. Bekey, *Autonomous Robots: From Biological Inspiration to Implementation and Control* (Cambridge: MIT Press, 2005), 1.

6. Bruce J. MacLennan, "Editorial Preface: Computation and Nanotechnology," *International Journal of Nanotechnology and Molecular Computation* 1, no. 1 (2009): i.

7. Bruce J. MacLennan, "Models and Mechanisms for Artificial Morphogenesis," in *International Workshop on Natural Computing*, ed. Ferdinand Peper and Hiroshi Umeo (Berlin: Springer, 2010), 25.

8. The "sociable robotics" project at MIT is a good example; see Cynthia L. Breazeal, *Designing Sociable Robots* (Cambridge: MIT Press, 2002). There is already an *International Journal of Social Robotics*.

9. Johann Wolfgang Goethe, *Faust*, ed. Albrecht Schöne, vol. 7, pt. 1, *Sämtliche Werke. Briefe, Tagebücher und Gespräche* (Frankfurt: Deutscher Klassiker Verlag, 1995) [hereafter *F*]. This chapter draws on a number of English translations of Goethe's *Faust*. Here, 1. 11585 is translated by Walter Arndt, *Faust: A Tragedy*, ed. Cyrus Hamlin (New York: Norton, 2001), and l. 1700 by Walter Kaufmann, *Goethe's Faust: Part One and Sections from Part Two* (New York: Doubleday, 1961).

10. This is already occurring; see Peter Warren Singer, *Wired for War: The Robotics Revolution and Conflict in the Twenty-first Century* (New York: Penguin, 2009).

11. Bruce J. MacLennan, *From Pythagoras to the Digital Computer: The Intellectual Roots of Symbolic Artificial Intelligence* (forthcoming).

12. Ludwig Wittgenstein, *Tractatus Logico-Philosophicus*, trans. David F. Pears and Brian F. McGuinness (London: Routledge and Kegan Paul, 1974), 5.43. German text: http://www.tractatus.hochholzer.info/ (accessed February 12, 2010).

13. These developments, culminating in the computational theory of mind, are explained well in Howard Gardner, *The Mind's New Science: A History of the Cognitive Revolution* (New York: Basic Books, 1985).

14. John Haugeland, *Artificial Intelligence: The Very Idea* (Cambridge: MIT Press, 1985), 106.

15. Trans. Kaufmann.

16. Johann Wolfgang von Goethe, *Zur Farbenlehre*, ed. Manfred Wenzel, vol. 23, pt. 1, *Sämtliche Werke. Briefe, Tagebücher und Gespräche* (Frankfurt: Deutscher Klassiker Verlag, 1991), §754, 245; "Color," in *Scientific Studies*, trans. and ed. Douglas Miller, vol. 12, *Collected Works* (Princeton: Princeton University Press, 1988), §754, 277.

17. For example, Mephistopheles' interviews with the Student (*F*, 1868–2048) and with the Famulus (*F*, 6620–84), Wagner on delivery (*F*, 524–27, 546–47), Homunculus to Wagner (*F*, 6987–98). Other examples of "empty noise" presenting the illusion of meaning are discussed by Alan Corkhill, "'Why all this noise?': Reading Sound in Goethe's *Faust I* and *II*," in *International Faust Studies: Adaptation, Reception, Translation*, ed. Lorna Fitzsimmons (London and New York: Continuum, 2008), 60–61.

18. Goethe, *F*, 534–37.

19. Goethe, *F*, Part II, Act I, "Pleasance" ("Lustgarten") and Act IV, 10242–60; Act IV, "In the Foothills" ("Auf dem Vorgebirg").

20. Goethe, *F*, 1910–17, trans. Kaufmann.

21. Trans. Arndt.

22. Trans. Kaufmann.

23. Bruce J. MacLennan, "Field Computation in Natural and Artificial Intelligence," in *Encyclopedia of Complexity and System Science*, ed. Robert A. Meyers et al. (Berlin: Springer, 2009), 72–77.

24. Charles Scott Sherrington, *Man on His Nature* (Cambridge: Cambridge University Press, 1955), 178. For the roots of this metaphor, see Henry McIlwain, "Neurochemistry and Sherrington's Enchanted Loom," *Journal of the Royal Society of Medicine* 77, no. 5 (1984): 417. He traces the metaphor and Sherrington's title, "Man on His Nature," to the seventeenth-century alchemical philosophers Henry and Thomas Vaughan. No doubt Sherrington also knew *Faust* well.

25. Harold Jantz, *Goethe's Faust as a Renaissance Man: Parallels and Prototypes* (Princeton: Princeton University Press, 1951), 114.

26. Jantz, *Goethe's Faust*, 115, 116.

27. Goethe, who was very aware of contemporary linguistics, toys throughout *Faust* with the connection, and often disconnection, between the surface structure of language (including its sound) and its meaning; see Corkhill, "'Why all this noise?'" 60–61.

28. Daniel C. Dennett, *The Intentional Stance* (Cambridge: MIT Press, 1987).

29. On the inadequacy of formal syntax and semantics for even disembodied intelligence, see Hubert Dreyfus, *What Computers Can't Do: The Limits of Artificial Intelligence*, rev. ed. (New York: Harper and Row, 1979).

30. Dreyfus, *What Computers Can't Do*, chs. 7–9.

31. Hans Christoph Binswanger, *Money and Magic: A Critique of the Modern Economy in the Light of Goethe's Faust*, trans. J. E. Harrison (Chicago: University of Chicago Press, 1994), 56.

32. Marie-Louise von Franz, *Alchemy: An Introduction to the Symbolism and the Psychology* (Toronto: Inner City, 1980), 258–60.

33. There is an extensive, half-century-long literature pro and con strong AI, which continues to be debated; I cannot hope to summarize it or representatively

cite it. For the Turing Test, see Alan M. Turing, "Computing Machinery and Intelligence," *Mind* 59 (1950): 433. This paper has been reprinted in many anthologies, such as John Haugeland, ed., *Mind Design II: Philosophy, Psychology, Artificial Intelligence* (Cambridge: MIT Press, 1997), ch. 2.

34. Jennifer Couzin, "Virology. Active Poliovirus Baked from Scratch," *Science* 297 (2002): 174; Hamilton O. Smith, Clyde A. Hutchison III, Cynthia Pfannkoch, and J. Craig Venter, "Generating a Synthetic Genome by Whole Genome Assembly: "X174 Bacteriophage from Synthetic Oligonucleotides," *Proceedings of the National Academy of Sciences USA* 100 (2003): 15440.

35. *"Phiole"* (*F*, 6824, 6865, 6871, 6879, 6902, 6904), *"Kolben"* (*F*, 6852), *"Glas"* (*F*, 6871, 6881, 7069, 7832, 8093, 8236, 8251).

36. The stages in the alchemical process were associated with colors and corresponding birds; see Alice Raphael, *Goethe and the Philosopher's Stone: Symbolical Patterns in "The Parable" and the Second Part of "Faust"* (New York: Garrett Publications, 1965), 56. "The 'peacock's feathers' were a widespread symbol in all alchemical literature, representing either the Philosopher's Stone itself or the stage in the Magnum Opus immediately preceding it." Ronald D. Gray, *Goethe the Alchemist: A Study of Alchemical Symbolism in Goethe's Literary and Scientific Works* (Cambridge: Cambridge University Press, 1952; Mansfield Centre: Mantino Publishing, 2002), 65. It is "regarded as a favourable portent in the Great Work" (Raphael, *Goethe*, 56). Paracelsus writes, "When you have seen the different colours, it is necessary that you persevere in the work . . . until the peacock's tail is quite consumed . . . and the vessel attains its degree of perfection." Paracelsus, *The Hermetic and Alchemical Writings of "Paracelsus," the Great*, ed. Arthur Edward Waite (London, 1894; Chicago: de Laurence, Scott, 1910; Kila: Kessinger, 1991), 1:87.

37. Carl Gustav Jung, *Psychology and Alchemy*, 2nd ed., trans. Richard Francis Carrington Hull, vol. 12, *Collected Works* (Princeton: Princeton University Press, 1968), par. 433.

38. Arthur Edward Waite, ed. and trans., *Turba Philosophorum: or, Assembly of the Sages* (1895; Kila: Kessinger, 2007), 42–43.

39. Jung's own magnum opus on this topic, including the symbolism of the *hieros gamos* ("sacred marriage") in alchemy, was inspired by Kerényi's essay on the Aegean Festival in *Faust*. Carl Gustav Jung, *Mysterium Coniunctionis: An Inquiry into the Separation and Synthesis of Psychic Opposites in Alchemy*, 2nd ed., trans. Richard Francis Carrington Hull, vol. 14, *Collected Works* (Princeton: Princeton University Press, 1970), xiii. "*Mysterium Coniunctionis* can thus be considered an exhaustive commentary on Goethe's *Faust*, especially as it concerns its central image, the coniunctio." Edward F. Edinger, *Goethe's Faust: Notes for a Jungian Commentary* (Toronto: Inner City, 1990), 67.

40. *F*, 6829. He soon expresses his abhorrence of begetting in the traditional way (*F*, 6838).

41. June Singer, *Androgeny: The Opposites Within*, 2nd ed. (Boston: Sigo, 1989).

42. Raphael, *Goethe*, 162.

43. Hans Jonas, *The Gnostic Religion: The Message of the Alien God and the Beginnings of Christianity*, 2nd ed. (Boston: Beacon, 1963), 111. For more on the Gnostic background of Faust, see Michael Mitchell, *Hidden Mutualities: Faustian Themes from Gnostic Origins to the Postcolonial* (Amsterdam: Rodopi, 2006), ch. 1. Simon and

Helena are associated with the Sun and Moon, and their alchemical union brings about the salvation of humankind "by making straight the true human within" (Mitchell, 25).

44. Elizabeth M. Butler, *The Myth of the Magus* (Cambridge: Cambridge University Press, 1948), 81–83. See also Philip Mason Palmer and Robert Patterson More, *The Sources of the Faust Tradition from Simon Magus to Lessing* (New York: Oxford University Press, 1936).

45. Johann Wolfgang von Goethe, *Faust, Part One and Part Two,* trans. and ed. Charles E. Passage (Indianapolis: Bobbs-Merrill, 1965).

46. Johann Wolfgang von Goethe, *Faust,* trans. Philip Wayne (Baltimore: Penguin, 1959).

47. In *On the Origin of Species* Darwin acknowledged Goethe as a predecessor in evolutionary thinking. John Gearey, *Goethe's Other Faust: The Drama, Part II* (Toronto: University of Toronto Press, 1992), 14–15.

48. Johann Wolfgang von Goethe, *Faust: Parts One and Two,* trans. George Madison Priest (New York: Covici Friede, 1932).

49. Bruce J. MacLennan, "Aesthetics in Software Engineering," in *Encyclopedia of Information Science and Technology,* 2nd ed., ed. Mehdi Khosrow-Pour (Hershey: IGI International, 2008), 1:72–77.

50. Donna Jeanne Haraway, *Crystals, Fabrics, and Fields: Metaphors That Shape Embryos* (Berkeley: North Atlantic, 2004).

51. P. G. de Gennes, "Soft Matter," *Science* 256 (1992): 495; Gabor Forgacs and Stuart A. Newman, *Biological Physics of the Developing Embryo* (Cambridge: Cambridge University Press, 2005), 2, 21–22, 133.

52. Bergson also remarked that, in contrast to the discrete separated spatiality of formal knowledge, "the essence of the psychical is to enfold a confused plurality of interpenetrating terms," "the mutual interpenetration and continuity that I find at the base of my own self." Henri Bergson, *Creative Evolution,* trans. Arthur Mitchell (New York: Modern Library, 1944), 280, 281.

53. Fumiya Iida, Rolf Pfeifer, Luc Steels, and Yasuo Kuniyoshi, eds., *Embodied Artificial Intelligence* (Berlin: Springer, 2004); Rolf Pfeifer and Josh C. Bongard, *How the Body Shapes the Way We Think—A New View of Intelligence* (Cambridge: MIT Press, 2007); Rolf Pfeifer, Max Lungarella, and Fumiya Iida, "Self-Organization, Embodiment, and Biologically Inspired Robotics," *Science* 318 (2007): 1088; Rolf Pfeifer and Christian Scheier, *Understanding Intelligence* (Cambridge: MIT Press, 1999).

54. Passage, *Faust, Part One and Part Two,* lxvi.

55. *Faust: A Tragedy,* trans. Walter Arndt, ed. Cyrus Hamlin, 525.

56. Alan Corkhill, "Language Discourses in Goethe's *Faust II,*" in *Unravelling the Labyrinth: Decoding Text and Language, Festschrift for Eric Lowson Marson,* ed. Kerry Dunne and Ian R. Campbell (Bern: Peter Lang, 1997), 69–72.

57. Douglas Lenat and R. V. Guha, *Building Large Knowledge-Based Systems: Representation and Inference in the Cyc Project* (Reading: Addison-Wesley, 1990).

58. Dreyfus, *What Computers Can't Do,* ch. 7.

59. Apparently I. J. Good was the first to suggest (in 1965) that a non-human "intelligence explosion" would occur after the first superhuman intelligence was created. Irving John Good, "Speculations Concerning the First Ultraintelligent Machine," in *Advances in Computers 6,* ed. Franz L. Alt and Morris Rubinoff (New York:

Academic Press, 1965), 31–88. In 1983 V. Vinge called this event "The Singularity." Vernor Vinge, "The Coming Technological Singularity," *Vision-21: Interdisciplinary Science and Engineering in the Era of CyberSpace*, proceedings of symposium at NASA Lewis Research Center, March 30–31, 1993 (NASA Conference Publication CP-10129).

60. Vinge, "The Coming Technological Singularity."

61. Bill McKibben, *Enough: Staying Human in an Engineered Age* (New York: Henry Holt, 2003); Bill Joy, "Why the Future Doesn't Need Us," *Wired Magazine*, April 2000, http://www.wired.com/wired/archive/8.04/joy.html (accessed January 5, 2010); Ray Kurzweil, *The Singularity Is Near: When Humans Transcend Biology* (New York: Viking, 2005); Hans Moravec, "Robots: Re-evolving Mind at 10^7 Times Nature's Speed," *Cerebrum* 3, no. 2 (2001): 34–49, http://www.dana.org/news/cerebrum/detail.aspx?id=3010 (accessed June 18, 2010).

62. Moravec, "Robots: Re-evolving Mind."

63. Johann Wolfgang von Goethe, *Faust: A Tragedy*, trans. Bayard Taylor (New York: Modern Library, 1950).

64. Moravec, "Robots: Re-evolving Mind."

65. Moravec, "Robots: Re-evolving Mind."

66. Trans. Taylor.

67. Johann Peter Eckermann, *Gespräche mit Goethe in den letzten Jahren seines Lebens*, ed. Christoph Michel, vol. 12, Johann Wolfgang Goethe, *Sämtliche Werke. Briefe, Tagebücher und Gespräche* (Frankfurt: Deutscher Klassiker Verlag, 1999), 365–66; translated as *Words of Goethe: Being the Conversations of Johann Wolfgang von Goethe* [tr. John Oxenford] (New York: Tudor, 1949), 310–11.

68. Edinger, *Goethe's Faust*, 62.

69. Edinger, *Goethe's Faust*, 62.

70. Eckermann, *Gespräche*, 365; *Words of Goethe*, 310.

71. Carl Gustav Jung, *The Structure and Dynamics of the Psyche*, trans. Richard Francis Carrington Hull, vol. 8, *Collected Works* (Princeton: Princeton University Press, 1969), par. 253.

72. Eckermann, *Gespräche*, 365; *Words of Goethe*, 310.

73. Denton J. Snider, *Goethe's Faust: Second Part* (St. Louis: Sigma [1886]), 110.

74. Snider, *Goethe's Faust*, 110.

75. Snider, *Goethe's Faust*, 110. In fact it seems that this is Hegel's extension of Spinoza's statement and intent. Simon Duffy, *The Logic of Expression: Quality, Quantity and Intensity in Spinoza, Hegel and Deleuze* (New York: Ashgate, 2006), 18.

76. Snider, *Goethe's Faust*, 111–12.

77. Goethe, *F*, 7836–41, 7849.

78. Snider, *Goethe's Faust*, 111–12.

79. Snider, *Goethe's Faust*, 112.

80. For example, *F*, 7067, 7068, 7826, 8093, 8104, 8231–36, 8245, 8459, 8466–67.

81. John Read, *Prelude to Chemistry: An Outline of Alchemy* (Cambridge: MIT Press, 1966), 143–45.

82. Aristotle, *On Sophistical Refutations; On Coming-to-be and Passing Away; On the Cosmos*, trans. E. S. Forster and D. J. Furley (Cambridge: Harvard University Press, 1978), bk. 2, ch. 2, 330b4; all subsequent references to *On Coming-to-be and Passing*

Away are cited as *Gen. corr.* According to Aristotelian physics, each of the four elements has two qualities: warm or cool, moist or dry (330b4–6).

83. Aristotle, *Gen. corr.*, bk. 1, ch. 8, 325b25–29.

84. Aristotle, *Gen. corr.*, bk. 2, ch. 3, 330b31–34.

85. Aristotle, *Gen. corr.*, bk. 2, ch. 2, 329b31–33.

86. de Gennes, "Soft Matter"; Forgacs and Newman, *Biological Physics.*

87. Aristotle, *Gen. corr.*, bk. 2, ch. 2, 329b31–33.

88. MacLennan, "Models and Mechanisms."

89. Trans. Passage.

90. Jung, *Mysterium Coniunctionis.*

91. See, for example, Lise Eliot, *Pink Brain, Blue Brain: How Small Differences Grow into Troublesome Gaps—and What We Can Do About It* (Boston: Houghton Mifflin, 2009). The title does not accurately reflect the conclusions; see A. Scott Henderson, "Unsexing the Brain," *Science* 327 (2010): 414.

92. Franz Hartmann, *The Life and Doctrines of Philippus Theophrastus, Bombast of Hohenheim, Known by the Name of Paracelsus* (New York: John W. Lovell, 1891), 303–6n2.

93. Bergson, *Creative Evolution*, 205.

94. See, for example, James Jerome Gibson, *The Ecological Approach to Visual Perception* (Boston: Houghton Mifflin, 1979); Robert Shaw and John Bransford, eds., *Perceiving, Acting, and Knowing: Toward an Ecological Psychology* (Hillsdale: Lawrence Erlbaum, 1977).

95. Dreyfus, *What Computers Can't Do*, 248–50, 253.

96. See, for example, Iida et al., *Embodied AI*; Pfeifer and Bongard, *How the Body Shapes the Way We Think.*

97. See, for example, Pfeifer, Lungarella, and Iida, "Self-Organization"; Pfeifer and Scheier, *Understanding Intelligence.*

98. See, for example, Andy Clark, *Being There: Putting Brain, Body and World Together Again* (Cambridge: MIT Press, 1997); Horst Hendriks-Jansen, *Catching Ourselves in the Act: Situated Activity, Interactive Emergence, Evolution, and Human Thought* (Cambridge: MIT Press, 1996).

99. Goethe, *Faust*, trans. Arndt, ed. Hamlin, 433.

100. William Page Andrews, *Goethe's Key to Faust: A Scientific Basis for Religion and Morality and for a Solution of the Enigma of Evil* (Port Washington: Kennikat, 1968), 66.

101. Jean Campbell Cooper, *An Illustrated Encyclopedia of Traditional Symbols* (London: Thames and Hudson, 1978), 188–89.

102. Porphyry's work is a commentary on the *Odyssey* bk. 13, ll. 96–112. For this metaphor, cf. Plato, *Statesman*, 273d–e.

103. Porphyry, *On the Cave of the Nymphs*, trans. Thomas Taylor (Grand Rapids: Phanes, 1991), 55.

104. Quoted by the translator in Porphyry, *Cave*, 70n22.

105. Henry George Liddell, Robert Scott, and Henry Stuart Jones, *A Greek-English Lexicon*, 9th. ed. (Oxford: Oxford University Press), s.vv.; Lucas Siorvanes, *Proclus: Neo-Platonic Philosophy and Science* (Edinburgh: Edinburgh University Press, 1996), 151.

106. Porphyry, *Cave*, 30.

107. Homer, *Odyssey*, bk. 13, l. 104.

108. Note, however, that Galatea and her sisters are Nereids, not Naiads.

109. Porphyry, *Cave*, 34.

110. Goethe, *F*, 8324–26. See also Corkhill, "Language Discourses," 71–72.

111. Trans. Arndt.

112. Trans. Arndt.

113. Goethe, "Polarity," in *Scientific Studies*, 156. Goethe, "Physikalische Vorträge schematisiert," in *Schriften zur allgemeinen Naturlehre, Geologie und Mineralogie*, ed. Wolf von Engelhardt and Manfred Wenzel, vol. 25, *Sämtliche Werke. Briefe, Tagebücher und Gespräche* (Frankfurt: Deutscher Klassiker Verlag, 1989), 143.

114. Trans. Arndt.

115. Goethe, *Faust*, trans. Arndt.

116. Scott F. Gilbert, *Developmental Biology*, 6th ed. (Sunderland: Sinauer, 2000), 20–22, 223–61.

117. Ricard Solé and Brian Goodwin, *Signs of Life: How Complexity Pervades Biology* (New York: Basic Books, 2000), 150.

118. *"Gestaltung," "Umgestaltung," "Unterhaltung,"* the generative activities of the Mothers (*F*, 6287–88).

119. D. A. Beysens, Gabor Forgacs, and J. A. Glazier, "Cell Sorting Is Analogous to Phase Ordering in Fluids," *Proceedings of the National Academy of Sciences USA* 97 (2000): 9467.

120. de Gennes, "Soft Matter"; Forgacs and Newman, *Biological Physics*.

121. MacLennan, "Models and Mechanisms."

122. Snider, *Goethe's Faust*, 196.

123. Goethe, *Faust*, trans. Arndt, ed. Hamlin, 239n7.

124. Gray, *Goethe the Alchemist*, 5, citing *Goethes Werke* (Weimar: Böhlau, 1893), I:27, 203–4.

125. *Aurea Catena Homeri: The Golden Chain of Homer*, trans. Sigismond Bacstrom (San Francisco: Sapere Aude, 1983), 4 (ch. 2).

126. *Aurea Catena Homeri*, 5–6 (ch. 2).

127. Aristotle, *Gen. corr.*, bk. 2, ch. 2, 329b29–31.

128. Aristotle, *Gen. corr.*, bk. 2, ch. 2, 329b31–32, bk. 2, ch. 3, 330a5–11.

129. Trans. Wayne.

130. For example, Leandro Nunes de Castro, *Fundamentals of Natural Computing: Basic Concepts, Algorithms, and Applications* (Boca Raton: Chapman and Hall/CRC, 2006).

131. Goethe, *The Autobiography of Goethe. Truth and Poetry: From My Own Life*, new ed., rev., trans. John Oxenford (London: George Bell, 1881), 185; *Goethes Werke*, I:27, 11–12.

132. Geoffrey Stephen Kirk, John Earle Raven, and Malcolm Schofield, *The Presocratic Philosophers*, 2nd ed. (Cambridge: Cambridge University Press, 1983), 21–29.

133. Kirk, Raven, and Schofield, *Presocratic Philosophers*, 24n3.

134. See the definitive work, Martin L. West, *The Orphic Poems* (Oxford: Clarendon Press, 1983).

135. Trans. Wayne.

136. Raphael, *Goethe and the Philosopher's Stone*, 130.

137. Euphorion and the Boy Charioteer are so identified in Goethe's December 20, 1829, conversation with Eckermann. Eckermann, *Gespräche*, 369–70; *Words of Goethe*, 314.

138. Raphael, *Goethe and the Philosopher's Stone*, 132.

139. Carl Gustav Jung, *The Structure and Dynamics of the Psyche*, trans. Richard Francis Carrington Hull, vol. 8, *Collected Works* (Princeton: Princeton University Press, 1969), par. 935.

140. David J. Chalmers, *The Conscious Mind: In Search of a Fundamental Theory* (New York: Oxford University Press, 1996).

141. B. J. MacLennan, "Consciousness: Natural and Artificial," *Synthesis Philosophica* 22, no. 2 (2008): 401–33.

142. See, for example, Jordi Vallverdú and David Casacuberta, eds., *Handbook of Research on Synthetic Emotions and Sociable Robotics: New Applications in Affective Computing and Artificial Intelligence* (Hershey: IGI Global, 2009).

143. MacLennan, "Robots React But Can They Feel?"

144. Anthony Stevens, *Ariadne's Clue: A Guide to the Symbols of Humankind* (Princeton: Princeton University Press, 1998), 113.

145. Carl Gustav Jung, *The Archetypes and the Collective Unconscious*, 2nd ed., trans. Richard Francis Carrington Hull, vol. 9, pt. 1, *Collected Works* (Princeton: Princeton University Press, 1968), par. 291.

146. Jung, *Structure and Dynamics of the Psyche*, par. 432.

147. Trans. Kaufmann.

148. Goethe, "Physikalische Vorträge schematisiert," 142; Goethe's "Polarity," 156.

149. Carl Gustav Jung, *Aion: Researches into the Phenomenology of the Self*, 2nd ed., trans. Richard Francis Carrington Hull, vol. 9, pt. 2, *Collected Works* (Princeton: Princeton University Press, 1978), par. 2.

150. Raphael, *Goethe and the Philosopher's Stone*, 123.

BIBLIOGRAPHY

Andrews, William Page. *Goethe's Key to Faust: A Scientific Basis for Religion and Morality and for a Solution of the Enigma of Evil*. Port Washington: Kennikat, 1968.

Aristotle. *On Sophistical Refutations; On Coming-to-be and Passing Away; On the Cosmos*. Translated by E. S. Forster and D. J. Furley. Cambridge: Harvard University Press, 1978.

Aurea Catena Homeri: The Golden Chain of Homer. Leipzig und Winterthur, 1775. Translated by Sigismond Bacstrom. San Francisco: Sapere Aude, 1983.

Bekey, George A. *Autonomous Robots: From Biological Inspiration to Implementation and Control*. Cambridge: MIT Press, 2005.

Bergson, Henri. *Creative Evolution*. Translated by Arthur Mitchell. New York: Modern Library, 1944.

Beysens, D. A., Gabor Forgacs, and J. A. Glazier. "Cell Sorting Is Analogous to Phase Ordering in Fluids." *Proceedings of the National Academy of Sciences USA* 97 (2000): 9467–71.

Binswanger, Hans Christoph. *Money and Magic: A Critique of the Modern Economy in the Light of Goethe's Faust*. Translated by J. E. Harrison. Chicago: University of Chicago Press, 1994.

Breazeal, Cynthia L. *Designing Sociable Robots*. Cambridge: MIT Press, 2002.

Butler, Elizabeth M. *The Myth of the Magus*. Cambridge: Cambridge University Press, 1948.

Chalmers, David J. *The Conscious Mind: In Search of a Fundamental Theory*. New York: Oxford University Press, 1996.

Clark, Andy. *Being There: Putting Brain, Body and World Together Again*. Cambridge: MIT Press, 1997.

Cooper, Jean Campbell. *An Illustrated Encyclopedia of Traditional Symbols*. London: Thames and Hudson, 1978.

Corkhill, Alan. "Language Discourses in Goethe's *Faust II*." In *Unravelling the Labyrinth: Decoding Text and Language, Festschrift for Eric Lowson Marson*, edited by Kerry Dunne and Ian R. Campbell, 57–73. Bern: Peter Lang, 1997.

———. "'Why all this noise?': Reading Sound in Goethe's *Faust I* and *II*." In *International Faust Studies: Adaptation, Reception, Translation*, edited by Lorna Fitzsimmons, 55–69. London and New York: Continuum, 2008.

Couzin, Jennifer. "Virology: Active Poliovirus Baked from Scratch." *Science* 297 (2002): 174–75.

de Castro, Leandro Nunes. *Fundamentals of Natural Computing: Basic Concepts, Algorithms, and Applications*. Boca Raton: Chapman and Hall/CRC, 2006.

de Gennes, P. G. "Soft Matter." *Science* 256 (1992): 495–97.

Dennett, Daniel C. *The Intentional Stance*. Cambridge: MIT Press, 1987.

Dreyfus, Hubert. *What Computers Can't Do: The Limits of Artificial Intelligence*. Rev. ed. New York: Harper and Row, 1979.

Duffy, Simon. *The Logic of Expression: Quality, Quantity and Intensity in Spinoza, Hegel and Deleuze*. New York: Ashgate, 2006.

Eckermann, Johann Peter. *Words of Goethe: Being the Conversations of Johann Wolfgang von Goethe*. [Translated by John Oxenford.] New York: Tudor, 1949. Originally published as *Gespräche mit Goethe in den letzten Jahren seines Lebens*. Edited by Christoph Michel. Vol. 12, Johann Wolfgang von Goethe, *Sämtliche Werke. Briefe, Tagebücher und Gespräche* (Frankfurt: Deutscher Klassiker Verlag, 1999).

Edinger, Edward F. *Goethe's Faust: Notes for a Jungian Commentary*. Toronto: Inner City, 1990.

Eliot, Lise. *Pink Brain, Blue Brain: How Small Differences Grow into Troublesome Gaps—and What We Can Do About It*. Boston: Houghton Mifflin, 2009.

Forgacs, Gabor, and Stuart A. Newman. *Biological Physics of the Developing Embryo*. Cambridge: Cambridge University Press, 2005.

Gardner, Howard. *The Mind's New Science: A History of the Cognitive Revolution*. New York: Basic Books, 1985.

Gearey, John. *Goethe's Other Faust: The Drama, Part II*. Toronto: University of Toronto Press, 1992.

Gibson, James Jerome. *The Ecological Approach to Visual Perception*. Boston: Houghton Mifflin, 1979.

Gilbert, Scott F. *Developmental Biology*. 6th ed. Sunderland: Sinauer, 2000.

Goertzel, Ben, and Cassio Pennachin, eds. *Artificial General Intelligence*. Berlin: Springer, 2007.
Goethe, Johann Wolfgang von. *The Autobiography of Goethe. Truth and Poetry: From My Own Life*. New ed., rev. Translated by John Oxenford. London: George Bell, 1881.
———. *Faust*. Edited by Albrecht Schöne. Vol. 7, pt. 1., *Sämtliche Werke. Briefe, Tagebücher und Gespräche*. Frankfurt: Deutscher Klassiker Verlag, 1995.
———. *Faust*. Translated by Philip Wayne. Baltimore: Penguin, 1959.
———. *Faust: A Tragedy*. Translated by Bayard Taylor. New York: Modern Library, 1950.
———. *Faust: A Tragedy*. 2nd ed. Translated by Walter Arndt. Edited by Cyrus Hamlin. New York: Norton, 2001.
———. *Faust, Part One and Part Two*. Translated and edited by Charles E. Passage. Indianapolis: Bobbs-Merrill, 1965.
———. *Faust: Parts One and Two*. Translated by George Madison Priest. New York: Covici Friede, 1932.
———. *Goethe's Faust: Part One and Sections from Part Two*. Translated by Walter Kaufmann. New York: Doubleday, 1961.
———. *Goethes Werke*. Hrsg. im Auftrag der Großherzogin Sophie von Sachsen. Weimarer or Sophienausgabe. 4 pts., 143 vols. Weimar: Böhlau, 1887–1919.
———. "Physikalische Vorträge schematisiert." In *Schriften zur allgemeinen Naturlehre, Geologie und Mineralogie*, edited by Wolf von Engelhardt and Manfred Wenzel, 142–75. Vol. 25, *Sämtliche Werke. Briefe, Tagebücher und Gespräche*. Frankfurt: Deutscher Klassiker Verlag, 1989.
———. *Scientific Studies*. Edited and translated by Douglas Miller. Vol. 12, *Goethe's Collected Works*. Princeton: Princeton University Press, 1988.
———. *Zur Farbenlehre*. Edited by Manfred Wenzel. Vol. 23, pt. 1. *Sämtliche Werke. Briefe, Tagebücher und Gespräche*. Frankfurt: Deutscher Klassiker Verlag, 1991.
Good, Irving John. "Speculations Concerning the First Ultraintelligent Machine." In *Advances in Computers 6*, edited by Franz L. Alt and Morris Rubinoff, 31–88. New York: Academic Press, 1965.
Gray, Ronald D. *Goethe the Alchemist: A Study of Alchemical Symbolism in Goethe's Literary and Scientific Works*. Cambridge: Cambridge University Press, 1951. Mansfield Centre: Martino Publishing, 2002.
Haraway, Donna Jeanne. *Crystals, Fabrics, and Fields: Metaphors That Shape Embryos*. Berkeley: North Atlantic, 2004.
Harnad, Stevan. "The Symbol Grounding Problem." *Physica D* 42 (1990): 335–46. http://cogprints.org/3106/ (accessed January 5, 2010).
Hartmann, Franz. *The Life and Doctrines of Philippus Theophrastus, Bombast of Hohenheim, Known by the Name of Paracelsus*. New York: John W. Lovell, 1891.
Haugeland, John. *Artificial Intelligence: The Very Idea*. Cambridge: MIT Press, 1985.
———, ed. *Mind Design II: Philosophy, Psychology, Artificial Intelligence*. Cambridge: MIT Press, 1997.
Henderson, A. Scott. "Unsexing the Brain." *Science* 327 (2010): 414.
Hendriks-Jansen, Horst. *Catching Ourselves in the Act: Situated Activity, Interactive Emergence, Evolution, and Human Thought*. Cambridge: MIT Press, 1996.

Iida, Fumiya, Rolf Pfeifer, Luc Steels, and Yasuo Kuniyoshi, eds. *Embodied Artificial Intelligence*. Berlin: Springer, 2004.

Jantz, Harold. *Goethe's Faust as a Renaissance Man: Parallels and Prototypes*. Princeton: Princeton University Press, 1951.

Jonas, Hans. *The Gnostic Religion: The Message of the Alien God and the Beginnings of Christianity*. 2nd ed. Boston: Beacon, 1963.

Joy, Bill. "Why the Future Doesn't Need Us." *Wired*, April 2000, http://www.wired.com/wired/archive/8.04/joy.html (accessed January 5, 2010).

Jung, Carl Gustav. *Aion: Researches into the Phenomenology of the Self*. 2nd ed. Translated by Richard Francis Carrington Hull. Vol. 9, pt. 2, *Collected Works*. Princeton: Princeton University Press, 1978.

———. *The Archetypes and the Collective Unconscious*. 2nd ed. Translated by Richard Francis Carrington Hull. Vol. 9, pt. 1, *Collected Works*. Princeton: Princeton University Press, 1968.

———. *Mysterium Coniunctionis: An Inquiry into the Separation and Synthesis of Psychic Opposites in Alchemy*. 2nd ed. Translated by Richard Francis Carrington Hull. Vol. 14, *Collected Works*. Princeton: Princeton University Press, 1970.

———. *Psychology and Alchemy*. 2nd ed. Translated by Richard Francis Carrington Hull. Vol. 12, *Collected Works*. Princeton: Princeton University Press, 1968.

———. *Psychology and Religion: West and East*. 2nd ed. Translated by Richard Francis Carrington Hull. Vol. 11, *Collected Works*. Princeton: Princeton University Press, 1969.

———. *The Structure and Dynamics of the Psyche*. Translated by Richard Francis Carrington Hull. Vol. 8, *Collected Works*. Princeton: Princeton University Press, 1969.

Kirk, Geoffrey Stephen, John Earle Raven, and Malcolm Schofield. *The Presocratic Philosophers*. 2nd ed. Cambridge: Cambridge University Press, 1983.

Kurzweil, Ray. *The Singularity Is Near: When Humans Transcend Biology*. New York: Viking, 2005.

Lenat, Douglas, and R. V. Guha. *Building Large Knowledge-Based Systems: Representation and Inference in the Cyc Project*. Reading: Addison-Wesley, 1990.

Liddell, Henry George, Robert Scott, and Henry Stuart Jones. *A Greek-English Lexicon*. 9th ed. Oxford: Oxford University Press.

MacLennan, Bruce J. "Aesthetics in Software Engineering." In *Encyclopedia of Information Science and Technology*. Vol. 1, 2nd ed. Edited by Mehdi Khosrow-Pour, 72–77. Hershey: IGI International, 2008.

———. "Consciousness: Natural and Artificial." *Synthesis Philosophica* 22, no. 2 (2008): 401–33.

———. "Editorial Preface: Computation and Nanotechnology." *International Journal of Nanotechnology and Molecular Computation* 1, no. 1 (2009): i–ix.

———. "Field Computation in Natural and Artificial Intelligence." In *Encyclopedia of Complexity and System Science*, edited by Robert A. Meyers et al., 3334–60. Berlin: Springer, 2009.

———. *From Pythagoras to the Digital Computer: The Intellectual Roots of Symbolic Artificial Intelligence*. Forthcoming.

———. "Models and Mechanisms for Artificial Morphogenesis." In *International Workshop on Natural Computing*, edited by Ferdinand Peper and Hiroshi Umeo, 23–33. Berlin: Springer, 2010.

———. "Robots React But Can They Feel? A Protophenomenological Analysis." In *Handbook of Research on Synthetic Emotions and Sociable Robotics: New Applications in Affective Computing and Artificial Intelligence*, edited by Jordi Vallverdú and David Casacuberta, 133–53. Hershey: IGI Global, 2009.

McDermott, Drew. "Artificial Intelligence Meets Natural Stupidity." *ACM SIGART Bulletin* 57 (April 1976): 4–9.

McIlwain, Henry. "Neurochemistry and Sherrington's Enchanted Loom." *Journal of the Royal Society of Medicine* 77, no. 5 (May 1984): 417–25.

McKibben, Bill. *Enough: Staying Human in an Engineered Age*. New York: Henry Holt, 2003.

Minsky, Marvin, ed. *Semantic Information Processing*. Cambridge: MIT Press, 1968.

Mitchell, Michael. *Hidden Mutualities: Faustian Themes from Gnostic Origins to the Postcolonial*. Amsterdam: Rodopi, 2006.

Moravec, Hans. "Robots: Re-evolving Mind at 10^7 Times Nature's Speed." *Cerebrum* 3, no. 2 (2001): 34–49. http://www.dana.org/news/cerebrum/detail.aspx?id=3010 (accessed June 18, 2010).

Morris, Charles W. *Signification and Significance: A Study of the Relations of Signs and Values*. Cambridge: MIT Press, 1964.

Palmer, Philip Mason, and Robert Patterson More. *The Sources of the Faust Tradition from Simon Magus to Lessing*. New York: Oxford University Press, 1936.

Paracelsus. *The Hermetic and Alchemical Writings of "Paracelsus," the Great*. 2 vols. Edited by Arthur Edward Waite. London, 1894. Chicago: de Laurence, Scott, 1910. 2 vols. in 1. Kila: Kessinger, 1991.

Pfeifer, Rolf, and Josh C. Bongard. *How the Body Shapes the Way We Think — A New View of Intelligence*. Cambridge: MIT Press, 2007.

Pfeifer, Rolf, Max Lungarella, and Fumiya Iida. "Self-Organization, Embodiment, and Biologically Inspired Robotics." *Science* 318 (2007): 1088–93.

Pfeifer, Rolf, and Christian Scheier. *Understanding Intelligence*. Cambridge: MIT Press, 1999.

Porphyry. *On the Cave of the Nymphs*. Translated by Thomas Taylor. Grand Rapids: Phanes, 1991.

Raphael, Alice. *Goethe and the Philosopher's Stone: Symbolical Patterns in "The Parable" and the Second Part of "Faust."* New York: Garrett Publications, 1965.

Read, John. *Prelude to Chemistry: An Outline of Alchemy*. Cambridge: MIT Press, 1966.

Shaw, Robert, and John Bransford, eds. *Perceiving, Acting, and Knowing: Toward an Ecological Psychology*. Hillsdale: Lawrence Erlbaum, 1977.

Sherrington, Charles Scott. *Man on His Nature*. Cambridge: Cambridge University Press, 1955.

Singer, June. *Androgeny: The Opposites Within*. 2nd ed. Boston: Sigo, 1989.

Singer, Peter Warren. *Wired for War: The Robotics Revolution and Conflict in the Twenty-first Century*. New York: Penguin, 2009.

Siorvanes, Lucas. *Proclus: Neo-Platonic Philosophy and Science*. Edinburgh: Edinburgh University Press, 1996.

Smith, Hamilton O., Clyde A. Hutchison III, Cynthia Pfannkoch, and J. Craig Venter. "Generating a Synthetic Genome by Whole Genome Assembly: X174 Bacteriophage from Synthetic Oligonucleotides." *Proceedings of the National Academy of Sciences USA* 100 (2003): 15440–45.

Snider, Denton J. *Goethe's Faust: Second Part*. St. Louis: Sigma [1886].

Solé, Ricard, and Brian Goodwin. *Signs of Life: How Complexity Pervades Biology*. New York: Basic Books, 2000.

Stevens, Anthony. *Ariadne's Clue: A Guide to the Symbols of Humankind*. Princeton: Princeton University Press, 1998.

Turing, Alan M. "Computing Machinery and Intelligence." *Mind* 59 (1950): 433–60.

Vallverdú, Jordi, and David Casacuberta, eds. *Handbook of Research on Synthetic Emotions and Sociable Robotics: New Applications in Affective Computing and Artificial Intelligence*. Hershey: IGI Global, 2009.

Vinge, Vernor. "The Coming Technological Singularity." *In Vision-21: Interdisciplinary Science and Engineering in the Era of CyberSpace*, proceedings of symposium at NASA Lewis Research Center, March 30–31, 1993 (NASA Conference Publication CP-10129). http://rohan.sdsu.edu/faculty/vinge/misc/singularity.html (accessed January 5, 2010).

von Franz, Marie-Louise. *Alchemy: An Introduction to the Symbolism and the Psychology*. Toronto: Inner City, 1980.

Waite, Arthur Edward, ed. and trans. *Turba Philosophorum: Or, Assembly of the Sages*. 1895. Kila: Kessinger, 2007.

West, Martin L. *The Orphic Poems*. Oxford: Clarendon Press, 1983.

Winograd, Terry, and Fernando Flores. *Understanding Computers and Cognition*. Reading: Addison-Wesley, 1986.

Wittgenstein, Ludwig. *Tractatus Logico-Philosophicus*. Translated by D. F. Pears and B. F. McGuinness. London: Routledge and Kegan Paul, 1974. German text: http://www.tractatus.hochholzer.info/ (accessed February 12, 2010).

Index

About the Contributors

Frederick Burwick is professor emeritus of English at the University of California, Los Angeles. He has taught courses on Romantic drama and directed student performances of a dozen plays. Author and editor of twenty-six books and over a hundred articles, his research is dedicated to problems of perception, illusion, and delusion in literary representation and theatrical performance. In *The Damnation of Newton: Goethe's Color Theory and Romantic Perception*, he examined the relevance of Goethe's *Farbenlehre* in his *Faust*. In *Illusion and the Drama*, Burwick wrote on Goethe's stage designs and his sketches for a production of *Faust*. Recent publications include his edition with James McKusick of *Faustus, translated by Samuel Taylor Coleridge from the German of Goethe*.

Andrew Bush received his Ph.D. in comparative literature and is now professor of Hispanic studies and Jewish studies at Vassar College. His publications include *The Routes of Modernity: Spanish American Poetry from the Early Eighteenth to the Mid-Nineteenth Century*.

Alan Corkhill is an associate professor/reader in the School of Languages and Comparative Cultural Studies at the University of Queensland in Brisbane, where he has been teaching and researching since 1974. He is the longstanding Australasian editor of the Canadian periodical *Seminar: A Journal of Germanic Studies*. He has published extensively on the interfaces between texts and philosophical thinking in German letters since the Enlightenment. His most recent book is *Spaces for Happiness in the Twentieth-Century German Novel*, and he is also co-editing a volume of essays on female happiness discourse in eighteenth- and nineteenth-century German literature.

Jörg Esleben is associate professor of German at the University of Ottawa. He is the co-editor of *Mapping Channels between Ganges and Rhein: German-Indian Cross-Cultural Relations.*

Lorna Fitzsimmons is associate professor and coordinator of humanities at California State University, Dominguez Hills, in Los Angeles. She is the editor of *Lives of Faust: The Faust Theme in Literature and Music: A Reader* and *International Faust Studies: Adaptation, Reception, Translation,* and co-editor of *The Oxford Handbook of Faust in Music* (forthcoming).

David G. John is professor of German, Department of Germanic and Slavic Studies, at the University of Waterloo, Canada. His publications include *Images of Goethe through Schiller's "Egmont," The German "Nachspiel" in the Eighteenth Century,* and *Johann Christian Krüger. Werke. Kritische Gesamtausgabe.* His most recent book is *Bennewitz, Goethe,* Faust. *German and Intercultural Stagings.* His articles include a wide range of topics in German literature and theatre, including "Stage Productions of Goethe's *Faust* in India," and "Goethes *Faust* in Manila: Ein interkulturelles Experiment."

Susanne Ledanff is senior lecturer and German program director in the School of Languages, Cultures and Linguistics at the University of Canterbury, New Zealand. Her recent book publication is *Hauptstadtphantasien. Berliner Stadtlektüren in der Gegenwartsliteratur 1989–2008.*

Bruce J. MacLennan is associate professor in the Department of Electrical Engineering and Computer Science at the University of Tennessee. His research is in artificial intelligence, autonomous robotics, artificial life, artificial morphogenesis, the philosophy of mind, and self-organizing systems. He has also taught courses on Goethe's philosophy of science and *Faust.* He has published two books and more than sixty refereed articles and book chapters. He is currently investigating archetypal patterns in mathematics and nature, and has a book in progress.

Robert E. Norton is professor of German at the University of Notre Dame. His publications include *Herder's Aesthetics and the European Enlightenment, The Beautiful Soul: Aesthetic Morality in the Eighteenth Century,* and *Secret Germany: Stefan George and His Circle.*

James M. van der Laan is professor of German in the Department of Languages, Literatures, and Cultures at Illinois State University. His publications include *Seeking Meaning for Goethe's* Faust, "Lessing's 'Lost' Faust," "Goethe, Narrative, and Science," and "Goethe, Hesiod, and Yeats on Progress." He is currently co-editing a volume on the Faustian sixteenth century.